Max Pemberton

The Impregnable City

A Romance

Max Pemberton

The Impregnable City
A Romance

ISBN/EAN: 9783744674034

Printed in Europe, USA, Canada, Australia, Japan

Cover: Foto ©Thomas Meinert / pixelio.de

More available books at **www.hansebooks.com**

The
Impregnable City

A ROMANCE

By

MAX PEMBERTON

New York

Dodd, Mead and Company

1898

INTRODUCTION.

THE story of a life; the story of an unknown
city; the story of men who dreamed dreams; the
story of mercy and of death, of darkness and of
light, of order and of chaos; the story of myself,
Irwin Trevena, who set down these things as I
have seen and known them.

CONTENTS.

iv CONTENTS.

THE IMPREGNABLE CITY.

CHAPTER I.

I COME HOME FROM THE PLAY.

THERE was a newsboy upon the pavement crying of an outrage at the Café Mirabeau, in Paris; but he stepped back as my cab struck the curb and came by good hap unharmed into the broad roadway of Cavendish Square. I saw his face for a moment in the aureola of a lamp, a pale face and wan; but the mists were quivering upon the wet streets, and his cry was dead in my ears almost with its first coming to me. Then we entered Harley Street; and there was no sound or voice upon the calm of respectability.

The hour was midnight, the day was the 10th of March, the year 1892. I had been to the Haymarket Theater as a relaxation from my want of a practice; and was now going home to my little house in Welbeck Street, there to dream of fame and of fees. Until that time I had neither. My brass plate, which told, *urbi et orbi*, that London University had found me a fit and proper person to attend at the deathbeds of my fellows, attracted neither the undeserving rich nor the unprofitable poor. I was a physician ministering to myself, to the loneliness of one life, and to its budding failure.

I write of these things, in themselves of little interest, that those who care to know of the strange events now to be recorded may accompany me in the narration from the very beginning; may be with me when men, as it were, rose up in my path from the unknown, and in the night of mysteries visions were given to my eyes. Out of the fog, lying wet upon Welbeck Street, the first vision came—a single brougham standing at my own door; a light burning in my consulting room, where light so rarely was.

How much I paid to my own cabman as I sprang to the pavement I shall never know. My latchkey was in the lock while the shillings were yet tumbling from the roof of his crazy cab; and I heard his "Thank you!" in the same moment that my servant cried to me that a gentleman wished to see me in my room. Beloved Donald!

the sight of a patient had almost been too much
for him. His hand trembled upon the latch; he
even asked if he should set glasses.

"Glasses!" said I. "Donald, are you mad?
How long has the gentleman been waiting?"

"An hoor—maybe two. Oh, sir, I thank God
for the nicht!"

"Did you give him the paper?" I asked,
changing my boots in the hall as we stood.

"Indeed and I did; but I'm verra well sure
that it was last week's."

"That's unfortunate. What's the man's
name?"

"I'm no' acquaint with it; but there's letters
clapped on to the hind end. You'll be making
haste to learn, maybe."

It was a hint, and I took it; but my hand trembled as my man's had done when he told me the
news. A patient—*my* patient; my *first* patient.
Hope, advance, notoriety, money—the dream of
that long-drawn moment gave these to me. And,
dreaming, I threw open the door of the consulting room,—that little chamber garnished for the
stranger with all the few baubles I possessed,—
and the interview began.

The visitor sat in a basket armchair, drawn

near to a crackling fire of logs. A shaded lamp
upon a cabinet at his side cast light upon his
face; and I saw that he was a young man, with
black hair of exceeding richness, and eyes which
were very gentle in their expression. He had
loosened a heavy cape which was about his shoulders, and I thought from the first that I had
never seen a human being of such physique or
fine proportion of body and limb. As I entered
the room he paused in the act of turning over
the very ancient copy of *The Illustrated London
News* which Donald had found for him, and stood
up to greet me—a magnificent sight, and not a
little startling. In the same moment I observed
that his cape was buckled with a clasp of mother-
of-pearl, and that letters of gold stood out upon
it in relief.

My first words to him were those of apology;
but he put them aside with a gesture, and began
to speak in a voice deep and pleasing as the note
of a bell.

"Pray don't think of me," said he; "my time
is entirely yours. You are Dr. Irwin Trevena, I
think; and there was in *The Lancet* four months
ago an article from your pen on the subject of
anæmia of the brain. I am not mistaken?"

" By no means," said I. " The brain and its diseases have been my special study for five years and more."

" I presumed so from your work; and that is why I am here," said he next.

" Not as a patient?" cried I, with a laugh; for he had the air of a man who was absurdly healthy.

" Not as a patient," he continued—" no, indeed. Your subject lies upon a yacht moored at this moment in the Solent. She has come to England to consult the first authority on the disease to which she is a victim. If you will be good enough to accompany me, we shall be with her before daybreak."

" The case, then, is serious?" said I.

" From one point of view only. The lady has come a thousand miles to see you. Every day she has said : ' In so many hours Dr. Trevena will be with me.' The confidence inspired by your work, which she read casually at Cairo, is more wonderful than anything I have witnessed. I know nothing of brain disease, doctor; but my ignorance tells me that it were well if this craving were satisfied. And I am sure, if it is in your power, you will respond to the wishes of one who has made of you an idol before she had opportunity to worship you in the flesh."

It was all said brightly, buoyantly, with the air of a man too serious to be deemed flippant, merry enough to inspire confidence. A more commanding, noble manner I had never met with; nor such a grace of speech and bearing. And I replied to him readily.

"If you will give me leave to change my coat, I will go with you now," said I.

"Of course," he replied; "and let me beg of you not to leave gold upon your table."

He said this with infinite delicacy. While we had been talking he had put a little pile of sovereigns upon my writing table, and now he pointed to them.

"I am not quite aware of the custom of your profession," said he, "but I know that for such a case as this the remuneration is by mileage. Southampton is seventy-eight and three-quarter miles from here. The yacht is a mile and a quarter from the shore. You will find eighty guineas there."

"I am only entitled to sixty," said I; "two-thirds of the mileage is the custom."

He waved off the protest with a motion of his

hand, and I left him. Five minutes later we stepped into the brougham together; but a new thought came to me before the horse had moved.

"Hollo!" cried I, "what are we doing? The last train to Southampton is at 9.45!"

"Don't think of it," said he; "we shall conjure one from somewhere."

"You mean to take a 'special'?" said I.

"It is waiting at the platform for us," cried he.

I said no more, but sank back in the soft cushions. My dream! It had come, then, come as I had dreamed it! Oh, I could have filled all the heavens with my thanks to God!

CHAPTER II.

IN WHICH I BEGIN TO DOUBT.

I WAS very full of sleep when our train came to Southampton, and my eyes were scarce open when my companion led the way from the station to the water. There was waiting for him at the quay a small ship's launch, such as sailors call a kettle, and in this we went quickly toward the open sea, the night being infinitely dark, and the white mists rising in bedewing clouds. Such hulls of great steamers as we saw rose up suddenly like phantoms in our wake; and the lanterns were as golden balls floating lightly above the spuming swell.

The journey to the yacht seemed to me overlong, but no rain fell, and the west wind blew softly upon my face. I was now warmed up to a considerable curiosity as to my patient, and the success which would follow upon my venture; and this drove from my head both observation of the two seamen who had charge of the launch and thought of talk with my companion. He

8

had slept during the whole of the journey from London; and even now, with the salt spray whipping his eyes, he could not find his tongue. At the last, however, and just as one of the two men cried: "Ahoy, there!" in a ringing voice, he stood up quickly and put his hand upon my shoulder.

"Dr. Trevena," said he, "welcome to the *Wanderer!*"

"We are there, then?" said I. "Well, I'm not sorry. The cold was beginning to quarrel with me."

"Once on board, and I'll take it upon myself to prescribe for that," cried he merrily; and no sooner were the words out than the shape of a great vessel loomed up over the black of the water, and the light of lanterns danced upon her deck, and shot out brilliantly from her ports.

He went up the ladder quickly, and I followed him to a deck shining white under the glow of silvery lamps. There were three of the crew there to receive him, all dressed curiously; and to one of these he spoke hurriedly in Italian. The man nodded his head for answer, and without further parley I was conducted to a cabin lying far aft, and there left with a word from the man who had brought me.

"Doctor," said he, "you'll find books, and you'll find cigars. Of the former I'm no judge, but I'll wager that the latter are the best you ever smoked. Try one while I speak to the patient."

"Whose name I have not yet the pleasure of knowing?" exclaimed I inquiringly.

"She shall tell you herself," cried he, with a laugh. "It will sound the prettier from a woman's lips. Meanwhile, if there is anything you want, here is the bell which brings the steward. Consider that we are your servants while you remain with us. And if I may prescribe as I promised, let me recommend a glass of green Chartreuse as the finest known antidote to cold."

"Well," said I, "since you call me in to consult, I must agree with the treatment. But I must not smoke until the interview is ended."

He went off humming an air from the streets in the same buoyant humor that he had at first displayed, and I sat down to examine the cabin. I judged at once that it was the music room of the yacht, yet a more exquisitely furnished place

I had never seen. The hangings were of tapestry, richly worked in scenes, which glowed with
color. The frieze showed innumerable ships
done in ivory in *alto relievo;* a gold corona lay
above them, and from many a nook there peeped
sketches and landscapes whose value needed no
buttress of criticism. A moonlight scene by
Joseph Vernet, a sketch after Greuze by Mlle.
la Doux, an undoubted Meissonier, the picture of
an Italian woman by Alma Tadema—these were
but a few of the many treasures my eye discovered
in its first rapid survey. And everywhere, in the
wondrous play of concealed lights, in the pillars
of ivory, in the white table inlaid with cunning
gold-work, in the fine organ, and the piano whose
case must have been worth two thousand pounds,
there was evidence of a colossal wealth and a
rare taste such as my travels had not hitherto put
me in touch with.

Here, then, was the home of my first patient.
As I sipped the warming liquor which a man in a
quiet livery of black had set upon the table I
could have been content to think that I lay in
bewitching sleep, and that all this had risen to my
vision as the mocking phantom of my brain. A
surpassing pleasure filled me—a delirious hope

such as comes to some of us before the thirties and failure have soured us. I was but twenty-eight, susceptible to the least sway of fortune, depressed by a word, elated by another. And what struggling practitioner had ever such luck to be called from obscurity to the light of practice like this, in the home of one whose fame or position could be no less singular than the signs of wealth I now saw about me?

I had remained in this state of exquisite content for many minutes but for the sudden conviction that the yacht was moving. A low tremor of the screw-shaft struck through the steel of the ship; the table quivered almost imperceptibly; and I, looking through the port at my right, observed the Calshot Light, and we were passing it. It occurred to me at once that the man who had come with me was a long time absent, and had made no mention of any voyage. I determined to speak with him, and went to the door for that purpose; but I found it to be locked, and with a great thrill of fear striking up into my brain my dream passed from me.

For many minutes I sat while the cold sweat gathered upon my forehead, and I felt my shirt damp upon my chest. I had read in tales of medical men trapped here or trapped there ; but thought them sure fictions. Yet here was I locked in a cabin in a yacht that was steaming out to sea, and no more sign of a patient than of daybreak. I asked myself a hundred times what the meaning of it was? who was the man who had carried me from London? whither was the yacht bound? There was not even echo to give me answer, and, for lack of it, I put my hand upon the bell, and held it there while minutes passed.

My fingers were still upon the knob when the answer came. The door was opened quickly and the man stood before me, now dressed in a coat of some white silky stuff, delicately embroidered with gold lace. He looked vastly handsome without his cap of fur ; and there was a merry smile upon his lips when he spoke to me.

" My dear doctor," said he, " a hundred pardons, but my steward is busy on deck. I was just coming to fetch you."

My complaint died away in my throat before his speech, and I could only gurgle a reply.

" The door," I stammered—" the door was fastened—that is, locked.".

He laughed aloud at the suggestion.

"So much for our patent handles," said he; "you should have lifted it."

I had shame beyond expression at the rebuke.

"And the patient?" I asked.

"Is ready for us," said he; "may I beg you to follow me?"

He led me through a corridor, dimly lighted with incandescent lamps, and so to the door of the saloon, as I judged it to be. There was a curtain of cloth of gold hung before it, and this suddenly he drew back, exclaiming:

"Here is your patient."

For a moment I saw nothing; then I knew that many lamps shone softly upon a table bright with gold and silver, that palms stood out in every nook and cranny, that luxurious couches invited to rest, that the odor of rich dishes came to my nostrils, that flagons of wine stood among banks of exquisite flowers, that the soft harmonies of voluptuous music fell pleasantly upon my ears. But the room was empty. He and I were alone to enjoy the feast that had been prepared, and as I made the discovery his gentle laugh and my exclamation rose up together.

"Well," said he, "do you think that an operation is necessary?"

I turned round and faced him.

"Mr.——" began I, but then remembered I had not his name.

"My name is Adam Monk, but to my intimates I am known as 'Rocco,'" said he. "I shall feel under an obligation if you will so call me."

"But," cried I, now full of anger, "you have taken a very great liberty with me. I demand at once to be put on shore!"

"Oh, doctor," said he, "whatever would you do on shore at this time of night?"

"Sir," continued I, "that is no business of yours. Will you please to explain this masquerade?"

"Explanations, doctor," replied he, seating himself most impudently at the head of the table, "should give way to the more serious things of life. Look, now, do you think I am a rogue?"

I looked at him closely, and my suspicions died away. Who that ever saw Rocco did not love him?

"At any rate," said I, "tell me something."

"With pleasure," cried he. "This champagne is 1874 Heidsieck. Let me fill your glass."

I could say no more. I sat down to the table, and began to eat mechanically. But the motion of the yacht, as she now rushed through the water, was unmistakable. We must have passed the Needles.

CHAPTER III.

THE supper we now enjoyed was, as I say, served perfectly; the wine was such as only a man of rare palate could buy. My companion, who called himself Rocco, was the most captivating talker I have known. He passed lightly from subject to subject, had anecdotes of all peoples and of all lands; but, for the most part, he spoke of southern seas, the wonders of their islands, the perpetual sunshine which was upon them, the beauty of their calms and the grandeur of their storms. Often I sought to draw him to the subject which was strong in my thoughts,— the reason he had brought me to his yacht,—but no words came from his lips; and he so avoided my snares of speech that an uncontrollable anger came upon me at last, and I broke into his talk with no little abruptness. It was at the very moment the steward set cigars and punch upon the table.

17

"Mr. Monk," said I, swinging round my chair to face him, "your supper is admirable, and I have enjoyed your company. It is none the less necessary that I ask you again, Why have you brought me here, and in what capacity can I serve you?"

"You can serve me, doctor," replied he, putting a match to his cigar, "by giving me your opinion of my steward's punch. I tell him there's too much borage in it."

"That's all very well," said I, "and you play your part capitally. But it's my turn now to give you tragedy for farce. I will do it in a question. What is there to prevent me going upon deck and bawling to the first ship we pass for assistance?"

He blew a cloud of smoke from his lips, and then sipped the steaming liquor.

"You ask me a question," said he, "and I will be equal ready in answering. What is to prevent you going on deck, doctor? Why, nothing in the world. Only"—and here he became thoughtful—"only, it might not be wise."

"Might not be wise!" said I, trying to conceal the uneasiness—nay, fear—I felt. "But surely you do not threaten your guests, Mr. Monk?"

"I threaten? God forbid! I am only trying to interest you."

"Then set my mind at rest, and let us end this play. Where are you taking me to?"

"Fill your glass and I will tell you."

I did as he commanded, but the effort of drinking went near to choking me.

"Now," said he, putting his elbows upon the table, "listen to this, doctor, and take my word that I am dealing with you as I would deal with my own brother. Your destination is, roughly, a little more than ten thousand miles from here——"

Before he could say more I rose from my chair. My legs trembled under me; an intense sickness and feeling of unutterable despair came upon me.

"If you take me that far," said I at random, "I am a ruined man!"

"Indeed!" said he; "but I was just thinking you were a made man."

I sat down again.

"How can that be?" I asked.

"In the simplest way possible," said he. "I am going to be very plain with you. You are a man young and full of cleverness; but for the moment you do not make three hundred pounds a year. Very well. During the time that you are with me you will receive a remuneration of one hundred guineas a week——"

"One hundred guineas!" I exclaimed.

"As I say."

"But for what?" I gasped.

"For using such skill as you have in the interest of one who is sick."

"And the name of him who sends for me——"

"You will learn in good time. Be content now to know that I am in his service—that I live for him, and would die for him. A man who is a king among men, doctor; whose secret power is felt in every court in Europe; who is the father of charity and truth and justice; a man who is poor, yet rich, weak, yet strong, a child in hand, but a monarch in act—that man summons you."

"And the country in which he lives?"

"Is a country whose name you will never learn."

I was silent for many minutes. My cigar went out in my hand. The whole of his story rang in my ears like the voice of a dream.

"Your friend is ill?" I asked, when minutes had gone.

"Indeed, no," said he; "his health is splendid."

"Then who is my patient?"

He turned round in his chair again, and, bending forward, he touched a spring in the panel of the wall. Two little doors fell back, to show me the picture of a girl, upon which a shaded lamp, bursting into light, cast a powerful glow. The face was not one to call for an immediate admission of power or beauty; yet, as I continued to gaze upon it, the canvas seemed to hold me with a fascination not to be described. It were as if the eyes of the girl searched my very heart. Never had I known so curious a spell or one so sure. I saw but the sketch of a child of seventeen or eighteen years; a child with long hair of a deep auburn wound about her body; a child with ivory skin and little color in her cheeks; a child dressed in a white robe and wearing at her breast the same clasp of mother-of-pearl and of gold that he who called himself Rocco had. I saw all this, I say, and yet I continued to gaze, and to feel a new and potent interest the like to which my life had never known. The picture spoke to me; a message came as from the very heart of her I looked upon; the thought that she

was to be my patient filled my veins with warm
blood; for many minutes I sat without speech or
motion; I forgot the night and its circumstance,
forgot even that another watched me.

.   .   .   .

"There is your patient!"

My companion spoke. I turned from the
painting with a start, to look at him. He was
like a man transformed. The tenderness of his
eyes was multiplied a hundredfold; there was red
in his cheeks; he bent forward to the picture as
if he would put his lips upon it, and in that
moment I read his secret. He was the lover of
her to whom I was to carry my skill. Perhaps
she was his wife. The thought stung me even
then, though I had never seen her; I was afraid
to look at the picture again. When I did so, I
saw that the upraised left hand of the girl was
without a ring, and the mood of depression
passed. In the same moment he touched the
spring of the panel, and the doors shut together.
The light faded; the vision was moved from
my eyes.

For some time the two of us sat without speaking, the smoke from our relighted cigars floating
heavily in the still air. He was the first to break

the silence, but his voice was now low, and his buoyancy had left him.

"Dr. Trevena," said he gently, "you are going to strange seas and to strange places. Sights will be given to you beyond anything you can imagine. You will learn of things of which dreamers may have dreamed, but which few men have seen. You are on the way to riches for which you might have worked a lifetime, and yet have missed. You are privileged to become the servant of one who is the beloved master of a people that adore him. Yet now, at the beginning of it, I say to you, Beware; shut all weakness from your heart; think of her to whom you will minister as a patient only. As you value everything that is dear to you, seek not to make her a friend, lest the heart be eaten out of you as mine has been—and the hearts of others more worthy of better things. I speak to you as a friend—I speak only of what I know. Beware, for the last minute has told me where you stand."

I shrugged my shoulders indifferently; but it was a shallow thing to do.

"I thank you," said I, "but the warning is scarcely necessary. Doctors, you know, are not usually weak in that respect.

The laugh that he gave was scornful, but he checked it at once.

"Forgive me!" said he; "it was said by one who wishes well to you. May I count now on your going through to the end of it without protest?"

The memory of the picture dictated my answer.

"Mr. Monk," said I, "you may count upon me to the end."

"You are wise!" cried he, rising from the table. "I have only one more favor to ask. We shall be together many months. Be among the number of my friends, and believe in me!"

He held out his hand, and I gave it a hearty grip. Then a steward appeared to conduct me to my bedroom.

I was now worn out with excitement and the hour; and though the cabin into which I was shown was in keeping with the luxury elsewhere to be observed upon the ship, I had no thought for it, but fell upon my bed, dressed as I was, and there lay, with throbbing eyeballs and burning head. In my ears there echoed the sound of the man's voice; before my eyes there floated the vision of the picture. To what home of wonders was I going? what play of Fate had drawn me suddenly to these mysteries and these phantoms? who was the master of men? where was his home? should I ever see London again? or had I been cut from life and friends and hope as though death had taken me? No answer could I find to these ever-changing thoughts—no answer but the tremulous play of the screw, the dull swish of the sea, the roll of the yacht as she rose and fell in the waters of the Channel. No answer, indeed, but fear and hope and foreboding, the sense of solitude, the despair of the night. And, worn and weary, at last I fell asleep, with the daylight streaming upon my bed, and the eyes of the girl watching me to rest.

CHAPTER IV.

THE " WANDERER " AND HER CREW.

THE whole cabin was full of sunbeams when I awoke, and a little clock, set in a pillar at the foot of my bed, marked the hour of eleven. As I lay looking upon it I began to wonder how such a thing had come into my room, and why Donald had not got me up at my usual hour. With my eyes half closed, and a great sense of heaviness in my mind, the fact that I was upon a ship, and in some way a prisoner, was not to be realized. I remembered only that it was my morning at the hospital, and that I was already late.

The striking of a bell almost above the roof of my cabin shattered the dreams of waking. Seven times the note rang out: and while the metal was still vibrating I had come to possession of my full senses; and memory of all that I had seen and done leaped swiftly into my mind. I recalled the coming of Adam Monk, his speech in my rooms in Welbeck Street; my journey to the yacht, the happenings thereon, and, more vividly

than these, the face of the girl I had seen in the
picture—and the beauty of it! The vigor of the
morning softened none of the impression which
the first sight of the painting had made upon
me. I had gone to my sleep with the girl's eyes
looking into mine; I awoke and thought still
that I saw them, and that they were very near
to me.

In this mood I sat up in my bed to survey my
cabin. There had been light of dawn when I had
thrown myself upon my bed; but I was then too
weary to take any observation of my surround-
ings. Now, however, with the whole room full
of sunlight, and the sweet fresh breeze of the sea
coming through the porthole, I examined the
place and sat in some astonishment to realize its
luxury. That I was in a bed in lieu of the more
common bunk, and was there curiously propped
up with pillows, gave me my first surprise; but
when I looked about, there were more wonderful
things than these. Close to my head were knobs,
by which I could command heat or cold or light
in the cabin; a blind of stained glass permitted
me either to let in the sun's rays or to exclude
them; a great couch, padded and cushioned,
offered, with an armchair in crimson leather, rest

for the day; a washstand, whose basin was seemingly of solid silver, was cunningly fitted against
the wall; there was a rack full of good fiction
almost at my elbow; and upon the little table at
the side of my bed a decanter of cut glass half
filled with yellow wine, a box of cigarettes, and
some siphons of soda water were placed for my
refreshment.

Of the decoration of the cabin I observed only
that its scheme was in light blue and silver, and
that a frieze of fine Oriental work, seemingly
done in metal, gave it an air of richness and
of light. The carpet was a Persian one, very
soft to the feet and glowing with color; and in
all the panels were depicted the faces and the
forms of sea nymphs and of nereids. Here, as in
the music room and the saloon, richness and the
sense of wealth plumbed my imagination to its
depths. Who, I asked, owned a yacht like this?
how came his home to be nameless, and ten
thousand miles from Southampton? What was
the mystery in which I was taking so curious a
part? who was Adam Monk, and why was he in
charge of the yacht and of myself? With the
clear brain of morning, I even found myself writing a diary in my mind, and the words of it are

still fast in my memory. For thus, had pencil been near to me, should I have set down my story:

"I, Irwin Trevena, doctor, practicing yesterday, the 10th of March, 1892, in London, am to-day a prisoner upon the yacht *Wanderer*, bound I know not for what port, owned I know not by what master of money and prince of men. Last night, as by magic, I was carried from Welbeck Street to the ship; strange sights were shown to my eyes; strange tales were whispered for my delectation in a saloon the like to which few yachtsmen have seen; I was feasted with great splendor; the strains of music fell upon my ears; there was set before me an entertainment which would have served for a king. And then I was shown the picture of a woman which impressed me more profoundly than I have ever been impressed before. To-day——"

But with the words "to-day" the mental diary ended, the door of my cabin opened, and a steward entered. He carried a tray, whereon were steaming coffee and bread in many shapes; and as he set them by my bed he wished me good-morning.

"Shall I send the barber, sir?" he asked.

"I am much obliged to you," said I. "Is your master up?"

"The gentlemen are now upon the promenade deck," replied he. "They wait for you there."

The man was immobile, very civil, yet quite uncommunicative. The hope that I had of obtaining from him any particulars as to the ownership of the yacht passed away at the moment of its inception, and I watched him while he raised the floor of my cabin and disclosed a bath of shining metal. By the time that he had filled this an Indian barber had come into the room and shaved me with wonderful adroitness. And when the pair of them had gone, I dressed with some haste. The steward had said that "gentlemen" wished to see me. Who, then, was added to the number of the man Rocco's guests?

These were my speculations when I opened my cabin door and stepped upon the deck; but as the glorious breeze snatched the handle from my grasp I forgot them. I saw now the whole of the yacht for the first time, and surprise was my chief thought. From the hurricane deck, to which I mounted, I looked down upon a raking ship of fifteen hundred tons burden at the least, and could but marvel at the sight. Three-

masted ; with two funnels, white and brass-bound ;
with spotless decks ; with capstans, wheels, and
metal-work shining like gold in the sun's rays ;
with luxurious chairs at all points on her higher
promenade ; with paneling of teak and skylights
of stained glass ; with a crew in dress of the
purest white ; with machine guns everywhere,
and little houses starting up, and rich rugs for
the feet, and snowy awnings against the sun,
there never was a fairer sight than the *Wanderer ;* nor will there be, I think, in the whole
history of yachting.

As I stood thus engrossed upon the promenade
the sea was tumbling and tossing in foam-capped
ridges about the yacht ; she was dipping her nose
into the spray, and rushing forward as a hound of
the deep. From my station I seemed to be a
tremendous height above the green hollows, and
to be in some pleasing manner a master of them.
I could see, but a great way from us on our starboard bow, the dark line of land ; fishing boats
lay rolling in the trough of the swell near to us,
and their brown sails flapped sharply in the rushing wind ; a big steamer, with smoke driven over
her prow by the breeze, was passing us, and her
passengers crowded to her deck-rails to give us

greeting.   And over all was the spirit of the
morning, the spirit of the sun's light, and of the
invigorating, exalting wind ; of the foam-flecks
breaking upon the face, and the sweet airs which
gave life.

From a contemplation of these things Adam
Monk himself now aroused me.   He came swiftly
along the deck, whereon there were some dozen
seamen dressed in spotless white, and very richly
clad for their work ; and with him there was a
young man shabbily begarbed in the oldest of ill-
cut clothes.   The youth appeared to be a for-
eigner, though his hair was of a deep red color ;
and I learned presently that he was an Italian.
Monk himself was in his gayest humor, and
greeted me almost with affection.

" Doctor," said he, " tell me that you've slept
well, or I'll have to hang someone.   Was it all as
you wished ? "

" It was more than I could have wished," said I.

" I'm glad to hear it, and glad to see you looking bright," said he next.   " I wish I could say
the same for my friend, here.   Let me introduce
you.   Signor Privli—Dr. Irwin Trevena.   He
doesn't speak a word of English, doctor, which
is a virtue in these days."

I bowed to the man, and saw that he was suffering from *mal de mer*.

"Well," said I, "my Italian is limited to three
words, and those I have forgotten; but, if I can
be of any service to Signor Privli——"

"Indeed, and you can't," said Monk lightly.
"I've done for him already. One basin to be
taken as required. But now tell me, are you
hungry?"

"I should be a wonderful man if I was," cried
I, "seeing the amount of coffee I have just
drunk."

"Then we'll have our breakfast in thirty
minutes," said he, taking my arm with a kindly
gesture; "let me recommend you to eat every
half hour at sea. The constitution requires it.
Meanwhile I'll show you the yacht, which you'll
be glad to see, since it must be your home for
the next thirty days and more."

"Thirty days and more!" cried I, again feeling my heart sink as the reality of my separation
from all that interested me was thus emphasized.
"Your destination surely is not so far?"

"I wish that I could bring it nearer, doctor,"
cried he, walking me slowly up the deck; "but
it's thirty days with the best of weather. My

only consolation is the thought that you'll forgive me when we get there. Believe me, you are
one of the luckiest men in existence. It is difficult to realize it, and you have only my word;
but to that I can add the evidence of your eyes.
Look down there, and ask yourself if you ever
saw a more contented crew."

We stood now by the bridge, and I saw at a
great distance the Eddystone Light, like a black
pillar above the sea. Upon the deck itself the
spectacle was one of profound order. Men of all
nations, but principally Frenchmen and Russians,
with a number of olive-skinned fellows who had
the air of Polynesians, stood soberly at their
places. Their white uniforms and scarlet caps
shone pleasantly in the sunlight; they worked,
when called upon, with a quickness and a skill
rarely seen except upon a man-of-war. The first
officer himself, now slowing pacing the bridge,
had the ruddy face and the yellow hair of a north-
country man, but was, I learned, an American,
long since distinguished for his seamanship. The
man by him was an Englishman, from Hull; an
Irishman was at the wheel; and I observed
others of my own countrymen here and there near
the forecastle. But chiefly, as I say, the crew was

made up of foreigners, and was not a little remarkable for the babel of tongues it commanded.

"These are our men," said Monk, when we had stood gazing upon the scene for many minutes. "I give you leave to ask any of them if they are happy. Aren't they a magnificent lot? Watch that great hulking Irishman, there; did you ever see a picture of finer health or build? There's not a complaint in the heads of the whole of them; and they serve the master you are going to serve, and adore him. Talk to them for yourself, and see how you find them."

"That I will with pleasure when the opportunity comes," replied I, not a little consoled at the sight; "but where and who is your skipper?"

"He will be at the breakfast table, where I think we might look for him. They're going to strike eight bells, and my appetite rings in response. We follow the French custom here, and take *déjeûner*. If you can't become a Frenchman I'll have things sent into your cabin every morning."

"You're very good," said I, "but your method is the only civilized one. An early breakfast is the last relic of barbarism."

The bell was struck as I spoke, and I caught a

glimpse of the Irishman who struck it, the man whom Monk had praised for his power and his health. It occurred to me at once that the face was ridiculously familiar to me. I had seen the man in Westminster Hospital six months before —a poor devil of a fellow, woe-begone, sick, and a pauper. He now stood before me a very giant in height and breadth, and ruddy with the vigor of the sea. When our eyes met, he gave a little start, and then put himself to his work again; nor did he look up as I went with Monk on my way to the saloon; and thus he passed from my view. But the sight of the man was like new wine to me, for it seemed at last that I had found one who was a friend, called from the life I knew, to be with me in this unsurpassable experience of mysteries, every hour growing deeper and more profound.

Five minutes later I was talking to Reuben Joyce, the gray-haired, gentle old skipper of the yacht, who greeted me as though he had known me all his life.

CHAPTER V.

THE MAN IN THE CAGE.

IT was the night of the ninth day, we being some twelve hours out from Porto Grande in the De Verde Islands, where we had taken coal. I stood alone on the lower deck of the *Wanderer* watching the glorious sky, shot with its myriad of rolling stars. The air was warm, yet not lacking freshness; the sea was almost golden in the path of the moonlight; there was a sound of fiddles and of fifes from the forecastle, where the men made merry; from the bridge the deep, resounding voice of Reuben Joyce, the captain of the ship, was to be heard at intervals.

I had gone forward after the usual satisfying banquet in the saloon, the feast being accompanied as ever by the music of the ship's band, to witness, at Monk's invitation, the junketings of the men, no less merry in their play than sober in their work. But my head was so full of thoughts that when I had seen one of their

dances, and listened to a song,—a wild, delirious,
haunting song, like to nothing I had heard in any
quarter of the world,—I wandered from the scene
to the lower deck of the ship, and so stood very
near to the hatch of the engine room.   Upon the
water there shone the glow of the arc lamps
beneath which the men were gathered; the sea
itself was dark and limpid and still; the breeze
was soft and sweet as a breeze from a garden of
roses; the thud of the engines was like the rise
and fall of a mighty hammer.   Oftentimes, when
the doors of the furnaces were opened, a great
wave of crimson light bathed the decks and funnels above me; it shone scarlet upon the faces
of the engineers; it died away to leave the darkness.   And all through it the yacht was rushing
ahead to a land whose name I was not to know,
to a people and a power stronger, as I had been
told, than any people or any power upon the face
of the globe.

Nine days now had I been a prisoner; for nine
days lived in the company of Adam Monk, of the
Italian Privli, of the officers of the ship.   Each
morning had been like other mornings; each
night as other nights.   Banquets, rich foods, rare
wines, engrossing books, sweet music—all these

were mine day by day and hour by hour; yet melancholy sat heavy upon me, the longing for my home ate at my heart. I seemed to be going even out of the world itself; only the memory of the woman's face, the spell that the painting had cast upon me, held me back from unspeakable despair and a depth of woe.

Ask me why, and I have no answer. Men in numbers would have given years of their life to have been where I stood. I was enjoying an experience such as the very rich only can know; I saw nothing until that time but kindness and affection and noble thought. Strange that in one moment the whole of my trust was to be shattered, the whole of my fearing to be renewed.

It befell thus; but no words could convey the terror of the thing as I saw it, there off the African coast, on that memorable night. I was standing on the lower deck, as I have said, when the low sound of moaning fell upon my ears. I listened, and the cry was repeated; I could hear it quite close to me—the bitter cry of a man suffering, almost the sound of weeping and of ultimate despair. For long moments I stood in a cold sweat, so fearful was the plaintive moan. I thought even that some dreadful deed was being done almost at my feet. Then the cry died away, and I asked myself what delusion had brought it to my ears.

While all this stupefying fear was upon me, and my hand had begun to tremble as a woman's, I observed, abaft the engine room, a staircase leading to the lower quarters of the ship. No sooner had I seen it than the cry was raised again, and it came to me that it was uttered down there in the depths of the lightless passage. There was no one to watch me. The hands were forward with the music. I knew that I was doing that which might bring me to danger; yet so weird and wild and full of suffering was the voice that I went quickly down the stairs, and all that was hidden lay instantly before my eyes.

The passage was narrow and of little height. A solitary oil lamp cast a flickering glow upon the low doors on either side of it. One of these doors had now swung open upon its hinges; and as I followed the dim light cast into the den now revealed, I saw the man. He lay behind thick bars of iron upon a floor of wood; his hair was long and matted, and fell upon his face in blinding curls; he had hands like the talons of a bird, and a heavy lock of iron bound his wrists together. Unable to stand, unable to lie, compelled to crouch upon his hams, fetters eating into the flesh of his ankles, pale as one dying, weak with exhaustion, his mouth dry with thirst, tears clotted upon his face—the vision of that man will linger with me to my dying day. And when he saw me, when he raised his head and cried again like a wounded woman, I felt pity welling up from my heart, and anger which scarce brooked control.

"Who are you?" I whispered, bending over him. "Tell me without fear; I am a doctor, and a stranger."

"God reward you!" gasped he. "I am Jack Williams, seaman. Look for yourself; they're killing me here."

"What have you done?" I asked. "Why are you in this place?"

"For going ashore," he moaned; "going ashore without leave. It's the rule, and I broke it. This is light to what's before me."

I had a flask of brandy in my pocket, and I put it to his lips.

"If it's possible to help you," said I, as I forced the liquor between his teeth, "you shall be out of here in ten minutes."

He laughed even in his pain.

" Sir," said he, in a minute, " how did you come upon this ship ?"

" I was brought here," said I back in a low voice, " brought here by a trick."

" Then take the advice of a man who's not got long to live—go ashore at the first port we touch."

" Do I stand in any danger?" I asked quickly.

For some while he did not answer me directly, but of a sudden with a swift motion he put his arm against one of the iron bars.

" Doctor," asked he, " will you help a poor seaman ?"

" What can I do for you ?" said I.

" Make it lighter for me!" cried he. " Put your knife in my arm here; you'll be knowing where ! "

I started back from him at the request, not a little amazed at the profundity of suffering which begot such a demand. I remember that I stood for a spell watching his thin yellow face pressed against the bars, the flickering lamp throwing a palmy light upon it. Then, quite quickly, the man was shut from my sight; the door of his cage was closed with force, and I turned sharply, to find the Irish seaman at my elbow. But he had his finger to his lips, and when he had done his work, he took me roughly by the arm and almost pulled me up the stair-case. At the top of it, and when we were again near to the engine-room hatchway, he spoke in a very low voice.

" Doctor," said he, " it's bad air you'll have found below."

The look with which he said this meant more than his words.

" It's very bad air for sure, doctor," continued he, after the pause; " and such a fine night on deck, too!"

At this I forced myself to speak, though my head was burning the ashes of a hundred specu-lations, while my hands were wet and clammy.

" Tell me," said I—" is not your name Dennis O'Brien? And were you not discharged from Westminster Hospital last September?"

" The same, your honor," replied he.

" And you knew me when I came on board?"

" Every inch av ye, sorr."

" Then you can speak freely with me. What is this ship? and why is that man there treated like a beast?"

He looked down the deck—dark, except in those intervals where the crimson wave floated up from the furnace doors. When he had assured himself that we were alone, he put his mouth to my ear and spoke again.

" Doctor," said he, " it's plain words I'll say to you. If you'd ride comfortable on this vessel, don't ask questions, and don't look for answers. It's me, Dennis O'Brien, that says it, and meaning good to ye."

With this word he made an end of it, and hurried quickly toward the forecastle, where the music had ceased. The whole episode had come about so quickly that, when I stood on deck again, I had difficulty to convince myself that it was real. Nor could I conceive what course it was my duty to take. That there was hidden upon the yacht work to make even an unemotional man shudder I knew; and, beyond this, the conviction that my own security was not the thing I had dreamed it to be came strongly to me. It was possible, of course, to go straight to the saloon and demand explanations; and if I had thought that such action would have helped the poor fellow who lay below in such sore straits, I should have listened to no counsel of personal risk. But the voice of common sense told me to hesitate. I was one man against forty or fifty; I had hope neither of help nor a seconder. How, then, could I assist another? I felt it to be out of the question and that it lay upon me only to wait and to watch—to wait and to watch, it might be, for my preservation against dangers which the imagination could but guess at.

Thus assuring myself, yet hot with excitement, with doubt, and with conjecture, I went toward the saloon, then brilliantly lighted; but at the very door of it I stood again to hear words which added infinitely to all the haunting speculations of that terrible night. They were spoken by Privli, the Italian, to Reuben Joyce, the captain of the yacht, and they were as good English as I would wish to hear.

Had not Adam Monk told me, on our first meeting, that Privli had not a word of my tongue? He had lied to me then.

CHAPTER VI.

I SEEM TO KNOW THE ITALIAN.

THE two men were standing near to the staircase which led to the promenade deck, but they did not observe me as I passed them, and I found Monk alone in the great cabin, where the tables were hid under banks of palms, and cut-glass bottles with many kinds of wine scintillated under the powerful lamps. The saloon was warm with the warmth almost of an African night, and Monk, who had thrown off his coat, lay all his length upon one of the couches. He looked up when I came in, and wore upon his face that pleasing smile which was his prevailing characteristic; but I had no heart to respond to his friendship; indeed, I could hold back my tale only with a great strain upon my self-control. This was hid from him, however; and, when he had pushed the cigars to me, and a steward had brought me iced wine, he began to talk of the concert which the crew had given.

46

"They're wonderful men," said he with animation. "You won't find better hands, aloft or below, if you sailed the world round to sign them. What did you think of their songs?"

"Oh, they sang very well," said I.

"It's evident you're not an enthusiast, doctor!" exclaimed he; "but we shall make you one in good time. Twenty-five days now, and good-by to the *Wanderer*. I always say that with some regret, for I love the yacht."

Instead of answering him, I put a question in my turn.

"Do you find the men invariably well behaved?" asked I.

He searched me with his eyes before he answered.

"As a whole," replied he, after a pause, "there are not sounder men afloat. I could name exceptions, though."

"How do you deal with them?" I went on, following up the confession.

"Deal with them? Why, thoroughly. How do you deal with a spoiled child who turns upon you? They are all spoiled here; and, when they kick against the process, they get justice. I should be sorry for you to see anything of that, doctor."

It was on my lips to tell him that I had seen his justice; but I held it back, thinking that I would sleep upon my perplexity. For his part, he turned the subject and began to speak of the South Atlantic, and so engrossing was his talk that I found myself listening to him with no remembrance of my trouble. When we parted, it was at one bell in the middle watch, and the yacht slept but for the quivering of her shell and the rush of foam in her wake. I told Monk when I left him that sleep was heavy upon me, and that I was going to bed; but when I entered my own cabin the notion of resting was far from me. This night I did what I had never done before: I locked the door of my room, and even peered into the crannies of it as children do who fear the dark. Exert myself as I could, the sight I had seen down there upon the lower deck came again and again to my eyes. In what way had the man offended to meet with such barbarity? how came it that he could thus be treated upon the yacht of one who was described as a prince of justice and of charity? And if such things were possible to others, how did I stand? It even dawned upon

me that the whole story of a strange country, and
of the woman whose picture I had seen, might be
a fabrication; that I might be carried to some
horrible work which I did not dare to imagine. I
determined at last that I would not think about
it; and in the quest of forgetfulness I found
myself lying upon my bed and reading an evening
paper I had bought in London on the very night
they carried me to the yacht.

To read a newspaper is an undertaking if your
brain be at work upon many troubles. You put
the care from your head, and read three lines;
you take up a new care, and add another three
lines to your achievement. I can bring it to my
mind that as I lay upon my bed there, and
skimmed the crumpled print, scarce a word I
read stuck in my memory. I was staring at the
paper, seeming to be absorbed in its page—in
reality a hundred miles away from it. No sooner
would I begin at the word "Police" than a new
problem would present itself to me. I turned
over to "Sport," and the speculation changed
with the column.

Anon I declared that I would read of the outrage at the Café Mirabeau, of that outrage of
which the newsboys cried as I left London; and I

began diligently with the five headlines, and the
picture of the café which had been wrecked by
one of the crazy fanatics then preying upon Paris.
The attempt appeared to succeed. I learned
that the mad deed was supposed to be the work
of Italians, that the police had taken one of them,
and would yet put hands upon the others. I
examined the published portraits of the men ; I
found myself looking into their faces as one who
studies character.

The flow of success continued unchecked until
the name of the Italian Privli, with us upon the
ship, came back to me. Then the paper
dropped upon my pillow. How came it that
Privli, who spoke English fluently, concealed the
fact from me ? What a curious head he had ! I
said to myself, and his hair was red. I remembered that one of the Italians wanted by the
police of Paris had red hair. Somehow, the
paper came into my hands once more. I searched
the faces again ; I looked at them right under the
electric lamp ; I held the print for more than ten
minutes and my eyes scarce left it. When, at the
last, I put it down, or, rather, let it flutter from
my hands, there was no longer left to me a
doubt.

Marco Privli, my fellow-guest upon the yacht, and the man wanted in Paris for the murder of innocent people, taking their recreation in a café, were one and the same person.

The thing was clear beyond dispute. The missing man was described to his finger tips; the rough newspaper portrait of him was the portrait of the Italian upon the *Wanderer;* height, clothes, hair, manner—these the French police had set out in their advertisement—which the English press had copied—with a fidelity and an accuracy which left little hope to the victim. Yet here he was, I made sure, upon this yacht; as securely hid for the moment as though he had been buried. And if the summary of his "past" which the account gave were accurate, no more despicable or petty scoundrel breathed God's air upon earth.

To say that I realized the moment of this discovery when I made it would be hopelessly to misrepresent my thoughts. The truth is that I had lived so many days in a sphere of mysteries, had reasoned with so much and to so little gain, that this new and amazing conviction cast a blight upon my mind and seemed to paralyze it. It was otherwise when I had spoken to the man

in the cage, for then the tangible reality of suffering had moved me to great fears for my own
safety; but when there was added to this the
knowledge that the ship was a haven for cutthroats, and that we had one of them aboard,
then, I say, I could bear with the argument no
longer, and I put it from me as a vain thing and
unprofitable. What it meant I knew no more
than the dead; the possible risk to myself person-
ally I did not care a straw about. Since the night
I had seen the picture of the girl my wish to go
through with the adventure had become stronger
every hour; it was not to be cooled because, for-
sooth, a common assassin was at my elbow, and
the men I made passage with could treat other
men as beasts. Nay, the curiosity begotten of
the whole problem was almost a charm; and the
desire to "know" and to satisfy myself in the
knowledge, above all, the desire to see my
"patient," burned upon me the more with every
knot the yacht made.

It is to be imagined what company of dreams I
had in my sleep that night. The sweet face of
the picture, the pitiful face of the man below, the
pockmarked visage of the Italian, the kindly eyes
of Monk—these looked upon me as the old ques-

tions went whirling through my head, and I tossed
restlessly in my bed. For the first time since I
had been aboard I was glad to get on deck with
daylight ; glad to sniff up the morning air, and to
fill my lungs with it ; glad to cool my brain with
the sparkle of the sea, and to warm my veins with
the breezy walk upon the deserted promenade.
There, at any rate, was neither danger nor haunting spectacle—there, where the boards were white
as ivory in the sunlight, and the men who trod
them masters of triumphant health. And all
about me upon the Atlantic herself, the countless
jewels of light glistening upon the green of the
waves, the play of sporting billows running and
tumbling in the gambol of the breeze, the sense
of sweetness and of vigor and of gentle warmth,
the sparkle of distant sails, and the assurance of
mastery of the deep which comes of a good ship
below one, conspired to put the ill of anticipation from me, and to carry me to those greater
thoughts which the majesty of the lonely ocean
rarely fails to inspire.

Until the change of the watch I remained upon
the deck. I had wandered, in fact, to the hatchway of the engine room, and was standing there
gazing down to that terrible pit of heat and fiery

light when the bells rung. As they were still reverberating a new batch of stokers, washed and trim, descended the iron ladder; and I was not a little astonished to see among them the poor fellow who had lain yesterday a prisoner in the cage. He was now pale enough, and his hair was still uncut; but it seemed to me that my discovery of him had at least brought him liberty; and his nod, a very friendly and humble one, confirmed me in the assumption. And I make sure that he would have spoken a word to me but for the sudden coming of Monk, who put his hand upon my shoulder at the very moment I went to ask the man how he did.

"The top of the morning to you, doctor," said he, "and whatever interests you in our coalhole?"

"A good deal," said I, thinking it no poor chance for giving him a plain word—"that man among others; he wasn't so well when I saw him yesterday."

To my surprise, he made no motion either of anger or surprise; but answered me with another question.

"Do you often concern yourself with rogues?" he asked.

"It depends upon their treatment," cried I, nettled at his imperturbability.

"Their treatment here is as they make it—but I confess that I was weak enough to set that man free as a small compliment to you."

"I appreciate that," cried I; "it was a merciful thing to do."

He shook his head doubtingly.

"Mercy," exclaimed he, "may fall like the gentle dews from heaven, but it often reaches very hard ground, doctor. That man has deserted this ship twice, and would desert again to-morrow if I gave him half a chance. But he won't get the quarter of one."

I thought it curious that there should be need thus to hold the crew of the *Wanderer* in such complete subservience; but I made no reply to him, and, observing my hesitation, he took me by the arm and the gamut of his irresistible spirits was sounded in his ringing laugh.

"My dear fellow," he cried, "you are always dealing with the abstract of life, when you should deal with the concrete. At this moment the concrete is hot coffee and the bread of Vienna. If there was no hot coffee and the bread of Vienna was not baked, you might wear that terrible frown of yours, but, seeing that the stuff is steaming in the saloon, why, *allons*, and the devil take the ' might be.' "

It was a fine argument, and I went off with him, carrying the rare appetite of the sea to the table. The man Privli was not in the saloon, nor did I see anything of him for many days; but I found the cheery companionship of Monk a thing not to be resisted, and in two minutes I was laughing with him.

"Now," said he, after he had poured me a creamy dish of the coffee, "drink that, and when you've drained the bumper we'll have some prune brandy. It's the worst thing for the liver existing, so I hasten to prescribe it for you."

"It will be my turn to-morrow," said I.

" Did you ever think," said he, bounding from subject to subject and falling to work upon the food with healthy vigor, " how curious is the first condition of the life we live now? None of us have any nerves. Our grandfathers drank them away for us. They took the port at night; we, the sons, get up in the morning and drink the soda-water—at least we should do so!"

"Well," said I, sipping the liquor which he now

poured out in a tiny glass that had unmistakably come from Venice, "this is a very good soda water anyway."

"You want cheering," cried he, "so I break my rule never to drink before lunch unless I have the inclination to. And look, now, doctor, we'll go and play it off with deck cricket and a squash ball—after which you will promise me to think about nothing, and to dream about nothing, until we touch our destination. Old man, isn't it a glorious life abroad here? Isn't it a whole existence to breathe this air and tread these decks?"

I nodded a full affirmative.

"Then imitate me and give yourself up to it. To the devil with to-morrow, and a shout for a good cigar! Oh, doctor, I wish I could sell you some of my spirits!"

I told him that he had done better, since he had given me some; and I made up my mind then and there that I would henceforth cast speculation to the dogs, and live the life offered to me until the yacht had cast anchor at her port, and I had come to the home of my patient, and to the master of these mysteries.

CHAPTER VII.

THE BEGINNING OF VERY GREAT EVENTS.

THE dome of the western sky was ablaze with a flame of golden light, chrome at the zenith, scarlet and infinitely red at the horizon, when the sun set upon our fourth day in the Pacific. Until that time my passage in the *Wanderer* had been an unbroken delight, a month of rest and placid ease, an experience pleasant beyond all my experiences. Day by day the same soft breeze of the unruffled sea, the same freshness and strength, the same amazing luxury, had soothed to the forgetfulness of cities and of men; had called us to that fullness of life which is to be had only upon a ship. Day by day we dreamed the hours away, while the foamless waves lapped upon our prow, and the music of the yacht's band was joined to the song of the Atlantic. Day by day I would play with Monk upon the lower decks, or listen to his merry chatter, or join with him on some new enterprise for the amusement of the men. And scarce a week seemed to have passed when we touched for coal at Monte Video; and, coming out of my mental sleep, I said: Here is the end, here is the scene of the work to which I am called. But the yacht remained no more than a few hours in the port of the Argentine; and, when she had taken coal, she began to steam due south again, and the haunting mystery still waited its solution.

It was thus that we passed the Straits of Magellan, with the restless swells of Cape Desire, and, after some hours of heavy rolling and bitter cold, came out at last upon the immensity of the golden Pacific, setting thence a course almost full north and west, and leaving the track of ships bound for New Zealand or for Melbourne. From that time we steamed alone. Hours passed and days and we sighted no sail; had for company only the great gold orb of the sun by day, the rolling world of stars by night. Yet in the very vastness of this queen of oceans the heart was uplifted in silent ecstasy, the mind brought to a great content, the whole man made new with the strength of the unbroken rest and solitude. Nor did I fail here to take to heart the advice of the admirable Monk, and to throw from me all thoughts but those of the present, be the morrow what it might.

I have made mention of our fourth day in the Pacific because it was the day upon which, for the first time since leaving London, there had been signs of bustle in the yacht. From eight bells of the morning watch until sunset men were busy scrubbing machine guns and all bright work, and generally getting shipshape, as though they looked for an early sight of their haven. Monk himself I had not seen since daylight; they told me that he was writing in his cabin; but my surmise that the end of our voyage was not distant was confirmed when I went down to make straight for dinner, and heard a little lad singing most musically the very strangest song I had listened to at sea. I jotted down the words,—for he sung almost at the door of my cabin,—and here is the rough note of them:

> " Where the mountains kiss the sky,
> Where the golden eagles cry,
> Where the stoutest heart may wither,
> Thither—thither
> Hasten, wind and wave, to speed me ;
> Hasten, hasten, spirit, lead me
> 　　To the land I love."

The boy sang gayly enough ; and when I came

into the saloon I found Adam—for so I had come to call Monk—in the best of spirits.

"Trevena," said he, "an extra glass of fizz to-night—there's no need to tell you the why and the wherefore."

"No," said I, "we're almost there, I'm sup-posing."

"Indeed, and we are; and if the weather holds, we let the anchor go in the middle watch."

Pleasant as the voyage had been, I was right glad to drink in his words; and we dined together in fine humor. For weeks past I had ceased to ask myself, "Whither am I going?" Now the question was inseparable from my thoughts, and in some measure welcome, since the answer to it could not long be held back. Another day would not break before I stood with the owner of the yacht and beheld the subject of the entrancing painting in the saloon; the sun would not rise until I had the key to the mys-teries, and the phantoms had shaped themselves. The assurance elated me strangely. I found myself responding gayly to Monk's badinage; the dinner assumed the proportions of a banquet; the noise of the seamen singing and of the bustle upon deck was in keeping with my mood;

the chorus, whose echo floated to us from the
fo'castle, rang in my ears, and I found myself
humming it :

> " When Jack comes home again, boys,
> Then sing with might and main, boys,
> Land ho !   Land ho !"

We decided to take our coffee in the open, and
no sooner had we come up the companion than
the immediate cause of the din which the hands
had set up was apparent. Shining like a star
upon our starboard quarter, yet a great way off, a
beacon rose up and stood out brilliantly above
the silent seas of the Pacific. Small it was when
we first beheld it, yet infinitely bright and cheering amid that desolation of waters ; and it seemed
to me to bear a message as from a friend. Nor
was the spectacle less welcome to the men
who shouted one to the other that they had
come home again, and sang with the hearts of
children because their voyage was ended. As
for my friend Adam, he could scarce keep still
a moment, and the ring of his voice was everywhere like the sound of a trumpet.

" Trevena," he said to me in one of these out-
bursts, " it's home we are, old man, and good

luck to you. If I don't give you a fine time yonder, you are at liberty to kick me."

" I can't thank you enough for what you've done here," said I ; " you've been more than a friend to me."

" Don't talk of that," cried he ; " wait until I gallop you on our heights, and then tell me what you think of us."

" And of the patient," I suggested.

But at this a cloud came upon his face, and I felt again that I did ill to mention the subject.

" Yes," said he, " you will see the patient—and when you see her, think of my words. I speak as a friend, and I say to you, Look out ! "

He turned on his heel and descended to the saloon ; but I, pondering upon his speech, continued to smoke upon the upper deck, and to wonder what mystery hedged itself about that lovely face I had seen in the picture that the mere sight of it should be a danger to men. Nor could I explain the thing in any way, and with its trouble for companion I remained to watch the star-like beacon growing every moment, and appearing as we approached it to rise higher and higher above the water, until at last it stood at a great altitude above the sea, and the path of its light was like a wide yellow road upon the ocean. I judged then that the lantern was upon some cliff at a great height above the shore; but the power of it was beyond that of any light I have known, and the arc it cast upon the waves scintillated with golden gems of dancing irradiance while we were yet many miles from land.

There was no sleep for any man upon the yacht that night. I myself walked the deck until long after eight bells; and even when I went to my cabin, the excitement of the hour kept my brain from resting. For the matter of that, the whole place was so full of the flooding white light which the nearing beacon cast that turn where I would the soft yellow rays followed me. Their deep shadows lay across my floor like slabs of blackened marble; they struck upon the walls in darkening bands; they made zebras upon my bed; and what with watching the light, and listening to the hubbub above and the ringing shouts from the bridge, my attempt to rest was a poor farce to play, and one I did not long attempt.

I had been below an hour or more when the vibrations of the screw stopped suddenly, and a curious silence fell upon the ship. It was broken by the sharp report of the small gun at our bows; and to this we got for answer the heavy booming of a great cannon. A moment later Dennis O'Brien, the Irishman, stepped into my cabin and greeted me with an expanding grin of satisfaction.

"Great news for yer honour," said he, bubbling over with his excitement; "it's there we are, and nowhere else at all—in our own pretty nest, an' no prettier afloat or 'shore. Will you be stepping up and wishing it the top of the morning? It's Mr. Monk that says the same which I'm telling you."

"I'll step up at once, my good man," said I. "That's a fine light you've got, I must say."

"Ye spake truth, sorr. That's the ould lady?"

"And who, pray, may the old lady be?"

"Indade, she just sits at the top of the estab-lishment and keeps her weather eye on the lot of us. The ould lady is divisible twenty miles from the oiland, sorr."

"We have come to an island, then?" exclaimed I, taking up his words quickly.

He looked a little crestfallen.

"Well," said he, "there's some as thinks it's an oiland, and some as differs; and, bedad, oiland or no oiland, it's the most queersome place on

earth, and yer honour can't do better than cast
your eye over it. Mr. Monk looks for ye to
come."

I drew a cape round my shoulders, and mounted
to the hurricane-deck. Reuben Joyce, the skipper,
was very busy upon the bridge getting the ship
warped in her mooring-ground; but Privli and
Adam were talking by the door of the smoking-
room, and the latter now busied himself to interest me.

"Doctor," said he, "your thirty-and-five days
are done. There is the home of my master."

He pointed, with the word, to a huge mound of
rock, rising sheer from the centre of the Pacific;
a vast pyramid, with steep, inaccessible, overshot
cliffs, in many places going up to a height of
two or three thousand feet; a promontory
stretching some distance from us to the westward,
but ending at our place of anchorage in a greater
cone, below the summit of which, as I stood talking to him, that wonderful, insurpassable electric
beacon again burst out.

In a moment the still sea around was alive with
fire. Every board in the yacht's deck stood out
white as in the sun's light. I could now observe
fully the wondrous towering face of the land I

had come to; I could note the barrier-reefs of
coral which shut out the greater island from the
full fury of the Pacific; I could understand why
we had a place of harbourage, though quite near
to us were crags and jutting ridges of rock innumerable; I could see small boats, but chiefly low
ones of a curious shape, almost like squat torpedo-
boats; yet of sign of habitation of the island, or
of the presence of any living being near the ship,
save those the ship had brought there, I could
not see.

Adam watched my astonishment for a spell
without adding to what he had said. The glorious tropic night suited his mood well; for he was
now in mighty good spirits, and when he did
speak to me his voice rippled with laughter.

"Look you," said he presently, walking me away
from the bridge, where the bells were ringing from
the engine-room, and the steam steering gear was
scarce a moment at rest, as they brought the ship
up, "look you, I know your thoughts, Trevena,
and I can read you like a star. You are saying,
'Here's a fraud of a man—a man who offered to
take me to one of the loveliest places on earth,
and who has brought me to this patch of barren
rock.' Well, I admit your case; but another

hour will serve to land us, and then you shall judge me."

"I must say," said I, "that the exterior of your place is not exactly bewitching, but I'll hope for a surprise when we get ashore. You haven't told me yet how you do get ashore. Those cliffs must be three thousand feet high, and inaccessible. You don't suggest hauling me up in a basket?"

"Not for a moment."

"Then the shore is on the other side of the island."

"Indeed, no; it lays exactly under the great light there."

"In which case," said I, "you have a tunnel through the rock?"

"Doctor," said he, "you're the most persevering man I ever saw. Won't you wait and enjoy something new without spoiling it. And look now, you said there was nothing pretty about us. Well, what do you think of that?"

He pointed to the headland upon which the beacon stood, and I saw that a strange thing had come about while he spoke. From a great natural spout, opening at an altitude of five hundred feet or so in the side of the black and iron rock, there was gushing a torrent of water, and with the water there was steam, which now floated up in wavy, snowlike clouds, and was thus lit with the rays of the mighty light until it reflected a thousand entrancing shapes of a glowing and a radiant colour. For ten minutes at the most the outpour continued. Then the steam clouds floated like gas-lit balloons away above the silent ocean; the spring that had burst out seemed to be quenched; the black volcanic rock stood naked again.

"Well," said Adam, "how did you find that?"

"It was a fine sight," said I.

"It was a welcome from one of our vapour springs," cried he; "you shall see more of them inside—and soon, by Jove! for there's the gun!"

The gun of which he spoke flashed across the sea from a bastion high in the face of the cliff. We answered it with three reports, and immediately after Reuben Joyce himself begged me to step ashore.

CHAPTER VIII.

I GO BELOW THE SEA.

THE skipper of the yacht was at the gangway when I came up to him. Dawn had now begun to break over the sea—a floating, tremulous dawn heralded by a restless movement of the swell—a dawn opening at last with long bands of softening light, which poured upon the gigantic rocks of the island before me until the land seemed to tower up from the sea, a very mountain of power and of defiance. But the ocean herself shone infinitely green in the morning; you could look below to ultimate depths, where the coral reefs were building and the deeper channels were scoured; you could watch the strange fish, the nautilus, the anemone; and there was a sense of delicious warmth in all the air—a sense that it was a joy to live, a delight even to breathe.

"Doctor," said the skipper, "you're going to make a queer passage, but a short one. You are going below the sea. I shall be with you in the ship, if that will be any consolation to you. Were you ever in this kind of craft before?"

The craft he pointed to was a low-pitched black vessel, looking very much like a torpedo-boat. She lay at the foot of the yacht's ladder; but of deck she had none, being round above her water-line, and possessing but one hatchway, which was full amidships. This appeared to have a cover of steel, but it was now unscrewed; and I stepped, at the skipper's invitation, into the small iron cabin, and waited for what was to come. But my heart was in my mouth; and I hope never to know a similar quarter of an hour so long as I live.

The second to step aboard was Adam; the third was Joyce himself. When we were all seated, the skipper went to a frame with many levers, but Adam began to banter me.

"Trevena," said he, "I wish I'd thought to have offered you a whiskey and soda before we started; if we get stuck below the sea here for a fortnight, you'll forget the flavour."

"That wouldn't trouble me," cried I; "and as you're with me, I'll make myself easy. It's quite certain that you would not go where any such catastrophe as a fortnight without whiskey was possible. Fire on!"

"But you've made your will?" asked he.

"Oh, two or three times," said I, "and you're the sole executor. I trust upon you to see that every creditor I have is honestly paid a farthing in the pound."

"Have done with it," cried the skipper; and at the same time he roared, "Let her go!" to those on the yacht, and touched one of the levers at his side.

The small craft now began to move toward the headland of dark rocks; the beautiful shape of the steamship that had carried me from Europe became visible from stem to stern. As we gained speed and began to ride through the long swells, regardless of the water we shipped, I could make out presently the various serrations and shapes of the mighty barrier of volcanic rock toward which we were rushing. Here glistening as with quartz and mica, there as with jasper and feldspar, the whole height of the cliffs of a sudden were struck by the flash of the sun, which leaped up above the waters and bathed them in the flooding golden light of a Pacific morning. The lapping waves now sparkled with a delicious radiance of light. The yacht behind us showed balls of fire whenever the sun touched her brass-work; nothing could have been purer than the flowing seas; nothing more elevating than that superb coming of day in that heart of the Southern Ocean.

We had gone half a mile, perhaps, and could already hear the beat of the surf against the rocks when the skipper spoke again.

"All hands below," said he; and at this he moved another lever, and the cap which fitted upon the top of our cabin glided into its place, and then was screwed down from below. I could now feel that warmed air was rushing across my face from some tube, the thud of pumps was audible in the fore-compartment of the ship. Nor was the sense of semi-suffocation altogether wanting; and the knowledge that I was screwed down in an iron-hole as securely as a man is screwed in a coffin sent a cold chill creeping down my spine. I had an inclination to cry out aloud, to jump up and demand to be released; and when at length I felt the ship sinking rapidly into the sea, and could watch the surpassingly green waters playing upon the black windows of the cabin, I believe that I gave up hope of seeing any land or any man again.

One stay I had in this supreme moment, and it came to me from the confidence of the others. As

the vessel sank and Adam sat back in his seat
and sang a fragment of the first chorus from "Les
Huguenots," the skipper, with immobile face,
looked through the spy-glass before him, and kept
his hand to the regulator. Once, indeed, Adam
touched me upon the shoulder. It was to point
out to me a great shark butting at one of the
lenses, his pilot-fish flashing by him like silver
streaks. A more horrible apparition could not
be imagined than that of this ferocious, threaten-
ing brute, which came at us with vast distended
jaws and eyes that burned with anticipation.

Anon the scene changed. The boat began to
slacken in her speed. In the place of the
unbroken green sea around us were walls of rock
and myriads of haunting shapes. I had a conviction that we were passing through a tunnel; yet
was this the least of the wonders, for the tunnel
was lighted by electricity, the lamps glowing
beneath the rushing water, and casting a golden
green light upon our lenses which surpassed in
beauty of hue any thing I have ever seen. Here,
too, were myriads of fish darting, sleeping, even
fighting; fish with hideous pointed heads, fish of
a hundred colours, glorious anemones, spreading
weeds, coral of amazing shape and form. It was,

indeed, as a scene from some marvel book that one had read; some creation of enchantment and not of reality.

The passage of the tunnel occupied five good minutes, so far as my rough reckoning goes. I could not speak to my companions as we went, for the thud of the engines, the squelching of the air from the tubes, and the rattle of the pumps which fed them, forbade all hearing. Presently, however, the ship began to steady herself; then came muffled through the water the dull reverberations as of some mighty gong ringing at the surface of the sea. A moment later I knew that we were rising; at the end of a minute Captain Joyce turned the hatch with the lever, and raised it off the ship. Once more I could breathe; once more assure myself that I was not screwed down in an iron coffin, which was to carry me to a living death.

"Now," said Adam, when the hatch was off, "I won't say you're there, doctor, because you're exactly two hundred feet from there. But if you'll look up, you'll see your destination."

I gazed up to see that we were in a huge pit upon a dark and still lake, a quarter of a mile long by a hundred yards wide. Steep, iron-like, inac-

cessible rocks bound us in on all sides.   There was
not even the sign of a ladder—only a small landing-stage with two men.

"Well," said I, "it isn't what I should call
Buckingham Palace, and you don't seem blessed
with many stairs.   Are we to climb up with our
hands and teeth?"

"Seeing that we haven't any dentists in the
island, I can't recommend that," cried he; "but
the light is deceiving you.   That black line above
us is the line of the lift."

"I'm glad to see it," said I, "and may I never
ride in a hansom cab like that again as long as I
live."

"If ever you're to leave here, you'll have to
make the passage again," cried he; "it's our front
door, and we've no servant's entrance.   For the
matter of that, doctor, it's a very good front-
door, too, as some of the governments will find
out if ever they come to rap upon it."

"Yes," replied I, "there can be nothing like it
in the world."

"Nothing!" said he; "and as we sailed the
world ten years to find it, we should know.   But
after you——"

"Is the Italian ashore?" I asked suddenly.

He bent forward and whispered to me:

"I wish he were twenty fathoms down below," and with no more ado we entered the lift and mounted through the gorge. Ten seconds later a flood of sunlight fell upon my eyes, and all the surpassing beauties of the Isle of Lights lay at my feet.

CHAPTER IX.

THE ISLAND OF LIGHTS.

THERE was at the head of the lift a company of soldiers, numbering fifty, perhaps, and clad in an exceeding pretty uniform of white and gold. They all carried swords with cunningly wrought blades shaped like the blades of cimetars; and I noticed that revolvers were stuck in their belts. A young officer, who had the look of a Russian, gave the word to "present arms" as we arrived, and immediately the men formed round us, and began to march with us toward our destination.

I have said that when I came up from the gorge of the sea the whole beauty of this wondrous island lay before my eyes; and I confess it was to the island that I looked now, rather than to the little company of men. From the sea I had observed nothing but the bare aspect of a mighty natural tower, rising sheer upon all sides above the waves. What a contrast, then, was the succession of hill and valley, of shining gardens and limpid lakes, which now fell upon my view. Trees

of all sizes and forms; palms whose spreading
leaves made tents in themselves; cypresses casting great waves of delicious shade; cocoanuts in
thousands; bread-fruit trees; long and infinitely
green grasses, shooting up in all the meadows;
orchids of the rarest, richest hues; creepers, climbing plants, roses in amazing profusion. Truly,
the first vision of that paradise, the first breath
of its sweetly perfumed airs, was an opening of
heaven to me, of the undiscovered land where the
golden age forever runs.

Of all these things I had now but the scantiest
view, for our guides hurried us along a fine path
of gravel bordered by sweeping shrubs of maize
and quaint firs and palms heavy in the leaf; and
so they carried us to a long white building which
was set on a high place, and commanded a view
of the whole valley beneath. As we went, Adam
told me at once what the object of the journey
was.

"The count," said he, "who is, I may tell you
now, the owner of this place, and of the lives of
all of us, will see you directly. When the interview is over, it may be that he will wish you to
see the patient. Take my advice, and say nothing
of the portrait I showed you upon the yacht."

"The patient is his daughter, is she not?"

"His only daughter. She was born in Vienna eighteen years ago. Count Andrea was then the chief minister in Austrian-Poland. The ingratitude of courts and the love of humanity drove him from the world. He came here after many years of wandering, and here he—and all of us— will end our lives. Oh, my dear Trevena! learn to love the count, if you would love the noblest, greatest man that ever trod God's earth."

"I will try, for your sake. Is this his house we are at now?"

"No other; and we needn't fear to wake him, for he always rises with the sun."

We entered the house as he spoke, or rather the courtyard of it, odorous with the perfume of a thousand flowers. It was a great circular chamber, with a gilded dome high above us, and a mighty basin of marble at its centre. Sun-fish, and others of gold and silver, and rich blues, and strange variegations, swam among the floating lilies and great bell-shaped shrubs of the crystal water. There were birds of gorgeous plumage, parroquets, white rooks, stately storks, kingfishers chattering and fluttering in the branches of the spreading palms; the soft sounds of fountains

splashing was like music to the ears. A few
servants, in rich liveries of white,—for white was
the prevailing colour on the island,—guarded the
entrance to other apartments giving off from this
entrance-hall; but scarce had we waited the tick
of a clock, when a serving-man in a richer dress
than the others beckoned us to follow him, and
when we had passed through two small and
simply furnished rooms we stood in the presence
of the count himself.

For a spell I could find it possible only to
observe the extraordinary richness of the room
in which I was, a room which surpassed anything
that I could conceive possible in the attainment of
artistic perfection. It was a long room, thirty feet
by thirty-five I should judge, and the scheme of
it was the faintest, most captivating shade of
green. From its roof there depended lamps in
silver filigree work, but the frieze itself appeared
to be of solid ivory, while the walls below were
almost smothered in the very choicest water-colour
drawings. For seats, there were lounges in gorgeous tapestry-work, and scores of little inlaid
tables were crowded with ornaments in Sévres
and Dresden and fine bronze-work. In one
corner I observed a great clock shaped like the

full figure of a man whose arms held up a dial, and I saw that a crucifix was nailed to the wall above the lounge whereon the count now sat.

Upon the face of this man, in whom I felt so potent an interest, there was glowing a soft light of the sun which fell through windows of the faintest stained glass. He seemed to be an old man, and somewhat infirm, and was dressed in the uniform of the Austrian Guard. His iron-gray beard fell almost to his waist; his hands were long and talon-like; his face was worn with furrows and wrinkles, and was white and bloodless. Yet his eyes spoke strongly of a fire of thought and action burning in his mind. They were eyes that could lie very still and peaceful, and yet could turn upon a sudden with the devouring gaze of one who reads you before you speak, who knows your thoughts almost as you shape them.

When we entered the room there were three attendants by the lounge of the count; but he rose on seeing me, and stood up as straight and erect as a man of twenty.

"Dr. Trevena," said he, in English as good as my own; "an old man welcomes you with all his heart, and thanks you for coming here."

With that he turned to Adam, and greeted him

with great affection; but no sooner were the words done than he raised his hand, and all withdrew from the room. Then he bade me seat myself.

"Doctor," said he, "before I talk to you, let them set us something. Try our home-grown coffee and our home-grown liqueur. I think they will differ from anything you have tasted in Europe."

He touched a gong at the suggestion, and a servant placed before us two porcelain cups full of very thick, rich coffee, and two small glasses of a liquor which was exceeding pleasant upon the tongue, having the flavour of nectarines strong about it. The count drank his coffee at a draught, and then, passing me a very fine Egyptian cigarette, he lighted one himself, and began to speak.

"You will have been asking yourself," said he, in a very gentle voice, "what sort of man I am, ever since you set foot upon my yacht. And I should not blame you if you came to a very ill opinion of me."

"Indeed, I have done nothing of the sort," replied I. "Mr. Monk has taken too good a care of your reputation."

"Ah," cried he, "that was like him.   And so he speaks well of me?"

"He does; no man could speak better."

"And he has hinted to you why I was led to commit what must have looked to you like an outrage?"

"He gave me no reason other than the need for my services."

"Exactly; that is the only reason.   I have here, doctor, a community of six hundred souls, which it is the ambition of my life to protect against powers and people that would injure them. Many of these men are hunted fugitives; some are undeserving of my help; others have become exiles in an honest attempt to better their fellow-creatures, to upraise the poor, to mitigate human suffering, to alter that woe of destiny which presses so heavily on all humanity in this fateful century.   These men are my children.   I have rescued them—some from the prisons of France, some from Siberia, some from New Caledonia, some from the Isles de Salut.   I take them from the world, and I admit them to the brotherhood of my wealth and of my home.   I have formed, as you may see, and as you will see in my own time, a city which is impregnable against the powers.

The ships of a thousand nations could not hunt me from this, my home, while my people are faithful to me. None the less is it necessary that I guard, so far as may be in my power, against every danger of the discovery of my retreat. For that reason I was compelled to bring you here by stealth. Is it a good reason?"

I think I must have nodded my head in answer, for the man's tale was so amazing that I could find no words upon my tongue. When he began to speak again his voice was yet softer than it had been, and he bent forward toward me as one who invites confidence.

"Doctor," said he, "if you forgive the means, the end is soon told. I have informed you that there are six hundred souls in this island, all very dear to me. There is one among them for whom I would shed every drop of my blood, and thank God if it could help her. I refer to my daughter, Fortune; the daughter of my dead wife, whom I married in Glasgow. Cut off here as I am, in a work which I believe to be the work of Almighty God, this child of mine is like a chain of roses round my heart. She is the softening link in every fetter of anger I am tempted to forge; she is the sweet, blessed influence of my life; she is—

ay, a thousand times—the angel in the house.
Need I tell you that she is your patient, and that
to see her I have brought you all these thousands
of miles?"

"Can you tell me anything of her symptoms?"
I asked.

"Alas! I have no terms which would help a
medical man. We have here with us a young
Russian—Kryganovski—whom I brought out of
Siberia two years ago, and he got some knowledge
of medicine at Moscow. He declares she is suffering from a very gradual decay of mental power."

"How does the decay show itself—any strange-
ness of action, aberrations, wanderings?"

"Not exactly; but great excitability of mind,
often a trance-like condition, enduring for twenty
or thirty hours. Sometimes she will weep for
days together; sometimes sit moodily, as if all
the world were dead to her. As the months pass,
doctor, I feel that she is, indeed, sinking into
her grave, and drawing me down with her. Save
her life and I will reward you as physician was
never rewarded yet. Restore her to me, and I
will be grateful as man never was. Give life to
her cheeks, and whatever wish your imagination
can conceive that wish will I gratify."

"One question more, and I will see her," said
I. "Have you any reason to suspect that affection—nay, love—for any man is at the bottom of
the trouble?"

He looked at me seriously as he spoke. Then
he brought his fist heavily upon the table before him.

"Dr. Trevena," said he, "the love of my
daughter is not for any man; let none dare to
speak to me of it."

Passion dominated the count, stood out lividly
in his eyes. It seemed to me, when I remembered
the impression the picture had made upon me,
that I stood in infinite peril in consenting for a
moment to see the child; but before I could say
ay or nay he had touched his gong, and servants
were ready to conduct me to her chamber.

CHAPTER X.

THE SUBJECT OF THE PICTURE.

THE count spoke a few words in German to the man-servant who now appeared before him; and when he had got his answer he led the way from the room. We passed quickly through another chamber, which was filled with books from floor to ceiling; thence we entered a little garden, which was full of odorous blooms and tropic palms. I learned that his daughter's apartments were at the far side of this acre of flower and fern, and as the count went he said some words to warn me against my welcome.

"My daughter," said he, "is not likely to prove a ready patient. She has theories of her own upon medical science, and believes that physicians can minister to ailments, but not to disease. I fear you will find her untractable and somewhat obstinate, doctor."

"The symptom of her trouble, count," said I. "These things are invariably to be set down to an abnormal condition of mind or body; they do

not disturb me at all. I have made it the purpose of my life to study the brain, and knowledge
begets confidence. If she is to be cured, I will
cure her."

"That shall be a great day in your life," said
he; and with that he entered his daughter's apartments and knocked upon the door of her room.

At the second knock the door was thrown open,
and we passed into the chamber of the girl. It
was a small room, but the beauty of it was not to
be questioned. I saw that it was hung in blue
and silver, and that a conservatory of unusual
size opened at the far end of it. Great couches
of ebony with tapestry covers, as well done as
the Gobelins tapestries at Windsor, served in the
place of chairs. There was a harp in one corner;
a grand piano, in satinwood, with panels painted
by modern French and English masters, in
another; an organ with silvered pipes was built
into the wall at the end which faced the conservatory. I observed that the room was lighted by
chandeliers of Venetian glass filled with wax
tapers, and that the electric light, used everywhere in the apartments of the count, was not
here to be seen. But the number of paintings
was no less than in the other chambers, and

flowers of great perfection and size sprang up in every nook and cranny.

All this, as I say, was to be seen at a glance; but my eyes were turned almost immediately from a contemplation of the mere material to that of the human now before me. The count's daughter lay upon a lounge drawn near to the open window. She was clothed in a morning gown of pure white, having a girdle of solid gold about her waist, and the mother-of-pearl clasp with the golden letters at her breast. Her auburn hair was knit up in a great coil, without ornament; and, save for the girdle of gold, no jewellery of any sort was upon her dress or her fingers. I observed at once the singular sweetness of her face even in repose; but the amazing eyes, which were alight with the fire of passion and of intellect in the picture, were now drooping and dull. Nevertheless did I feel that the strange, unavoidable, inexplicable spell which the painting had cast upon me was renewed, intensified, made more real in the presence of the living woman to whom my skill was to minister.

When we entered the room there were two persons with my patient. One was a young girl dressed much after the fashion of a London

hospital nurse; the other was a man, perhaps of
twenty-five years of age, a fair-haired man, and
one of great stature. The count introduced him
at once; but he turned upon me a savage look,
and I saw that my presence was not welcome to
him.

"Dr. Trevena," said the count, "this is my
friend Kryganovski, of whose services to my
daughter I have made mention. He will now
gladly leave the case to you. Let me introduce
you to it."

The words were spoken flippantly; but the
man's exceeding love for his daughter stood
marked in his look—nay, even in his gesture. As
for the Russian, he drew back with sullen ill-will,
and immediately left the room. Then I turned
to the couch and to my patient.

"I make the acquaintance of your daughter
with infinite pleasure, count," said I; "it is my
hope that I may now have a long conversation
with her."

"In which case I am better away," said he. "I
shall await you in my room, doctor."

Thus were we left—the girl and I—the nurse
alone witnessing our interview. I drew a couch
near to hers, and looked into her eyes. She was

very pale—pale to loveliness; her skin was clear as paper or cream; there was a flush, almost a hectic flush, of red upon her cheeks. Nor for some minutes would she look at me, turning away with that which was near to rudeness, and playing with a little mandoline which she held in her hands.

I was the first to break the silence.

"I am hoping that you speak English," said I, at a venture.

"Oh, indeed!" she cried; "and suppose I did not, how funny that would be!"

"But you speak it admirably, I find," said I next.

"I was ten years in London," she exclaimed; "long enough to get an accent."

"London is my home," said I, encouraged but a little. "I have come from London to see you."

"What a waste of time!" cried she, striking a chord upon the instrument. "Doctor, if you'll take my advice, you'll go back there at once."

"Well," said I, "now that I see you, I think you are right. There is nothing whatever the matter with you."

It was a word at hazard, but it did more than a thousand questions could have done.

No sooner had I said it than she turned upon

me those wondrous eyes of hers, and I saw that
they were full of laughter.

"Oh, doctor," she said, "tell me that again."

"With pleasure," said I. "You appear to me
to be perfectly well, but you want change. If I
could prescribe for you as I would, I should order
a dance once a week and a picnic every other
day as good things to begin upon."

"And you don't want me take feeding things
out of ugly bottles?" she asked; "you don't want
to feel my pulse, or put a piece of wood upon my
chest?"

"Some day," said I, "we will do that, just to
remind you that I am a doctor; in the meanwhile
tell me about these trances of yours. I have
heard about them from the count, and am
interested."

The brightness left her face when I spoke of
trance; and her eyes lighted up with a look
which was one of fear and loathing and of very
great pain.

"My trances!" exclaimed she; "oh, doctor,
they make me shudder to think of them. When
one comes upon me I am like a dead woman—a
dead woman who can see and hear and know all
that is happening near to her. What I suffer

then, I could never tell you. Sometimes
struggle for hours, yet cannot raise my hanc
The feeling is dreadful; it is death, and a thou
sand times worse than death. I fear often tha
they will carry me out while I still live and bur
me; and that thought nearly drives me mac
What could my gratitude to you be if you cure
me of this awful illness!"

Her face had flushed crimson while she spoke
and she lay panting upon the couch, a swee
picture of beauty and of weakness. I availe
myself of her outbreak to take her hand in mine
but my own fingers trembled at the warmth c
her touch, and for some moments I could scarc
count the beat of her pulse.

"Your trance," said I, speaking with wha
gentleness of voice I could command, "may b
set down to a general lowness of condition. I
you will permit me one moment, I will listen t
your heart. I think we can cure this with ver
little trouble."

She did not resist and I placed my stethoscop
upon her chest. Her heart was organically sounc
but was doing its functions very ill; was, in fac
at a great ebb of weakness. In the same way,
found that her lungs were whole, though she ha

wasted in her anæmic condition, and was thin
and weak. It seemed to me that I could cure
her if only she would be reasonable; and I
thought that I had made such good progress that
I might hazard the subject of medicines. Nay,
my desire to save her became stronger every
moment I was with her; and in the searching
glance of her eyes I drew the deepest inspirations
from my skill.

"Tell me," said I suddenly, "you would do
much to have no more trances?"

"I would do anything!" she cried. "Keep me
from that awful sleep and I will be as obedient
as a child."

"You would even take some tabloids I will
make up for you?"

She pulled a wry face.

"I thought you prescribed dances," said she.

"Certainly; dances for sweets, iron for bitter.
But, of course, if you won't take it, you must
have more trances."

She shuddered at the thought.

"You are like the rest of them, after all," said
she; "you can do nothing without blue bottles
and a twelfth part to be taken three times a day.
And they said you were so clever!"

"Well," said I, "whether I am clever or no, you shall tell me when I have been here a month and if you don't learn to like me a little then, I will go back to London."

She turned upon me with an interested look.

"Tell me about England," cried she; "it will be better medicine than any you could make for me. Remember, doctor, that I am shut up in this place for life; shut up with murderers and felons and hateful men, who live upon my father and would take his life to-morrow if they dared. Oh, it is a dreadful punishment! What have I done to deserve it?"

"Does your father never take you to Europe?" I asked.

"He will never leave what he is pleased to call his kingdom," replied she. "He will stay until he dies, or those who live upon him kill him. There is no hope for me. I am buried here forever."

She began to work herself up into a state of great excitement at the thought, and the hysteria which was her chief ailment, came upon her with tears and wild weeping. In her abandonment to grief she was no less pretty than when I had first seen her; and her amazing auburn hair now fell all about her body, and her breast rose and fell like the sea with her emotion. It lay upon me then to use all my skill to soothe her, and I put my hands upon her brow, and began to exert my whole mind to quieten her. I found that she was a good subject for hypnotism, for presently she ceased to weep, and fell into an even, satisfying sleep; and when I had willed that she should sleep for some hours, I crept from the room and left her to her nurse.

But already my mind was burning with an uncontrollable longing for her; and, as I came into the garden before the count's house, it seemed to me that, if he could have read my heart, the affair had ended there and then.

CHAPTER XI.

I FACE A GREAT DANGER.

WHEN I came into the garden, my head full of hope and fear and of many emotions, a glorious sun of morning was pouring upon the multi-coloured flowers, and lighting with a thousand hues the gushing waters of the fountains. I could look from the high paths of the garden over the verdurous glades and shady forests of the island : and I did not fail to observe the shimmer of white houses, and of other great buildings shin-ing as with brick or marble in the powerful rays. Here were spires and domes of infinite beauty, minarets as of mosques, the Gothic nave of a great church, a building of Grecian design which seemd to be a theatre, the iron gates of a wooded park, the mirror-like surface of lakes, the spray and foam of vast fountains. It was a scene to engross, to fascinate—a scene to recall the memory of fabulous lands, to bring the mind to a great joy in the possession of life and sight.

I stood, for some minutes after leaving the

chamber of Fortune, wondering at the beauties
unfolded before me. It may be that mingled
with my meditations were feverish and disquiet-
ing anticipations of the immediate future. I
knew then that, whatever should come to pass,
the face of the count's daughter could never be
blotted from my memory; that neither the hazard
of suffering, nor the danger of my environment,
could compel me to think of her as I had thought
hitherto of women I had known. And in this
reflection I began to ask myself what was my
duty to the count; how I stood with him who
had been so ready to give me his confidence.

The sound of a step upon the path turned
me from my problem in social jurisprudence. I
looked up, to see Kryganovski, the Russian, waiting as if he would speak to me. But he had
strong passion written upon his face; and when
he had made a gesture and had advanced two
steps toward me, he of a sudden turned upon
his heel and left the garden. The action was
surprising, at the least; and it occurred to me
that the man resigned his case with ill will; but
I put the matter from my mind, and with no
more delay I sought the count.

He was waiting for me in his library. I divined

that he had been pacing up and down looking for my coming; but he restrained himself from any outburst of wild questioning, and uttered the simple monosyllable:

"Well?"

I answered him as he would have wished.

"Count," said I, "it is early to promise, but I believe that I can cure your daughter in a month."

At this saying he fell upon his knees in prayer, and for some moments his eyes were full of great thankfulness and gratitude. When he rose up he took both my hands in his and held them for long minutes, while all his anxiety took shape in many questions.

"You can cure her," said he. "Then you do not fear paralysis of the brain?"

"Such talk is child's nonsense," cried I. "She is suffering from pure hysteria."

"And you have prescribed for her?"

"I have promised to; but it suddenly occurs to me that we want drugs."

"Nay," said he; "there is no drug in the pharmacopœia which I have not in my cabinet."

"That is great news; it would be too much to suggest that you have tabloids."

"Indeed, I have a complete case of them. I

will now put it into your care. When you have
looked at it, let me beg of you to rest, for I hear
you had a long night upon the yacht."

"I will take you at your word; my eyes are
full of sleep. I don't think I have closed them
for twenty hours."

He was now very light of heart and cheery in
his talk, and he led me to his medicine-chest;
and when I had admired its completeness he rang
for them to show me to the suite of rooms that
had been placed at my disposal.

"Doctor," said he, "welcome again, and the
thanks of all my heart for your service. It will
be my work to make your life here a pleasure,
and a happy remembrance. To-morrow I will
begin to show you some of the wonders of my
kingdom. You have learned already that it is
a land of many beauties, of unfailing sun and
flowers; and whatever it contains, of that you
are to consider yourself master."

He bowed to me with all an Austrian's courtesy,
and his servant led me through the gardens again,
and so to a broad road, whereby, when we had
walked a few hundred yards, we came to a low
bungalow, which I learned was to be my home.
It was furnished with a splendour equal to that

I had seen in the count's own house; and I found
that I could see from my windows, through a
chasm of the cliffs, the Pacific and the outlying
coral reefs which defended the island. Here, in
a bedroom lighted by the electric light, and full
of books and flowers and wonderful grasses
springing up from porcelain pots, I lay upon a
great bed of ebony-wood, and even with my mind
resting upon the strange things that had happened to me, I fell into a fretful sleep, and
dreamed again of the consultation, and of the new
force which had come into my life. For thus it
was, always from this time, that the eyes of the
child were ever looking into mine, and, waking
or sleeping, I seemed to feel the touch of her
hand, her sweet breath falling softly upon my
cheeks.

My fatigue must have been great, for I slept
the afternoon through; and when I awoke at
sundown I had no inclination to rise from my
bed. At that hour servants brought me a lavish
dinner, and set it out with a fine show of silver
and of cut-glass; others kindled a fire of sweet-
smelling logs upon my hearth, for it fell cold at
the first of the night; and when they had my
assurance that I would not join the count's party

until the morning, they withdrew and left me to
myself.

I partook slightly of the food brought to me
before the departure of the serving-men; and
now lit one of the cigars of which an inlaid cabinet at my bedside was full. The cigars were of
the finest tobacco, and, by the taste of them, such
as only the Rothschilds in all Europe may smoke.
There was a cup of the exquisite coffee set upon
my little table, but I had turned down my light,
and the flicker of the log fire alone cast a dull
and restless glare upon the painted ceiling and
fine panelling of my chamber.

In this half-rest and half-light I lay thinking
for more than an hour, while the perfect tobacco
quieted my nerves and brought upon me a great
state of content. At that time all the wonderful
things that had happened to me since I left
London passed rapidly through my thoughts. I
remembered my last night in Welbeck Street, my
journey upon the yacht, my first amazement at
the picture of Fortune, the mighty electric light,
my journey below the sea, and it was as though
it had all passed a year ago, rather than within
the forty days. Then I remember thinking how
curious it was that the count should have found

an island which could be reached only by a tunnel beneath the sea. I recalled the dread of that passage in the submarine boat; I dwelt upon the count's threat that he would hear no man speak of love for his daughter. And in the same thought I confessed to myself that I loved her.

How it was I cannot tell, but as these reflections came to me, the image of the Russian, Kryganovski, suddenly flashed upon my vision. It occurred to me that the man's eyes were full of hate when I entered Fortune's room in the morning. Was it possible that he, too, had been a victim to her waywardness and her beauty? If so, his anger was to be explained; it remained to be proved if it was to be feared.

My cigar had gone out as this speculation troubled me, and the moon had risen, its light flooding through the windows of my bungalow. I could see away over the island, where many lamps and lanterns were as stars among the woods and gardens; I heard the music of a string band floating up from the valley. The sweet harmonies soothed me to sleep. I had begun to doze lightly when the sound of a footstep in the veranda waked me with a start.

For some moments I did not move, thinking

perhaps that a servant came to see how I fared.
Yet I thought it curious that whoever visited my
room should come so steathily.   And this feeling
was stronger when, anon, there fell across my floor
in the moonlight a warning shadow.   Plain as
day it was, and easily to be recognized—the
figure of a tall man, and that man Kryganovski.
I could even see that he had no hat upon his
head, and came step by step with the cunning
and the quiet of a footpad.

"What did the man want?" I asked the
question again and again, as his shadow passed
from one window to another, and became fixed at
last within a hand's-breadth of the door.   There
he stood; and it was ridiculous to see how queer
a shape the silhouette of him had as he peered
through the glass, and seemed to be listening.
For my part I determined that I would not inter-
rupt him, and I feigned sleep; but I began to
fear exceedingly when I remembered that I was
not armed, and had no weapon, not so much as a
common knife, within my reach.   And during the
whole of it the Russian stood at the door, until,
his shadow suddenly vanishing, I knew that he
was coming toward my bed.

Of my feelings during that long-drawn moment

I can tell you nothing. So far as recollection
helps me now, I recall only that I lay as one fas-
cinated. There, in the light of the moon, the
man was crawling toward my bed, hate and
resentment shining from his eyes. I could see
the blade of a knife gleaming below his right
hand. I remember that he wore a mess jacket,
and that his shirt had burst open at the stud-
hole. But for the moment I was unable to lift
a hand or to utter a cry. I was rigid with the
fear of death, tongueless, incapable of doing
aught but listen to the rapid beatings of my
heart.

In this state I lay until the man was almost
upon my bed. With a sudden motion he raised
himself from his stooping posture, and made a
quick step toward me; but this was the breaking
of the spell upon me. With a loud cry for help,
I sprang from the bed, and the blow which he had
aimed struck the clothes as they fell from my
grasp. Before he could strike again I was at the
door; but he had, by what means I know not,
secured it behind him, and thus was I left at his
mercy. From this it was idle to expect anything.
The fiercest passion existing, the passion of
uncontrollable jealousy, was upon him, and he

sprang at me again as I stood fumbling at the
lock. So well aimed was his blow at this second
attempt that his knife cut the skin of my neck,
and then buried itself deeply in the wood of the
panel. There, as it stuck quivering, I grasped
him with all my strength, and for long moments
we swayed together, sending small tables rolling
upon the floor, and the blooms in showers upon
the soft mats beneath our feet. Nor did I doubt
for a moment what the end of it would be; for I
felt that he had three times my strength, and was
crushing the life slowly out of me. Thus, foot
by foot, we staggered across the room, and fell
together at the last quite near to the fire of logs
and branches burning upon my hearth.

Now, how the notion came to me I cannot
divine, but that heavy fall saved my life. As I
lay within a yard of the fire, it occurred to me
suddenly that I could make a weapon of one of
the lumps of wood then aglow with flame.
Almost with the thought, my right hand pulled
a brand from the hearth; and, while the Russian
knelt low in the endeavour to choke me, I trust
the burning wood in his face; and, with a great
cry of pain, he put his hands to his eyes and fell
upon the floor. In the same minute the door of

my room was burst open and a dozen men, with swords in their hands, were between us.

During the height of the hullabaloo, it was impossible for me for a space to make myself understood. The Russian was bawling out with the pain in his eyes; the troopers seemed ready to kill him as he lay. And we were just in the thick of the noise and the din when the count himself, and Adam with him, came running up the veranda.

"Trevena," said Adam, speaking first, "in God's name, what has happened?"

"Your friend the Russian can best explain that," said I.

At this the count turned upon the man a look which meant much.

"Take him out," said he, stamping his foot, "and let the others come to me."

They picked up the man and hurried him from the room, while all overwhelmed me with their questions. Ten minutes later the sound of a great bell boomed over the island.

"They are ringing his death-knell," said Adam to me in a whisper; "he will not see another sun."

CHAPTER XII.

A NIGHT OF WAKING.

I HAVE said that there was a babbling of tongues and much noise in my room during the whole of this episode; and it may be set down to this cause that I did not, at the hearing, understand fully the meaning of Adam's words. Nor had I any opportunity to answer them, for the count had taken my hand in his, and again and again he begged my pardon for the outrage of which I had been the victim.

"I would have given my hands full of jewels, doctor!" he cried, with a great pity welling up in his voice, "never to have seen this man. He owes his very life to me. I fetched him out of Siberia when he lay dying of fever. You see how he has rewarded me. What can I say or do to atone for the crime of which he has been guilty?"

"It was an ungrateful act, I must admit," said I in reply, "but we must take a large view of it. I hope you will not punish him on my account."

"Nay," said he, his face becoming very serious, "that is impossible. The safety of all my people can never be placed at the will of an assassin. He shall have justice—no more, no less; the justice which I pray Almighty God may be given to all of us."

"May it be tempered with mercy is my earnest hope," I answered him; but I saw that there was sadness in his eyes; and when he had wrung my hand again, he left me alone with Adam.

I judged that it was then near to ten o'clock at night, but all my weariness had left me, and my nerves were much shaken by the shock of the adventure. I knew that I could not rest for many hours, and I suggested to my companion that we should get what fresh air we could in the valley before the house. He was very ready to fall in with my views: and when he had sent for wine, and we had lighted cigars, he put his arm through mine and we passed into the garden. The night was then glorious, the shimmer of the moonbeams fell soft upon the silent pastures and the perfect palms; broad shadows of mighty trees lay spread out in lakes of silver radiance; the murmur of fountains came up on the breeze; a band was still playing in the park before the great building which I thought to be a theatre; there was the sound of human voices and of laughter, a joy of the night such as I had never known.

We had walked some way silently enjoying our cigars, and had turned down toward the place whence came the music, before either of us spoke. But the subject of the punishment of the Russian ran strong in my head, and when we had entered an umbrageous park, where ebony trees and acacias and fine oaks stood, all lit by the perfect light, I began to talk of the affair.

"Tell me," said I, "what will happen to Kryganovski?"

Adam took his cigar from his mouth, and when, very slowly, he had knocked the ash from it, he answered me:

"He will die."

"Die!" cried I; "but not for one offence?"

He thought for some time before he answered. When he spoke it was as friend speaking to friend in all confidence.

"You cannot understand," said he, "you, who come here to find things of which men in Europe have never dreamed. Look, Trevena; I will talk to you as I would to my own brother. You have seen the count; you have learned something of his life; but you must know him more fully. He is a man as gentle in heart as a child; he has given his money, his time, nay, all his years, to befriend men who are outcast from humanity. Show him a felon lying stricken with fever in Cayenne, tell him of a man suffering in Noumea; an exile, worthy beyond his fellows, who is groaning under the lash in Siberia, and he will not rest day or night until he has brought that man here, to clothe him, to feed him, to set before his eyes delights which few could imagine. Do you think that all such are worthy? Is it possible to humanity to be lastingly grateful? Will there be no blackguards, no hypocrites, no assassins in a company of two or three hundred drawn often from the dregs of criminality? Indeed no; we have them all here; and, for our very existence, we must deal with them as they would with us, did it lay in their power. Some day, of course, we shall have to fight with the warships of Europe; the time will come when this island must prove its strength. How should we fare then if traitors were among us when the enemy was at our gates? I leave you to answer me."

"Have you no prisons?" I asked.

"We have the securest prison in the world, but it is not for murderers. For them, as you will see before dawn, there is only one way. It is a terrible way. Yet I am sorry for Kryganovski, for I knew his secret. And he is not the first man who will die for love of a woman."

I had guessed it long, but I said nothing. The man who was to perish had loved Fortune. I read it in his eyes at our first interview, but my pity for him, as the conviction came home to me, was intense.

"Can nothing be done to save him?" cried I. "Will they not give me his life if I ask it?"

"They will never give you that; the law here is as hard as those rocks above us. It knows no mercy, it is meted out to the highest and the lowest. I, myself, who am loved by the count as though I were his son, had died to-night if I had done as this Russian."

He said no more at the moment, for we had come upon a well-planted square, lighted by many trembling arc-lamps. The building I had seen from the higher ground was now before me; a vast temple, with porch and columns and frieze in Doric fashion, and great splendour of gilt and painting in its entablature. The doors of it were closed, but there was light by which to see its magnificence and its amazing proportions; and I observed quite near to it a café, before the glass windows of which a number of men and women were seated at small tables sipping wine or lager beer. In the centre of the square a band of Hungarians played a wild and a haunting melody; and what with the colours of the lanterns, which swung in the trees, the sweetness of the night, and the exhilaration of the music, it was impossible to deny either the gaiety or the novelty of the scene. Nor did I forget as I looked upon it that I was in the Southern Pacific, many hundred miles from life and from civilisation.

That there were women in the square surprised me; but they proved to be of all nationalities, as were the men who accompanied them. I saw Russians drinking spirits as freely as they drank vodka in northern latitudes; Frenchmen with glasses of absinthe before them; Germans sipping foaming beer; Italians thumbing cards; Hungarians nodding to the rhythm of the music. But of Englishmen I saw none—that is to say, there was no face which, on my first remarking it, appeared to be that of a fellow-countryman—

nor were any of the women in any way suggestive of London. In this first assumption I was wrong, however, for hardly was I at the door of the café when a very stout man, with iron-gray hair and cheeks of abundant fulness, left his chair and waddled toward me.

"I beg your pardon," said he, with a high and fife-like voice; "but you are the doctor who arrived last night, I think? I should be obliged if you would prescribe for me."

"With pleasure," said I. "From what do you suffer?"

He rolled into a chair and wiped his forehead with a handkerchief of exceeding size.

"I suffer—oh, my dear sir!—I suffer everywhere; and the port wine in this place isn't drinkable; it's poison!"

"Then why do you drink it?" I asked naturally.

"I must live. I am not a subject for beer, doctor; beer kills me. Surely I am a very miserable man."

I was about to answer him, but Adam put his arm in mine and drew me away.

"Look here, Dyer," said he, speaking to the man, "we're too busy to listen to your ailments to-night. I've told you what to do. Run up to the lighthouse every morning before breakfast, and live on brown bread and lemons."

He carried me away without any other explanation; but I heard the fat man gasping, "Brown bread and lemons!" as we went, and there was the deepest disgust in his voice. When we were out of hearing I asked who the man was.

"He," said Adam, lighting another cigar and calling to a waiter to bring us whiskey, "he is the biggest humbug in this community. His name is Jacob Dyer, and he has left two or three hundred widows and orphans penniless in London. The count met him at Tahiti, where the detectives were looking for him, and he was weak enough to give him shelter."

"And is there anything the matter with him?"

"As much as with me. He eats enough for five men and drinks enough for seven. We can't keep a drug in the medicine-chest for him. He takes everything, from rhubarb to quinine. It's a pity that his instinct always keeps him off the poisons."

He laughed in his old way; but he checked himself after the first outburst, and became very grave. The tragedy of the night sat heavily upon us both. The music of the band seemed ill-placed and jarring.

"They must stop that noise in a minute or two," said he suddenly. "I wonder they haven't heard. News such as we have is generally quick to get abroad. Ha! here they come!"

A horseman rode up almost as he spoke, and, reining in his little Hungarian pony at the band-stand, made a sign to the leader. In the same instant the music ceased, and the bell of the cathedral, which lay a good half-mile from us, began to boom dolefully. The men and women, who had been chatting idly, rose from their seats at the first stroke of the hammer, and gathered together in excited talk. A few of them left the square and struck upon a road which appeared to lead to the summit of one of the hills. The example was contagious, for others followed; and even Adam and myself were drawn as by an irresistible power to the heels of the throng. Only the women stayed, huddled together with blanched faces; and so we left them as we passed from the glare of the arc-lamps to the darkness of the rugged road upon which the light of the moon no longer shone.

Though no one told me absolutely, I knew

well, as I began the march up the steep and
rocky hill which the excited crowd now trod,
that I was to be the spectator of a tragedy.
Had I been alone, and calm enough to reflect, it
might be that I had drawn back; but the strange
influence of the scene, the force of the general
example, the whole excitement of the night and
of my environment, led me on, as I have said,
irresistibly.   And so it came that I found myself
at last, when we had continued to climb the side
of the hill for more than twenty minutes, out
upon a rampart buried in the very face of the
gigantic cliffs, and so looking down sheer upon
the still water of the Pacific.   Two thousand feet
below me the sea shone like a silver mirror.   I
could gaze over upon the coral reefs, or down
to the harbor, where lay the yachts and the iron
ships I had seen on my first coming.   I could
observe the foaming breakers of the remoter
ocean thrashing the barrier of rock which stood
between our lagoons and the unchecked waves.
And all around me, their muzzles peeping from
steel turrets built into the rock, were guns of
great size, or houses for ammunition, or flags for
signalling, or stations for watching.   The electric
light, standing out a thousand feet above us, of a

sudden enriched the whole scene with unsurpassable rays. It cast upon the faces of the men
about me a glow at once paling and illuminating,
so that awe seemed to come upon the throng,
and they stood motionless, scarce whispering or
lifting a foot to change their standing places.

As for myself, I was as one bewitched. I had
thought to come out to see a man die; but here
was no instrument of death, no prisoner. Only
a rampart, with a stone wall three feet high at its
seaward side; a rampart ending at last in an
open platform of rock, in no way defended by
rope or balustrade. Soon it was apparent that
the tragedy was to be played upon this platform.
The dirge of a drum rolled upon the air; a few
soldiers with drawn swords drew up upon the
unwalled rock; a priest holding a crucifix walked
with slow step; Kryganovski followed him with
bent head and bloodless face. Once upon the
plateau, the priest knelt to pray; and then I saw
the count himself. He stood motionless, his
body erect, his hands gripped one upon the other.
And when the priest had made an end of his
devotions, the old man spoke with a voice clear
as a bell and plain to be heard by every observer
of the weird spectacle.

"Felix Kryganovski," said the count, "I have few words to say to you, for this is no hour of reproach. When you were friendless, I became a friend to you; when you were in prison, I brought you out; when you were dying, I nursed you to life. As Christ commanded me, I made you my brother; I took you into my house; I loved you, and sought your love. What have you given me as your thank offering? For my affection, hate; for my friendship, ingratitude; for my gifts, crime. Shall such a one as you live among my people? Nay! May God judge between us—that God before whom you are now to appear, and to whose mercy I commend you. Oh, my son, my son! pray for that forgiveness in heaven which you may not find on earth! Pray to your Maker as I pray for you."

He ceased to speak, but tears were streaming down his face, and he had fallen upon his knees. Many of those about me imitated him in the act, and for many minutes there was the murmur of supplication there under the glow of the outstanding beacon. But the Russian himself did not kneel; he only covered his face with his hands, and when he had remained thus for the space of five minutes I saw the count make a signal, and a file of men with muskets stepped forward upon the rock. They had come too late, however. Quickly, and with a word of defiance upon his lips, Kryganovski sprang high into the air and leaped from the height to the sea. We watched the body turning over and over as it hurtled toward the still lagoon; we saw his hands outstretched and his clothes spread with the wind. Then, with a dreadful crash, he struck the water, and fountains of foam hid him from our sight.

But a shudder passed over the observing throng, and there were white faces to see as the men turned and went down toward the city.

CHAPTER XIII.

I FIND MY PATIENT WORSE.

ON the morning following the death of Kryganovski I was awakened at a very early hour by
the heavy fall of rain upon the broad leaves of
the palms in my veranda. I had enjoyed profound rest for a few hours after the scene upon
the ramparts; and though I had no more fears
for my safety, they had placed a sentinel before
my house; and this was their custom until I left
the island. But I had slept unconscious of his
presence, and remarked it only when the hum of
the rain, which came down in sheets upon the
land, forbade me to lie longer.

I have said that I had slept with profound rest,
but this, I think, was the outcome of the reaction
of excitement and of my long walk in the night.
When I awoke there was acted again in my mind
the whole of the grim business which I had witnessed; I found that my temples were hot and my
eyes burning. This set me longing for a bath,
though I had no notion if one were to be had in the

house; but when I had touched my bell, a servant
came and pointed out to me, at the rear of the
bungalow, a plunge of some size, built of marble,
in a little room whose windows were of stained
glass.   In this basin I bathed to my content, and
was then shown a large and exceedingly comfortable chamber, giving off from my bedroom, which
had been marked as my dwelling-place.   It was
arranged entirely for a man of bachelor's habits,
with lounges and Eastern mats and a profusion
of books, and there were even tennis racquets and
guns, and a grand piano near the open windows.
Here I discovered that my breakfast was spread;
a meal of many dishes, accompanied by the coffee
—of which I shall never cease to sing the praises—
and much cooling fruit, but particularly melons
and oranges and grapes of astounding size.

At the end of my meal, there being no message
from the count, I began to think upon my plans
for the day.   I had now grown somewhat used to
my position, and I could remember without hurt
that I was a prisoner.   Nor is this any matter for
wonder, since I thought day and night of my
patient; and, more than this, was in a very El
Dorado, a land overflowing with milk and honey
and all the sweet things of life.   Nay, I brought

myself even to a state of great content, and of
hope that there would be no sudden awaking to
these days of visions; and in this mood, for the
desire was now strong upon me, I determined that
I would see Fortune at the earliest moment.

There being a servant at hand, the fulfilment
of this wish was no difficult affair. I penned a
note and sent it across to the count's house; and
then I went to stroll upon the veranda before
my dwelling, and to watch the pitiless rain swel-.
tering upon roof and pasture. To my astonishment the veranda was not empty. The man
Jacob Dyer—the fat man with a partiality for
medicines—sat upon a chair smoking a cigarette;
and when he saw me, he had great joy of it.

"Oh, my dear doctor," cried he, waddling
toward me, "what good fortune to catch you! I
have been waiting here an hour."

"Well," said I, "you've been getting the fresh
air, anyway. What's the matter this morning?"

He dropped with a thud into the basket-chair,
and began a whole history.

"You don't know, perhaps, that I was a great
man in England," said he. "Ah, but I was! I
remember the day when my name was at the top
of sixteen companies."

"Might I ask," exclaimed I maliciously, "why it is not at the top now?"

"Enemies, my dear doctor," said he; "enemies and greed. There was a time when I made forty thousand in a week. How the champagne corks flew!"

I did not like to suggest that the directors flew subsequently; but I put it another way.

"Things broke badly for you after a while, didn't they?" asked I.

"Badly! that's no word for it. There were three hundred writs out against me in a fortnight. I could have papered a church with them."

"You should have set up as a decorator," I suggested.

"Ah!" said he, "it's sport to you, but it was death to me. I knew I couldn't face the conspiracy of rogues who had fawned upon me, and I left England, house and wife and child, and eleven hundred dozen of wines. There wasn't a finer cellar than mine in the kingdom."

He groaned audibly at the thought; but suddenly brightened up.

"Would you feel my pulse, doctor," he cried.

I felt it; it was like the pulse of a dock labourer.

"Is it very high?" he asked.

"It's very stringy," said I. "What you want is to live on fish and cold water for a week."

"Fish and cold water!" he gasped. "Lord! I should be a dead man. Fish and cold—— Do you think my lungs are all right?"

"If you'll reduce yourself about five stone in weight I could tap them," said I. "Why don't you begin by walking ten miles before breakfast?"

"Ten miles!" he cried. "Ten—— Doctor, you wouldn't make fun of an invalid. You'll give me some medicine. Don't you think if the count sent to London for some old port I might recover?"

I told him that it was possible, and was growing weary both of him and of his supposed ailments, when the messenger returned to say that Fortune would see me at once. At this I rose and told him that our interview must end.

"I suppose it must," said he; "but it's a pity, for you can know nothing of my case yet. Will you want to see me again to-day?"

"No, indeed," I replied.

"But you'll give me a tonic?"

"I have given you one. Fish and cold water. Let me know in a week how you like it."

He was speechless with amazement when I left
him; but the remembrance of the interview
awaiting me robbed me of all pity; and without
so much as a glance back, I passed down the
road and through the gardens which lay before
the other house. I found Fortune quite alone,
her nurse being occupied elsewhere; and when I
I entered her room she was standing, with an
exceeding dark look upon her face, before a bowl
of orchids. I judged that she had some trouble,
and attempted to divine it.

"Let me ask," said I cheerily, holding out my
hand with the words, "if we have slept well?"

"If *we* have slept well? How can I possibly
know that?" she answered, without so much as
looking up from her flowers.

"Come," said I, "don't be angry with me.
You are not so well this morning."

"I was in a trance for ten hours last night.
How could I be?"

This was serious news. I drew a chair near to
the table upon which the flowers stood, and took
her hand; but she snatched it from me and continued her occupation.

"Come," said I, "are we not to be friends?
Tell me about this trance."

For a while she did not answer me; but when her words came, there was a torrent of them. And while she spoke she turned her back upon me.

"I slept," said she quickly, and with low voice, "when they were killing my friend: but I heard the drum which beat over his grave, and the voices of those who went to see him die. Then I thought he was calling to me, and my brain was on fire, though my limbs were stiff and I could not raise a finger from my bed. He was my friend; the only one here who awakened my interest or had my sympathy. I would have begged his life at my father's feet, but I was dead through the night; my cries were fancies. I lay there like a thing of marble."

She ceased to speak for a moment; but, suddenly dropping her flowers, she cried most piteously:

"Oh! will no one take this pain from me? I cannot bear it; my heart is breaking!"

With this wild cry she dropped upon the couch, her hair falling over her face and catching up the tears which glistened upon her cheeks. I thought then that nothing more beautiful had ever come before my eyes; and my heart was full of tenderness for her.

"Indeed," said I, "if you will only accept my friendship, I will not rest until this shadow is taken from your life. But you must give me a little trust."

At this she turned upon me a look full of anger.

"Oh," said she, "you must not ask for that. It was because you came here that he died. I can never forget that. He loved me, and love is very precious to every woman. How can I bear to see you when I remember this?"

"Are you not laying to my charge acts in which I was as powerless as a child?" said I, feeling a great gloom come upon me at her accusation.

"Do not ask me," she cried waywardly. "Leave me to myself. You see how weary I am. Why did you come here to remind me of what is past? Why did you rob me of a friend?"

My face flushed at her injustice, and I rose to do as she wished.

"I came here," said I, "at your father's wish. I will not answer your reproaches, for you will answer them yourself before to-night. Only remember that I still think of you with all friendship, and have already forgotten what has passed between us this morning."

She gave me no reply, lying as she had fallen, her hair shining golden upon the couch, and her cheeks heated and bright with colour. And so I passed from the room, to find that the rain had ceased and that the sun was shining upon the island. But all things were dark to my eyes, and my head swam as though I had received a blow.

CHAPTER XIV.

A RIDE UPON THE HEIGHTS.

THE count was in the garden when I left his daughter's room. I found him pale, and by no means the erect man he was when he had spoken last to Kryganovski; for he now walked with labor, and there was a restlessness of hand and eye which only an unusual output of nervous force might explain. But he was no less ready to question me, or to hear of my work.

"Doctor," said he, "your face writes the bulletin for me; you have ill news."

I shrugged my shoulders, and in the act found time to make my tale. It lay upon me, even in those early hours, to ape indifference; yet I would have given years of my life to have told him all—then, at the beginning of it; to have said to him, "Let me go, while I have strength to leave her." And he was no man to hear lies; he, whose lightest word rang with love and confidence.

"The news is ill," said I, when at last I spoke; "but it is not grave. Your daughter lays the

Russian's death to my charge, and will not see me."

"I expected it," said he, though sadly. "These angers of hers are my constant anxiety; but they pass like a cloud. Before sundown she will regret with tears what she has said."

"In any other case, possibly," replied I; "but this seems to have been a mutual and a very strong friendship. You cannot ask her to forget that in a day, count."

"Nay," said he, "there could have been no friendship on Fortune's part with a man like that. She is a judge of men, doctor; she has a mind which reads things hidden even from me; she has that instinct of confidence or distrust which is one of the rarest things in life when it is true. She may weep because a man died, for death is a terrible thought to her; but she will come to say, 'It is just,' and then she will forget."

Down in my heart I prayed that he had spoken a true word; but I hid my feelings from him, though I could see now that the sun shone and that the cloud had passed from the sky.

"If you are right," said I, after a pause, "there is nothing for me to do but to wait until you send for me——"

"She will send for you herself," replied he; "indeed, she owes it to you. In the meantime, I have thought that you would like to see us as we are, and to know more of your temporary home. Our good friend Adam waits for you with horses at your own house. If you have any curiosity, he will gratify it. I beg of you hesitate in nothing, for I have you strong in my esteem, doctor, and would speak with you as with a son. An old man's weakness alone keeps me from that duty of hospitality which I owe to you. The night was a night of suffering to me, as you know. Ingratitude is a two-edged weapon, and I bear its wounds to-day."

His voice quavered as he spoke the words, and he took his leave of me almost tenderly. But I went my way with a great load lifted from my mind and all my hope returning. A wild hope it was—nay, a supreme folly in the knowledge of the count's words. Yet what man, into whose life the sweet face of one woman has come, ever stood to battle at the feet of reason or to wrestle with the logic of fate? And I was as other men in these moments of sweet thoughts and joyous dreams. And love was as the sun to me—rising to warm me in the day of faith; sinking to leave my heart cold in the night of fears. Nor would I have had it otherwise, though I had known that the hour was near when it would set forever.

At the door of my house I found Adam, and with him there was a man of fine build and breadth—a young man, though his hair was absurdly white and thick. The stranger was introduced to me as "Silver" Lincoln, and I judged at once that he had got his title from the want of colour in his curls. He proved to be an exceedingly pleasant fellow, an American gunner, who was then in charge of the great Krupp guns upon our ramparts; to which office he added that of provisional skipper of the count's cargo steamer. He rode with us now because, as he said, there had been complaints from the prison, and it lay upon him to look into things. He was mounted upon a sturdy Hungarian pony, and he held by the bridle a similar mount for me; but before we rode, Adam took me to my bedroom, and there showed me a number of pairs of light-brown riding-boots, from which I was to choose, with breeches of cord, and a white coat. This last, with the broad-brimmed hat of straw, I found a great service to me, for the sun fell hot upon the valleys, and was scarcely to be endured until we had reached the higher places of the uplands, which opened to the sea breeze.

From the crest of one of these hills I was able for the first time to see nearly the whole face of the Isle of Lights. At a rough reckoning I made it out to be some nine miles long by five miles broad; but there was a range of mountains at the end opposite to the great beacon which somewhat had the sweep of it, and I could not be certain what land lay beyond. For the most part, its white bungalows were grouped about the square in which I had heard the band play; but there were other houses near to the cathedral, and not a few upon the further hill-sides, where they stood in umbrageous gardens, and often almost hid by trees.

Elsewhere the land was cultivated and green with pastures. Its woods of cocoanut palms were as fine as any I have seen; there was a wealth of orange plants and of breadfruit trees which indicated possibilities against siege. I remember the sweet potato flourishing to luxuriance with the yam and the taro; and upon the ripe green pastures were goats and sheep, and herds of small cows. But I was not a little astonished at the number of white men who were

at work in the plantations; and it was this sight
which first set me questioning Adam.

"They're busy down there," said I, as we all
reined in upon a glorious sweep of grassland, and
had the island spread like a map below us.

"I guess we all work," said Silver Lincoln,
biting the end off a new cigar. "The man that
comes here to play tramps a hard road."

"That's so," said Adam; "it's no sinecure for
the strong and able. In the first place, every
man has to do his two months a year of military
service; then he has to earn his living in the
fields or in his house. Whatever his gift is, that
we let him follow. If he paints, we send his
pictures to Europe for him; if he writes, we
publish his books in London, Berlin, or Paris; if
he's a worker at a trade he may practise it here,
and we sell his goods in America, or buy them
from the common fund. And whatever he makes
above a pound a week is for his own pocket."

"That must be a farce," said I, "seeing that he
has no means of spending it."

"He has every means. We have shops in the
city there as fine as any in Regent Street.
What we don't keep we send to Europe for, and
the profit goes to the chest which will endow this

place as a refuge for men until the Day of Judgment."

"Or," said Lincoln, with a shrug, "until the boys get up to rob the mine, and clear off to Europe with the yellow stuff."

My eyes must have asked Adam a question, for he raised himself in his saddle and pointed to a low range of wooden buildings lying under the great black headland which towered above the lighthouse. It was at a spot where the volcanic rock split open, to show a spring leaping from ridge to ridge; and there I discerned the dark figures of men moving, and steam rising as from an engine.

"In that valley," said Adam, speaking earnestly, "there is enough gold to buy a fleet. It lies in the volcanic rock like leaves in a book. And it tells you without words how this city has sprung up."

"The count claims it, of course?" said I.

"He claims a tenth for himself and his child. The rest is spent for the benefit of every man here—and in the cause which we serve. But, as Silver says, it is worse than drink to some of us, and the day will come when that valley will ring with shot."

He rode on as though he did not care to dwell upon the thought, and we were all silent as we cantered over the breezy downs toward the further end of the island, where I had seen the range of mountains. When next one spoke, it was the American, Lincoln, who took nothing seriously, and could not long keep his tongue still.

"Doctor," said he, "I'm going this way to show you a queer thing. Did you ever feel moved to see a prison?"

"It depends upon the prison," said I.

"Well, I guess you wouldn't track one like ours if you walked from Tobolsk to Bordeaux," cried he. "It's just the queerest prison on earth."

"Is it far to go?" I asked.

"A quarter of an hour to the foot of the pass, and twenty minutes after among the hills. You can hang on by your eyebrows, I hope? It isn't quite a carriage-road up yonder."

I said that I would try, though I have no stomach for precipices, and at this he put his pony to the gallop.

"I guess we'll feed in the plantation there," cried he; "the boy I sent to meet us with the cocktails must have been holding on to swear-words this hour or more."

We were now following him in a blinding gallop; nor did we draw rein as we descended the hill, thundering on like men that ride a race. For the matter of that, we were in the plantation while I was still debating the nice probabilities of a broken neck; and there we found a young Polynesian who had spread lunch upon the grass. I learned that many of these natives had been carried from neighbouring islands to do menial work in the city; and Adam told me more of the economics of the community as we lay beneath the breezy shade of a mighty acacia tree, and listened to the bubble of a stream which here fell from the mountains to the glades below. But when an hour had passed, and we had lighted cigars, we were in the saddle again, and began to mount toward the pass, which was now clear to be seen at a great height above us.

For some way the road lay over grassland, very pleasant to ride upon. Then, abruptly, we struck a rocky track, boulder-strewn, and not a little remarkable for the steaming fountains of hot water which burst up from many fissures and crevices. One of these springs especially called

for my astonishment. I had never seen water
carried to such heights, or uprising with such
beauty. Clear as crystal where it broke from the
ground, of a thousand fires where the sun's rays
filtered through it, the whole fountain was capped
with foaming clouds of steam, which, in their
intense whiteness, had the aspect of mountain
snows. And yet the heat from the water struck
upon us while we were many yards from the
spring, and the ground was hot to the hand at a
great way from the pool.

When we had passed the springs I began to
mind me of the American's saying that the
road was not a carriage-track. We now came
out upon a ledge that had not the width
of a decent bridle-track; and, moreover, it
was rugged and much blocked with stones.
Upon my right hand a precipice rose up like a
wall; upon my left I could look down a thousand
feet to a ravine of iron crag and of darkness.
And at this I found my head swimming, and had
a temptation to throw myself from the saddle—a
foolish thought which many have known upon a
mountain. But the others smoked with no concern of the position; and in their confidence I
got my own, and let the pony do as he would.

We rode thus, my fears would have said for a week, my watch for ten minutes. At the end of it we struck two paths, one descending steeply as though to the very bowels of the earth; the other rising again, but with a gentle slope and much breadth. This latter path we followed for a hundred yards or more, but here we were not alone. Of a sudden a sentry challenged us; armed men were to be seen on every height and plateau of the rock. I watched them down there upon the lower road; they seemed to come upon me at every turn. Nor was explanation of their presence needed; for scarce had we ridden from the dangerous place when the prison of the Isle of Lights, with all its suggestive miseries, lay before my eyes.

CHAPTER XV.

THE VALLEY OF THE CAPTIVES.

THE prisoners lay in a well of the hills; in a ravine girt about with vast walls of iron rock. It was as though nature had dug out this open pit among the mountains for the very security of those upon the island. Upon three sides the insurmountable precipice rose up to a giddy altitude; upon the fourth side the wall opened above a great abyss, into which a torrent fell from the face of the chasm. And in this trap—this heated stony, barren amphitheatre—sixty men were shut from air and life and from the hope of men. I saw them, as the sun fell hot into the valley, lying in all attitudes; some prostrate and asleep; others that hugged their knees, or squatted, beast-like, upon their hams; others again, that paced the valley as caged brutes. For the most part they were clothed in rags, but a very few were near to being naked, and such faces as were upturned I would not willingly see again. Here were men of all ages; old men with the features of ghouls;

young men burned brown with the sun; cripples limping in silent agony; weak men who could scarce drag themselves from stone to stone. I saw the blind tottering upon the rocky floor; I saw human beings whose faces were nigh hidden with the growth of matted hair that fell upon their shoulders; I heard cries of despair and of anger; I observed the wretched captives fighting among themselves, as though their burden were not already sore. And as the scene of misery and of suffering became plainer to my eyes, it seemed to me that my journey over the mountains had carried me from a land of humanity and light to the very gates of hell itself.

Something of this thought must have showed itself upon my face; for when we had stood a little while to watch the prisoners, Adam began his apology.

"Well, doctor," asked he, "what do you think of it?"

"I guess he thinks next to nothing at all," interposed Lincoln, with a forced laugh.

"You have answered for me," said I; "it's a sight which any man with feeling would wish not to see. And," I continued, "it is no human work."

Adam's eyes were turned sharply upon me as I spoke. He was very ready with his defence.

"I can't follow you," said he quickly. "These men are mere criminals, thieves, and cutthroats. We do not work for darkness, but for light. Loose your prisoners there, and all that we have done in five years falls in a day. These men were offered a life of freedom and of pleasure. They rejected the offer for a life of cheating, of roguery, and of crime. On our part, we defend ourselves from them, as you see; and if pity does not enter into the bargain, lay it to the interests at stake. And let me tell you, doctor, that if one of these men got away upon the sea, there would be warships in our harbour within a month."

The thing was plainer as he put it; but Silver Lincoln took up his words.

"Yes," said he, "I guess we live in a powder-mine here, and we've got to keep a tall eye on sparks. Not that the carrion down there are worse off than men under stone and slate, as you shall presently see. For the matter of that, they're too well fed, to my way of thinking, since half of them are little better than cutthroats, and the other half wouldn't exactly take prizes in a Scripture class."

"Do they work at all?" I asked.

"About as much as a pug dog," said Adam; "but that's their lookout. They can earn their liberty by work; most of them prefer not to earn it."

"And what about their quarrels?"

"When they're mild," said Lincoln, "we look on and whistle. When they begin the killing, we tie them up to a post and knock the dust out of their backs. It's not exactly Fifth Avenue to go in among them, but you get used to it. I'm going in now, if you care to come, doctor."

I could scarce believe that he meant the thing; but he remarked my incredulity, and continued:

"There's no danger when I'm there; but don't look as if you had nitro-glycerine in your pocket, or they may be nasty. Rocco here is worth a regiment. The last time he went in he gave one of them a box on the ear—and they carried the man out on a plank."

He turned his horse at this, and without so much as waiting for my "ay or no," he rode down the lower road which had seemed to me, when first I saw it, to penetrate the bowels of the hill. Here, presently, there was a great softening of the sun's power, the rays filtering down through the narrows of the chasm, so that when we had ridden a little way we stood in a dim light like the light of a cathedral. At the same time it was quite possible to observe that the path carried us to the foot of one of the heights which nature had set as a wall of the prison; and I found, after five minutes of the descent, that a tunnel had been cut through the hill to give access to the valley of the captives. The tunnel was shut at its further end by a massive door of solid steel, before which two sentries stood; and with them we left our horses while we prepared to enter.

I have said that I had little liking for this emprise from the first suggestion of it; I had less when we stood at the gate and the keys rattled in Lincoln's hands. Nor did his words bring me to a greater confidence.

"When she's open," said he, "don't be a week before you're on the other side. There was a rush here last month, and some pretty shooting. They saw me on the hill, and twenty of them came through like a storm the moment I showed my face. I had to stretch five of them myself, and one was flattened out when the gate shut. Ugh! I can hear his bones crunching now."

The tale was pleasant, but no sooner was it told than he unlocked the gate, and cried, "In you go!" The next moment the door swung again upon its hinges, and shut behind us with a clash which set cold running upon my spine. We had passed in a moment from the dark to the light; from the chill of the tunnel to the arid floor of the burning valley. And no sooner were we thus within the prison than a clamour arose, and men, haggard, and dirty, and hollow-eyed, swarmed about us with fierce threats and gabbled oaths— even with tears and with entreaties. Here, below, the picture was no less one of pity than when viewed from the heights; the prisoners were no less ragged than I had thought them to be; the pit no less revolting. Nor was it possible to stand in that den, with the hot breath of the angry horde upon one's cheeks, and to feel that life was worth a moment's purchase.

For a spell after we had entered the pit no coherent word or definite complaint was to be heard. The press about us was so great, the babel of tongues so deafening, that we could but hold together and force our way onward. Yet even in the heat of the clamour I could hear that men cursed us, or prayed to us, or defied us; and that others raised cries for pity and begged of our charity food and drink. Soon the weaker cries gave place to the angry taunts of the bolder and more fearless ruffians. The stronger men began to jostle us and to find pleasure in the work. A huge fellow, with a face burned brown in the sun, and a few rags upon his legs for clothes, cried with fine hilarity to his companions that they should give us a welcome; and, suiting the action to the word, he snatched from my mouth the cigar which I had lighted.

It was in this moment, I think, that my hope of coming out of the prison without harm was at its full ebb. The jest of the leader had put courage into the others; and, at his example, the whole of the crew began to close up, while a few even picked stones from the rocky path. And I am convinced that, if my companions had not shown themselves to be men of very singular bravery, we had all died there before any aid could have reached us. But there never was a man with less knowledge of fear than Adam Monk; nor was Silver Lincoln a whit behind him in nerve and resource. Indeed, scarce had the giant of a prisoner stuck my cigar between his lips before the American had hit him with his hand

and sent him headlong upon the stones. And while he did this Adam whipped a revolver from his pocket and covered the nearest man that held a stone.

"Put that down!" cried he, in a voice that rang loud through the valley.

The stone fell from the man's hand; but he uttered no word. And again the cry went up, and a second man let go the missile he had snatched from the road. One by one the whole gang dropped their weapons and slunk away from us. Their threats died upon their lips; they ceased to plead; the weak were dumb as the strong, and in a meaning silence we gained the further end of the valley and the buildings of the prison.

These I had not seen from the road above the pit, for they lay beneath the cliff upon the hither side. I found them to be rough sheds of wood, with pegs for stringing hammocks, and tables covered with iron bowls and cups. They were very dirty, and the roof of the first shed had tumbled in, so that the rain of the morning had streamed upon the bedding and the floor. It was to mend this that Lincoln had now entered the prison, and when he had made his inspection we turned away very gladly toward the gate, feeling, I do not doubt, like tamers of beasts that have played a part, but yet must face the greater danger of leaving the cage.

As the thing stood, the peril was the greater because it was not to be seen. The prisoners had slunk away from us as we entered their dirty huts; they were squatting upon the rocks, or feigning to be in sleep, when we passed out. One man, indeed, came after me and whined piteously for tobacco, but he was of the honest fellows, since no sooner than I had given him a cigar than it was torn from his mouth, and ten ragged scoundrels were chewing its leaves. Him I did not fear; but the sleepers and the silent gang that dogged our steps, or hid behind the boulders, promised no good to us, and the feeling that a word or gesture might bring them from their holes was as unpleasant as any I have known.

At a distance of a hundred yards from the gate the danger of which I had been conscious for many minutes became apparent. Of a sudden a heavy stone whistled past my head and shivered itself upon a boulder; a second and a third followed, though the hands that cast them were invisible, and no voice broke the silence. Soon

the attack became a bombardment. I felt a piece
of rock strike me upon the shoulder; a second
missile cut my hand to the bone. The men, who
had laid in hiding to this moment, now sprang
out in numbers, and rushed toward us with yells
and oaths, while at Lincoln's cry, "Run for it!"
I took to my heels and bolted ignominiously for
the shelter which seemed, at the height of the
peril, to be so far from us.

Never have I run a race like that; never
stumbled upon a path so difficult. Yet to have
fallen would have been to die as a hunted brute
dies when the hounds come upon him. And
while I knew this, while in my mind I kept telling myself that I must keep my legs, I yet
tripped almost with every stride, and was twice
near to being flat upon my face. At every false
step the pursuing mob raised a louder cry of
satisfaction; they shouted one to the other to fell
us with the stones; a few, who had been lower
down the valley, headed us like men heading a
runner at football. These, however, were of no
account; whether the look of Lincoln or of Adam
took the courage out of them, or whether they
thought that the others would do the work, I know
not; but they gave way at our approach. Nor

could I see at what distance we ran ahead of the stouter gang behind—only this, the roar of their voices was almost in my ears, and by the sound of their steps I judged that some among them were upon our heels. At that time, I waited to feel hands grasp my shoulder, or to be struck while I ran; but in the heat of the pursuit they forgot their weapons, and were content with the hope of capture.

We were, as I have said, at a distance of a hundred yards from the gate when the rush began. We had run, perhaps, fifty yards when the end of it came. Twice I had felt the touch of a hand upon my arm, twice had shaken it off, and, turning with the effort, I saw that the mob was no more than ten paces from us. For leader there ran the hulking fellow who had been struck by Lincoln, and he held upraised a stone, with which he might have felled an ox. Nay, I am sure that he was upon the point of cracking my skull when, as by magic, help came to us. From the high path above the pit a volley rang out with rolling echoes that floated away from peak to peak, until all the mountains seemed to speak. I looked up, to see the sentries gathered upon an open plateau, their rifles smoking in their hands;

I heard a pitiful cry of pain, a louder cry of anger. For ten seconds the captives stood swaying between desire and hesitation; but the moments saved us. We were at the gate while they debated, and, though fifty stones smashed upon it as we turned the key, we had come to safety before the horde had found its legs again.

CHAPTER XVI.

FORTUNE SPEAKS WITH ME.

IT was five o'clock in the afternoon, a very pleasant hour upon the island, when I was back at my house again. The ride down the valley had been one of silence, broken only by the apologies and reproaches of my companions; and of Lincoln's promise that the backs of many of the captives should suffer before the morning. For the six men who fell at the volley, two of them dead and four wounded, no word of pity was spoken; and I, who had done what I could to forget the episode within the prison and to assuage the pain of those that lived, had done it against the wish of the others. And I was not a little astounded then at their want of humanity; though at a distant day I came to realize the noble aims of all who worked with the count, and their strange creed where mercy and severity walked side by side, and the death of man was reckoned as nought if only life might be given to man.

At the gate of my bungalow I left my friends, who went to play polo in the park. They offered me a mount for the game, but I declined, since I had the hope that some message from Fortune might await me. I promised, at the same time, that I would go down to the great hall for dinner; for I had learned already that the count imitated in many things the social customs of our English universities, and liked his people to dine together. The spectacle promised well, and with the determination to assist at it, I entered my own room and called to my servant for tea.

I could not find courage to ask the man if any message had come from "Mademoiselle," as many upon the island called the count's daughter; but there was no letter upon my table, and I sat down to draw off my riding-boots in very poor humour. Yet, when I had thought upon the matter for a little while, it seemed to me ridiculous either to look for a message or to expect that one would be hastened. What possible interest could the girl have in my coming or going? how should she feel constrained to write to me? To her I must have appeared as some crack-brained physician come to pester her as the others had done. She had seen me but twice; and I knew that then I had acquitted myself very poorly. My very tenderness for her might well have been misconstrued; my anxiety regarded as the eagerness of one who would cloak poverty in skill with richness in word. And the more I reckoned with it, the more did I bring myself to see the false position in which I stood, and how blindly I was pursuing the pleasant phantoms I had conjured.

All this, I say, was plain to me, just as it has been plain to countless men and women in the first stages of their love. For it is then that calmer thought ranges upon the one side, and against us, all the obstacles that the brain can create, and sets upon the other no reassuring image either of chance or of hope. Until that time Fortune had spoken no kind word to me; I knew that my coming to the island had been an episode to amuse her; that, if I left it, she would scarce ask why. In the bitterness of the knowledge, I fell to asking: Who is the man in whose arms she will lie? upon whose lips will her kisses fall? But this was pain to think upon, and I put the question from me, though it haunted me like an ill dream which pursues us when we have waked and would forget.

In the abstraction of these gloomy thoughts, I had pulled off one of my great brown boots, and was beginning to tug at the other when a sound at the open window caused me to look up suddenly. And then I saw what I had never looked to see, though I had lived a hundred years upon the island. Fortune herself stood by the casement, the golden light of the setting sun streaming upon her hair, her girlish face aglow with amusement. For a moment she stood watching me, with a rippling laugh and eyes lighted with surprise; but before she could draw back, I had limped to her as I was, and had taken her hand in mine. There she suffered it to rest, but her cheeks flushed with colour, and she looked up into my face as one who reads another's mind, and from whom no thought is hid.

"It was good of you to come to me," said I, and then, somehow, the words stuck in my throat, and I stood silent before her. But still I held her hand.

"I hoped you would not have returned," said she quite simply. "I wanted to leave a letter for you."

"Let us read it together," cried I, "or I will begin by guessing what you have said."

"Oh," said she, now drawing back her arm, "you would never guess."

She put her hand into the breast of her dress, and showed to me a tiny letter, which she held up gleefully, like a schoolgirl at her play.

"Well," exclaimed I, "let me try! You begin with 'Dear Doctor.'"

She laughed joyously.

"Indeed," said she, "I could guess better than that myself!"

"But you must begin somehow. Suppose we say, 'Dear Sir'?"

"Suppose we do!" cried she roguishly. "And then?"

"Well, then," continued I, "we say that we are very sorry——"

She tossed the curls which peeped out beneath her sun-bonnet from her eyes, and looked at me defiantly.

"Do I look very sorry?" she asked.

"I do not see a single gleam of penitence in your eyes," replied I, gazing, I admit, very earnestly into them.

"But I am sorry," said she quite suddenly, and ceasing to laugh. And then she continued quickly, "I did not mean to tell you so."

"I quite understand that," said I. "Suppose we change the subject, and have tea together— out in the garden there?"

She clapped her hands with delight at the thought, and so acquiesced.

"I'll go and lay the table!" she cried; "and the nurse can wait on us. Don't tell her that I said I was sorry."

She ran away to her maid, who was waiting in the garden, while I sat down to struggle with my other boot. A moment after she was back again.

"There's my peace-offering!" she cried, and so flung upon the floor the bouquet of orchids she had been carrying, and scampered off again.

I picked up her flowers, and when I had locked them away in a drawer, I followed her to the little pavilion which was built in my garden, and served me for my siesta at the heat of the day. It was a tiny cabin of bamboo and matting, in many ways like a Japanese house; and here was she already busy with the cups and plates they had sent from the kitchen. I saw, to my great comfort, that the excitement of the visit had enabled her to shake off the weakness of the morning; and though she looked very fragile in her dress of white, and her cheeks were heated with her work,

I knew that the interest of her occupation was the best medicine I could prescribe for her.

When I came upon the scene the tea was already steaming in the pot, and cakes were set in a china dish which she had produced as by a miracle. The way she scampered about, her dress flying here and there to show her tiny feet and perfect ankles, her hair tumbling over her shoulders, her fingers busy, now with flowers, which she snatched from the bushes around us, now with the arranging of her treasures, was worthy of a country girl; and I could scarce believe her to be the same delicate creature to whom I had talked that very morning. None the less was the spectacle delightful, and when we sat down together, and she waited upon me with mock humility, I vowed that it was the best moment of my life.

For some moments we talked of nothing but frivolous things—of the beauty of the garden, of the sweetness of the sea whose billows we could make out over the headlands, of the delicious warmth and the perfume of the roses. But after a while she asked me what I had done to pass the morning, and this led up to more serious conversation.

"In the first place," said I, "I spent a miserable hour thinking over your unkindness; then I spent another wondering when I should see you again."

She mused over this, resting her head upon her hand. When she spoke she looked me through and through with those searching eyes of hers.

"I spoke hastily," said she, "but I was unhappy. And I did not tell you the truth. The man who died was no friend to me nor to my father. Some day he would have betrayed us, as many others here would do, and will do when the opportunity comes. Yet I liked him, for he was sympathetic and kind when he chose. Love is not necessarily sympathy. My father loves me, but he does not understand me. He thinks I am still a child who is too young to have opinions. It was different before he met Count Tolstoy and set up to help the world. Then he had only me; we lived for each other. Now he preaches peace, and must preach it with the sword. This beautiful home of his is a home of death. The men he loves despise him; the few who are faithful work in a hopeless cause; it is all a mockery, a house of sand which the first evil wind will shatter.'

She spoke with an eloquence which was a delight to hear; and I confessed to myself that her words had the ring of a sound common-sense which was wanting in the romantic optimism I had heard since I set foot upon the island. Nevertheless I hid my thoughts from her, lest I should add to her foreboding.

"Come," said I, "you are taking a gloomy view of things. I can never believe that men who are surrounded by every luxury will deliberately exchange their condition for that of the exile and the felon."

She laughed a little ironically.

"Men," said she presently, "are driven through life by two ambitions—the ambition to act and the ambition to enjoy; the first is the stronger of the two, but they cannot gratify it here. Do you think that those who have passed half their days plotting and planning for what they call freedom will now be content to forget all because the trees are green and the sea breeze is sweet, and the flowers bloom everywhere? No, indeed; that is a foolish hope, a blind dream, which only a man of my father's goodness and nobility could enjoy."

I did not answer her, but presently, when we

had sat a while, she exclaimed, with heart-drawn
earnestness:

"Oh! if they would only trust him, he could
defend them here against all the world!"

She was looking out to sea when she spoke,
and her words were the outcome of that pride
in the island which must have filled every man
who had a sparkle of imagination. Cut off from
all approach by its insurmountable cliffs, to be
entered only by that wondrous tunnel below the
sea, inaccessible, remote—boasting brave hearts—
Count Andrea possessed, indeed, the city of the
world, the one stronghold which might defy the
nations—the fortress of the sea—the like to
which mankind has never known. And to feel
yourself a subject of such a man, to stand upon
the ramparts with the great ocean thundering
thousands of feet below you, to realise the
grandeur and the strength and the nobility of it
all, was to draw a new breath of life, to lift up all
your being even above the fear that life might
cease to be.

All this passed through my mind while we sat
silently together and watched the crimson sun
sink behind the headland. It seemed strange
that in such a paradise, in such a garden of vernal

delights, in such a noble city, the passions of
men, their ambitions and their unrest, should sow
the seeds of destruction, perhaps even of death.
I could not bring myself altogether to think that
she was right in her sombre view of things, and
I made mention of the many faithful men who
served her father; above all, of Adam Monk,
who was a man among men. At the mention of
his name she looked up quickly, and spoke with
so much confusion that all the castles I had built
fell tumbling to the ground, and the bitterness of
jealousy came upon me.

"Adam," said she, "is one of the dearest of
our friends. He is brave, and he would give his
life for us. If all were like him, my father might
be a king indeed."

"He is a lucky man," I exclaimed sadly, "of
whom you can speak like that."

"Oh," cried she, "I have too few friends to be
asked to spare my praises. And I am happy, for
to-day I have found a new one."

The word was meant to console me, for I must
have cut a poor figure with my gloomy face; and
while she spoke it, she bent over toward me, and
I found—nor could I tell you how—that I was
holding both her hands, and that her hair was

touching my forehead. And I held her close for many minutes, a fragile, sweet figure that a press of the hand would have crushed.

"Let me be your friend always," I whispered; "let me serve you, and be near you while I have life!"

And then she gave me a low word, and, quickly withdrawing herself from my arms, she ran down the garden like a hunted thing, and was gone from sight. But all the air seemed full of the sweetness of her breath, and I heard her voice in the rustling of every leaf.

Yet how contrary is the reasoning of man! for scarce had she gone when I began to ask myself again, What is Adam to her? and to find that the question troubled me.

CHAPTER XVII.

I HEAR OF TREACHERY.

THE boom of a gun from the headland aroused me from my reverie. I had been told that this was the signal for dinner, the first gun being fired half an hour before the community sat down; and I went at once to my room to dress. Though I had been in the island but a few hours, they had provided a wardrobe for me; and I was soon getting into my new clothes, being not a little amused at the cut of the coat, which was like a military dress jacket, black, and frogged with braid. When I was dressed it was almost dark, and the lanterns and electric lamps already shone like stars in the city below; but the road to the great hall was well lighted, and I had not taken twenty steps upon it when I met Jacob Dyer, the fat man, waddling quickly to his dinner.

"Ha, doctor!" said he; "why so fast? If you'll give me your arm, we'll go together."

I declined the invitation curtly, seeing that the man weighed something like twenty stone.

"Do you feel any better?" I asked him ironically.

"Not much, not much," replied he, making ludicrous efforts to keep up with me. "I tried the fish and the lemons. Oh, Lord, I can taste them now!"

"And the cold water?" I shouted.

He made a wry face.

"Cold water!" cried he. "Would you have me catch typhoid? You don't understand me yet. I came up to see you this afternoon, but you were occupied. Ha, ha, doctor! I've found you out."

The thing was said with an ugly leer. I would have given a thousand pounds that he, of all men, should not have seen what passed between Fortune and myself, and I stopped at his words to hear more of them.

"How do you mean?" said I. "Who was occupied?"

"Oh," said he, "I couldn't explain! but it was a very pretty occupation. Look here, my friend, if somebody knew, there'd be the devil to pay. But I shan't talk; I can keep my tongue still,

thank God! And I tell you what—some day
we'll scuttle out of this hole together, eh? ' Why,
man, they'd pay twenty thousand in Europe to
know what's going on here!"

It was the blankest, boldest, most childish
treachery that one could have heard, and it confirmed entirely the foreboding which I had heard
from a mere girl thinker; but the old rogue
blurted it out without a shadow of concern. For
a moment I felt disposed to knock him down as
he stood; then discretion got the better of me,
and, pretending not to understand him, I said:

"Hadn't you better choose another time to talk
about these things? The second gun will go in a
minute, and you'll lose your dinner."

"The devil I shall!" he said, quickening up his
steps until he almost ran. "That's always my
luck—*hors d'œuvre* gone and soup cold. No
wonder I'm not active. But you'll give me a
tonic in the morning?"

There was no need to answer him, for the gun
boomed as he spoke, and I hurried to the square
and so to the Temple, which was ablaze with
light and resounding with the babel of tongues.
Here I found a company of nearly five hundred
people of all nationalities sitting before tables to

which exquisite flowers gave colour and multi-
tudinous candles gave light.   Pretty women in
evening dress, men in the quasi-military uniforms,
jewels of great worth, a vast display of silver, the
very size of the hall itself, contributed to the
impression of the scene.   It was impossible to
enter a building such as that—a building with
walls half hid by statues, with a roof ablaze with
gold and painting, with a high table lighted like
an altar, with a multitude of men and women
gathered from all countries and all cities—and yet
fail to realize that here was the home of one who
was a king among men, a prince among a people
unknown to civilisation, blotted from the page of
the world's life.

My own seat was at the high table, where only
men sat—a dozen grave and reverend seigneurs,
who were, I learned, the count's advisers, and
styled themselves the Council.   Though Fortune
was not in the hall, Adam was near to me, and
he gave me hearty greeting; but I could—such is
the shame of love—scarce look him in the face.
I know now what a wrong I did him; indeed, I
might have learned it then in his kindness to me,
for he would not see my coldness, but heaped
attention upon me.

"Trevena," said he, "it just seems that we brought you here in time to learn all about our own troubles. This will be a poor dinner to-night, for we've bad news and serious things to occupy us. Some of these infernal scoundrels have been trying to sell us to the French Government. One of their letters was intercepted this after-noon."

I thought instantly of Dyer and his words.

"Do you know the man's name?" I asked.

"The particular man, yes; but the mischief of it is that there may be a dozen with him."

"In which case——"

"In which case we should smell powder down here."

"What do you mean to do?"

"We have done all we can already. You'll hear all about it when the women have gone—that is, if you care to stay. It's not a pleasant business, though; and, if I were you, I'd move on to the café. It's the irony of this place that we never hold up our usual mode of life whatever happens. Like Ugolino, we may eat our chil-dren; but the band plays all the time and men do not forget to laugh."

"Of course," said I, "the women are not enfranchised here. They seem much too pretty to have votes, though they may have voices."

"We regard the women," replied he, "as women should be regarded. We respect them, we marry them, we look to them for all that belongs to the tenderness of life. But we are not yet imbecile enough to put bits into our mouths and to let them drive us."

"How did they enter into such a scheme as this?" I asked, setting him a question that had often occurred to me.

"They came into it," said he, "when we found that it was not good for man to be alone. If a citizen here wishes to marry, he must first prove himself, and then work his way up until he is what we call a minor senator. After that, if he knows any woman in Europe with whom he would care to risk his peace, we go to her and ascertain what her view of the matter is. Very occasionally we have allowed a man to spend six months in Paris or Vienna, purposely to marry; but most of them have women in their mind's eye when they land here, and we finish the business for them in the great church up yonder."

"And the children?"

"You have yet to see the children's garden;

though, for the matter of that, we send the youngsters to Europe to be educated the moment they are old enough to leave their mother's knees."

"It seems to me," said I, "that the children will be one of your difficulties in the near future. Meanwhile, let me ask another question: How comes it that you tell me all this? why am I admitted here—I who am a mere stranger, who might go back to Europe to-morrow and set all London ablaze with a fine account of your proceedings? It seems to me very poor prudence."

"It is just the best prudence possible," said he; "for oh, my dear Trevena, you will never see Welbeck Street again."

I started back and looked at him. It was as though he had struck me a blow.

"Good God! you would not make a prisoner of me?" I gasped.

"You will make a prisoner of yourself," said he, giving my arm the suspicion of a kindly squeeze. "Don't misunderstand me. You are going, of your own free will, to cut yourself from the world and from your friends, to make yourself as a dead man, to blot London from your memory. And you are going to bless your stars that you are able to do so. For my part, I would give half my life to stand in your shoes to-night."

As he said the thing a look of infinite, overwhelming sadness came into his eyes. I was cut to the heart to see him so; yet I knew not what to say—how to speak of my own hope, which he, I doubt not, had divined from the first. For his words told me plainly that he loved Fortune; and love to such a man was no thing apart from his existence. I, however, could find no tongue to pursue the subject; and so we sat in some constraint until dinner was ended and coffee had been served.

Until this time, I confess that the entertainment had bored me. My thoughts were away to the garden; to the little pavilion where first I had held Fortune in my arms. But when the women rose to leave us, and the great doors clanged behind them, I became aware that a scene of surpassing interest was about to be enacted. Of the hundreds of lights by which the vast chamber had been illuminated, a paltry twenty were now left to relieve the gloom. Anon, servants quickly cleared the high table at which we sat, and placed upon it six candlesticks and a

jewelled crucifix. From a gallery at the further
end of the building the notes of an organ were
heard, then the voices of a choir singing the Latin
hymn, "Veni, Creator Spiritus,"—sweet voices
well tuned in softest harmonies. I heard the
hymn, standing with the others; and I saw what I
might have looked to see in such a company, men
upon whose faces jeers were written, men smiling,
men still biting cigarettes between their lips, men
fingering glasses, men impatiently waiting the
end of it, even men praying. But the figure of
the count, erect with the power of his devotion,
absorbed in silent ecstacy, lifting his whole heart
to his God, was the noblest and the most beautiful I have ever seen.

As the notes of the hymn died away this
leader of men offered up, with touching expression, the prayer "Deus qui corda fidelium." But
at the word "Amen," the whole company sat
down, and a deadly stillness fell upon the Temple.

The few servants in the hall now moved
warily, as though the suggestion of sound were
an offence. Men who had been smoking laid
down their cigars; a few came from the further
end of the building that they might hear more
clearly. It was a fine thing to look at from the

high table upon the hundreds of faces, some flushed, some pallid, some betraying the fears of expectation. When, at last, the count rose to speak, so great was the tension that his whispered words seemed to echo back to us from the very vault of the roof itself.

The man was born an orator; of that I have never had a doubt. Though the first sentences of his speech, delivered in the French tongue, were pitched in a very low and solemn tone, his voice gathered strength presently; and, from a plain statement of the history of the island from the beginning, he went to a sonorous *tour de force* of invective, which rang like a trumpet-call through the vast building. While I could make no note of his expressions, many of them yet linger in my memory, and recur to me whenever my mind turns back to that night, as it will turn in the days when many who were gathered there lie rolling in the grave, and many sweat in the labour of prisons. I remember that he appealed to them to say if justice had not been done; if mercy had been wanting to his counsels; if their happiness had not been his abiding hope and aim. In measured and pathetic sentences he asked again:

"What man among you is my enemy? What man is my friend?"

A hundred leaped to their feet to cheer him as he spoke; and, moved by their applause, his voice fell like the ebb of a gale, and he made his great appeal to them.

"My children," he cried, "if I, the servant of the servants of mercy, have wept when you have wept; have hungered when you have hungered; have rejoiced when you were glad, think not that of this I ask your help or claim your gratitude. But, oh! if in this your home you have ears for the cries of your brethren in distant prisons; if your eyes can look across the waters to the cities where men fall that humanity may rise; if you would stretch out your hands to those that sink; would heal the sores of the outcast and the exile —then, I say, rise up and put upon you the armour of Christ; fight the good fight with the sword of truth; cut down the weeds of treachery; stand firm in your resolution until the day of account shall come and you shall render up the trust to which you are here called and appointed."

He sat down with this peroration, and so powerful was the spell he had cast upon us that for a while you might have heard the tick of a

clock. Ten seconds went by and no man spoke;
then the storm of applause burst out with deafening vigour. Whatever might have been the aims
of many of those present, I could see that few
heard this old man without being moved to love
and affection for him; and now the whole room
stood up to honour him; and in the zeal of their
enthusiasm, Frenchmen and Russians and Span-
iards rent the air with their cries. You could hear
the deep and sonorous "*Hoch !*" of the Prussian,
the shrill "*Viva !*" of the Italian, the wild shouts
of the Parisians—even the familiar "Hear, hear!"
from the handful of Americans, whose piercing
voices atoned for their want of numbers. And
though the old man stood again when the cries
had been prolonged for many minutes, he could
neither moderate their enthusiasm nor obtain a
hearing.

When at last some approach to order was
obtained, and the men had reseated themselves, it
was not the count, but one of his twelve councillors, who addressed us. He also spoke in
French—the tongue in which the business of the
island was transacted—and while he made no
pretence to oratory, every word from his lips was
listened to with a profound attention, which

marked the import of his mission.   For that matter, he began his speech by reading to us a letter which, he said, had reached the island that day, being brought by one of the yachts from Valparaiso, whence came our post.   The epistle had been written by the oldest friend the count knew in Paris—the Duc de Marne, some time president of the French Jockey Club.   It was a very short note, and, so far as my memory serves me, was in these words:

"JOCKEY CLUB,
        "BOULEVARD DES CAPUCINES,
                    "March 3, 1892.

"MY DEAR FRIEND: I return here this morning to find awaiting me a little note from an old acquaintance which sets me ill at rest for you and your hopes.   Let me entreat you, as I entreated you here six months ago, to study the happiness of your friends in so far as your own welfare is a part of that happiness.   Oh, my dear count, whither is this dream leading you?   And who is this meddler who has written to our mutual friend, the Minister of Marine, offering, for the sum of one hundred thousand francs, to disclose facts which should help France to keep her prisoners more securely in those islands to which she has consigned them? Are these also facts in which you have an interest? I fear it. Again I say, beware! Paris would now be talking of the letter if we had forgotten you as you seem to have forgotten us. But that is impossible, and I hasten to reassure you. The minister has been persuaded that the affair is a hoax. Need I say by whom? Be assured only of my regard and affection for you."

This was the letter which the councillor now read, with no more concern than a man might read an advertisement. The effect upon those who listened is not to be described. Had the dead spoken the awe and mystery of it would not have been more potent. Nor was a word spoken until the count stood and addressed a question to the reader.

"Before we read more, brother," said he, "I will ask if any man among us can answer the inquiry of my friend the duke: Who is he who has written this thing? If there is such a man, I charge him speak!"

He looked round the vast hall, awaiting an answer; but no answer came. Then he went on again, and his voice was now strong with anger. The words ring in my ears yet:

"If there is such a man, let him stand here before me."

For the second time he had no response but the restless shuffling of feet and play of hands, the movement of men who feared almost to breathe.   Now, however, he laid his watch upon the table, and with the act he said:

"Brother, when a minute shall have passed, will you read the postscriptum of that letter for us?"

What happened in the seconds of grace I am unable to tell you.   With the others, I found it impossible to take my eyes from the count, who stood there, erect, motionless, the type of some avenging figure behind which mercy had been cast.   Yet it seemed an hour of painful tension— nay, an age of curiosity which was hardly to be borne—before the councillor spoke again.

"Gentlemen," said he, with the old tranquillity, "the name of the writer of the letter to the French Minister of Marine is happily given to us by Monsieur le Duc.   That writer was Gustave Deutesme."

The whole room seemed to swing about at these simple words.   The hundreds whose eyes

had been fixed upon the count now looked
sharply round toward a small, dark-visaged man,
who crouched back in a chair at the further
end of the hall. Even from the high table the
pallor of his face was plainly to be seen.

"Gustave Deutesme," cried the count, "come
forward that we may hear you."

The fellow rose at this invitation, and muttered
something perfectly inaudible to the majority of
the company. A loud cry of "*Plus haut !*" put
a speedy end to his mumblings, and then the
count spoke once more.

"Gustave Deutesme," said he, "whatsoever you
have to say, let it be said here before me."

A dozen hands were now ready to push the
man up the hall, and with lurching gait and a
pretty assumption of indifference, he stood presently within five paces of my chair, a hollow-
chested, feeble fellow, with the stubble of a black
beard showing dirtily upon his chin, and a face
that would have lost nothing by a wash. And
when he defended himself he put his hands in the
pockets of his trousers, like a defiant schoolboy.

"I never wrote that letter, Monsieur le Comte,"
said he; "someone has played a trick upon me.
You are deceived."

The count looked at him with unutterable scorn.

"Oh," said he, "you have a defence, then, monsieur? You suggest that the letter was not written by you?"

"Certainly not. I hear of it now for the first time."

"And if we could get it from Paris, it would acquit you of blame?"

The man gave the very slightest start of surprise at this; but he kept the courage of his tongue when he answered:

"I have no doubt it would."

The count's reply was a dramatic one. He bowed to the councillor who had already spoken, and exclaimed:

"Brother, may I trouble you for the letter which M. Deutesme wrote to the Minister of Marine?"

A note was passed across the table to him, and, while he held it up, he addressed the whole company.

"Gentlemen," said he, "here is the man's signature upon a sheet of writing-paper delivered from our library on January 8th in the present year. The number of the sheet, as stamped with the secret mark, which allows us to trace any communication sent from this place, was 280. I find that sheet 280 was, on the day in question, given to M. Deutesme."

He paused a moment, looked down at the wretched man withering there before the damning accusation. But he did not lose his self-command, and when he continued, his voice was almost gentle.

"It remains," said he, "to ask you, according to the rules which govern us, what is to be done to this man who would have contrived the misery of us all but for the will of Almighty God? You have heard him now, standing before us with a lie upon his lips and treachery in his heart. You have listened to his defence; you are able to judge of the whole nature of his act. I await your verdict."

Such a roar of execration as went up at the end of this appeal I hope never to hear again. Every man in the hall leaped to his feet to cry for the offender's death. Had there been weapons at hand I believe Deutesme would have fallen where he stood; yet such was the ferocity of the cry that he put his hands to his ears and bent his head as though a storm were beating

upon it.   When at length the hurricane of voices
fell, he accepted his doom as a thing not to be
avoided; and, with a smile of forced irony, he
spoke his farewell.

"Count Andrea," said he, "I have a parting
word for you.   These friends of mine wish me to
die.   Very well; I die to save many.   The plant
may be cut down, but the seed remains.   Beware
of the new crop.   I give you six months to finish
your play, monsieur.   And you, gentlemen,"—
here he turned to face the company,—"bah! I
spit upon you!"

It was his last speech.   Scarce had the words
passed his lips when two doors of latticed brass-
work, which stood upon the left-hand side of the
hall, were thrown open, and we could see a company of troopers drawn up with torches in their
hands in the garden.   While the fresh breeze of
night swept into the building, and the candles
sputtered and the light waned, the doomed man
went out from among us.   Silently he went, and
in silence the gates of brass shut him from the life
he had lived and from those he would have
betrayed.   And no man spoke during the long
minutes of waiting in the gloom of the now-
darkened hall; nay, you could have counted

hearts beating until that supreme moment when we heard a gunshot from the hill, and men muttered, "He is dead!"

As the report of the gun shook the glass of the building, one man in the hall fell fainting to the floor. I looked down the chamber and saw the prostrate figure of Jacob Dyer. They were throwing water in his face when I passed out to the delicious freshness of the night.

CHAPTER XVIII.

I AM TAKEN FROM THE ISLE OF LIGHTS.

As I sit in a gloomy room in London, and the fog lies over the city like a pall, and the lights in the houses shine dimly in the suffocating haze, and the very chamber seems full of mist, I ask myself again and again if I can bear with the bitterness and the pain of memory which the continuation of my story must now put upon me. For I come to write of days of darkness and of anguish; of days when I would have welcomed death, and yet struggled in a feverish war with life; of days when a curse seemed upon me, and I had reached the ultimate depths of despair. And, writing, I must once more live through the scenes of peril and of pain, must suffer again in memory as I suffered then in mind.

I had been upon the Isle of Lights three months, when I was wakened from the visions which had shut from my recollection all thought of other days and other scenes. The summer had passed like the page of an entrancing book;

the grim events which had come about in the
week of my landing had been blotted from the
minds of every man. Day by day the sunlight
fell generously upon that paradise of palm and
pasture; the sweet breezes ever blew from the
sea; changing delights soothed to ecstasies of
rest and of content. I saw men firm in the love
of men; I watched the gathering of harvests, the
diligent labour of those who served, yet were
happy in their service. Though I was cut off
from all that had seemed to me good in life three
months before, I had no word but those of thanks
for the offence; no hope but that I might end
my days in the friendship of the man who had
called me from obscurity to this all-beautiful city
of the sea.

You may judge from this if things had pros-
pered with me. Of a truth, I often told myself
that my lucky star shone upon the island from
the first hour of my arrival. And when June
came, and Fortune's cheeks had got their colour
again, and I could feel the new flesh upon her
arms, and watch the coming of her strength, I
knew of nothing more that I could ask for or
expect.

Until this time the secret of our love had been

our own save for that one episode when Dyer witnessed me with her in the garden. While I had told her often that it lay upon me to speak with the count, she had pleaded so tenderly for delay, the hours had been so short to us, that I had held my peace, saying each evening, "To-morrow!" and, when to-morrow came, finding new difficulties and new dangers. For the matter of that, I knew not by what means I should ultimately face one who had told me with such anger that no man should speak to him of love for his daughter. And in the peril of discovery I continued to dwell, putting the hour of reckoning from me as our lips met, and she, who was life to me, hid herself in the shelter of my arms.

It was near to the end of June, as I have said, upon a day when the sun shone with blinding light, and fields were golden with their crops, that the beginning of the end was. I had risen early to enjoy my morning gallop upon the hills, and when I had breakfasted, I saw Fortune in her room. She was cured now; of that I had no doubt. For weeks she had been free from trance, and had slept well; the vigour of her mind was given back to her; she had recovered a childish gaiety of spirits. I knew that my work was done,

and trembled often when I asked myself: What
if the count also should awake to this knowledge?

We talked but little on this morning of which
I speak, for the maid was occupied about the
room; and Fortune told me also that she looked
to see her father at an early hour. Thus it came
about that my visit was consistently professional,
both in duration and in manner. Upon the point
of my departure, however, she whispered to me
that she would be riding in the woods about the
hour of five, and might possibly be found at that
time in the wild coppice which we called "The
Silent Thicket." I nodded to the hint, and went
off hopefully to play tennis with Adam under
the shade of the great acacias which surrounded
our ideal court in the home park.

Weeks of close intimacy had but shaped and
made strong my friendship for this truly honest
man. Though he carried deep down in his heart
a sorrow which I alone could estimate, he hid his
trouble successfully from the world about him,
and laboured to inspire all with his own enthusiasm and ambition. There was good even in
the ring of his laugh; courage even in his jest;
nor could you associate with him without being
the better for his presence and his example. He

of all men in the island was the one I called most truly "friend." The count stood apart from us— an ideal, a mystery, none the less beloved and esteemed. Silver Lincoln was an admirable companion, but a man at whose mind you could not get. The rest were for the most part foreigners, from whom I stood aloof. But to Adam I spoke my whole heart, and he, in turn, was content that I should call him brother.

Of the Italian, Privli, I had seen but little during my residence at the bungalow. He was a sculptor by profession, and they had set him up a studio on the far side of the island. As for the fat financier, Jacob Dyer, he did not long pester me. It is true that he feigned to be dangerously ill a week after my arrival, complaining that all power had left his legs; but I blistered his back so relentlessly that he kept out of his bed two days, and was vastly improved by the exercise. After that he lost faith in me as a physician; nor did he venture again to hint that we should write to Europe. The death of the Frenchman, Deutesme, had taught him a lesson which he could scarcely forget.

This, then, was the state of things at the island when, upon that memorable day, I went to play

tennis with "Rocco" beneath the shade of the
acacia trees. We finished three sets before mid-
day, and then separated for our siesta and our
lunch. For my own part, I did not venture out
again until the church clock had struck five; but
at that hour I called for my pony and set off
toward the woods. "The Silent Thicket" lay
upon the hillside, three miles from my house;
but the sturdy little Hungarian carried me there
in twenty minutes; and no sooner was I in the
delicious shade of the pine wood than I observed
Fortune gathering the blossoms with which the
sparkling turf was everywhere carpeted. She
had tied her pony to a tree; and now, when she
saw me, she came running like a wild thing, her
hands full of flowers, her curls all flying in the
wind, her eyes alight with pleasure and with
merriment.

"Dearest," she said, "I have been waiting, oh,
hours!"

"Come," cried I, "you only had tea at five
o'clock. They told me so."

"Well," exclaimed she, as I dismounted to kiss
her, "it seemed hours!"

"Who rode up here with you?" asked I; for
she was never allowed to ride to the woods alone.

"The groom did," she exclaimed, with a pretty laugh; "but I told him his pony was lame, and he has gone back for another. It will be an hour before he's here again."

I kissed her a second time, as a reward for her diplomacy; and this reward was renewed, I fear, many times before we came to the heart of the thicket, where, in a little glade-like valley, all shaded as a bower, we sat down to talk. On her part, there never was one that loved with less restraint or such courage of her affection. She would lie in my arms, all fearlessly, as though there she had a right to be; would put her lips to mine with the burning kisses of the sweetest passion; would cling to me in the moments of her depression, as if I could heal her wounds and shield her from every word of evil. And I—nay, I loved her with my whole soul from the beginning! and she was dear to me beyond anything in the world.

In this utter surrender to our dream we sat in the valley of flowers that summer day; and, from what cause I know not, a shadow of gloom fell upon both of us. Twice I had tried to tell her that it was no longer possible to hold back knowledge of the matter from her father; twice she had silenced me with a press of her lips upon my own. And as she lay with her head pillowed on my chest, and her arms about my neck, it was impossible to argue with so beautiful a thing, impossible but to hope that some power beyond our own would scatter the clouds which hovered upon our lives. This I told her—though I knew that the words were childish and the hope a dream.

"Dearest," she answered me when I had spoken, "you fear for your honour; but was it by honour's ways that they brought you here? No, no! there is no honour to be spoken of—only our love. For my sake, let us be as we are! Let us not exchange the present for a future we cannot read. Only let us love!"

I bent down to kiss her, but my lips had not touched her face when I saw the count, her father, riding up on the hill path at the farther side of the valley.

He was mounted upon the thick-set gray cob which carried him in all his rambles over the island; and he wore, though the first chill of sun-set had not fallen, a light cape above his uniform. As he continued to follow the bridle-track, and looked neither to the right hand nor to the left, I could not be sure that he had seen us; yet the voice of reason told me that it was idle to reckon with so shallow a chance, and I watched him with burning eyes until he disappeared in the darker place of the lower woods.

It is not often possible, I think, to find our tongues in the moments of deeper misfortune. While I had reckoned up instantly in my mind the whole meaning of this unlooked-for calamity, I yet remained dumb. But a startled cry broke from Fortune's lips, and she withdrew herself quickly from my embrace, making, at the first, no sort of effort to conceal her distress. Only when the gray cob had disappeared in the shadows of the thicket did she come to me again, and, as I pressed her to me, I could feel her whole body trembling, and the silent tears which she shed were warm upon my face.

"Dear love," said I then, for I had no heart but to console her, "there is still the hope that we were not seen; and, if we were, well he must have known what he knows now before many days had passed. I will ride back and speak with him at once."

It was finely said, as I believed, but she did not hear me; and, laying her head down upon my arm, presently she gave way to wild, hysterical weeping, which was more bitter to me than even the thought of what awaited us down there at her father's house.

"Irwin," said she, when at last she looked up through her tears, "it is my dream. Last night in my sleep I saw this wood, and the grass of it was all burned up and the trees withered. Then I looked across the sea, and there was a light shining away—oh! so far; and while I could see the light it seemed to warm me like the sunshine. Then it went out suddenly, and I started up trembling with the cold."

She was shivering even as she spoke, and her face wore that haunting look of suffering which I had seen on the first day I came to her. It was vain for me to invent plausible possibilities, or to suggest that we might find the count in no such terrible mood as our fancies had painted him; she would not be comforted, and lay in my arms as if they were powerful to protect her from the ill of it.

"They will take you away from me!" cried she, again and again. "Oh, my love! they will leave me lonely. I have you alone in all the world! God help me!"

It was very pitiful to see her distress; yet I was in no better case myself, and my head reeled with the anticipations which crowded upon me. As for the thought that they would separate us, that I could not bear, and I put it from me, to remember—and to console myself with remembrance—that the count, unless he were a pure fanatic, must come to reason in the matter. It is true that I had heard on all sides of his unchangeable aversion to any mention of his daughter's marriage; but, after all, such a marriage was inevitable sooner or later, and, though there might be much trouble before us, I did not doubt that I could overcome it. The worst part of the matter was that we had to stand before him with the secrecy of the affair already against us; but, as Fortune had laid it down, that was, in some measure, his business, and I had a card to play against any of the sort he might be disposed to lead.

All these things were plain to me as we rode down the valley together; what consolation I had of them that I shared with Fortune. She had now fallen into a quiet state of resignation, scarce speaking to me or looking away from her pony's head. I found that we had been long together

in the glade of the woods, and there were lights
glowing in the gardens as we descended the hill
above the park. Indeed, the whole of that rare
scene, so full of the charm of wonderland, is
vividly before my eyes as I write of it; and at
this none may exclaim, for I looked upon it, in
all its beauty and perfection, for the last time.

At the door of my bungalow we separated, for
upon this she insisted. She turned her eyes
toward me with the love all written upon them
and what word I said to her I know not, for as
she went down the white road to her father's
house it was as though she had gone out of my
life. Once again I saw her before the days of
my exile, but then she could not speak to me;
and from that hour the island ceased to be my
home. I say the island ceased to be my home,
but it ceased by my anticipation only. In my
rooms nothing was changed; my clothes were
spread upon my bed; my man waited to help me
to dress. And yet as I must choose to see it all
was different; the very gunshot which called
me to dinner was like an echo of pleasures passed;
the music which floated up from the valley was
discordant to my ears. Do what I would I could
not shake off that foreboding which had gripped

me; and desiring only to be let alone I sent the man to other business and threw myself upon my bed to think.

The count, if he were going to act, would act at once I did not doubt. As I lay there listening for footsteps, or starting at every sound, it had been no surprise to me if he had stood by my bedside. When an hour had passed I had worked myself up into a state of excitement which was wearing as an illness, and this despite all that reason could adduce to moderate my unreasonable panic. And yet I remained alone—there was neither message nor messenger.

Tossed thus between argument and fear I heard eight o'clock strike, and nine. It must have been near to ten o'clock before the uncertainty was broken by the sound of a quick step upon the boards of my veranda. A moment later Adam, dressed as he had come from dinner, was sitting at my bedside. The ill news he bore was plain upon his face; there was scarce need for him to deliver it.

"Adam," said I, "thank God you've come!"

He shrugged his shoulders.

"I've no pleasant errand," said he, "but I thought it had better be me than another."

"He knows everything, then?" I exclaimed.

"He might have known it two months ago, if he had any eyes," he exclaimed; "it's the hiding of it that's cut him; but it would have been the same, anyway."

"I must see him at once," cried I, sitting up; "I owe it to him."

But at this he put his hand upon my shoulder, and his manner was that of friend to friend.

"Irwin," said he, "is it the time for such talk? And is he the kind of man to see at a moment like this? Oh, my dear fellow, think of it! Do you know that I've been wrestling with him for the last hour to save your life? Did not I tell you three months ago that he was something less than sane? You have chosen to prove the matter, and here's your answer."

"What is to be done, then?" I asked, feeling an overwhelming despair rush upon me.

He gave me my answer in a single word.

"Dress," said he.

I put on my coat, and waited for him to speak again.

"Now," said he, "we will call the man to pack your bag."

"My God!" said I; "you mean to send me off, then?"

He pretended not to hear, but went to the bell.

"Adam," said I, "I believe you mean well to me. Help me to see the count."

"You can see him," said he; "but if you have a grain of love for his daughter, you will do as I am telling you."

I was angered at his calmness, and suddenly blurted out:

"And if I don't choose to go?"

He laughed for the first time.

"In that case," said he, "I shall just carry you. Do you think I would come here on this errand if I did not want to serve you? Why man, reckon it up. Is it any great heroism to argue a fine point with a madman? Will the *rôle* of martyr suit you? Come, gather your wits together, and don't be long about it. It's the toss of a coin whether I get you away even now."

"Surely," said I, "he will come to reason in a day or two."

"That may or may not be," replied he. "I don't pretend to read your future. But, as God is my witness, I will be your friend, Irwin."

"Then what do you propose?"

"I propose to run for the open sea until the gale falls—in other words, to send you for a cruise."

"For how long?"

"Until, as I say, the gale has fallen."

"Then you will bring me back?"

"If it is wise to do so."

"And meanwhile you will put me ashore to tell your story to every man I meet?"

"I will take the risk of it, with the girl as a hostage. You are a likely man to bring ruin upon her home."

I was silent under the sting of it. Presently I asked him timidly:

"Am I to see Fortune again?"

He paced the room twice before he answered me.

"Well," said he, at last, "if it can be, it shall be. But you've not many chances to throw away. And, anyway, you musn't stop here, where he'll be looking for you."

The man had now put what things they had given me into a big travelling-bag; when he had received instructions to carry it to the creek, we followed him from the house. I could hear the band still playing in the square before the great hall, and the lanterns in the gardens were glowing with a hundred colours; but the music had lost its harmonies, the scene its potent charm. Like a man walking in a fitful sleep, I passed down the road which lay before the great pavilion.

There was a light burning in the count's study when we came to his gate, and, the blinds being up, I could see the bent figure of the man as he sat at his writing-table. He appeared to have no occupation other than that of gazing out upon the darkness of the garden; and though we stood to watch him for some minutes, he never moved so much as a hand. I had a strong impulse at the sight to disregard the apprehensions of my companion, and there and then to demand speech with one who deemed that I had wronged him; but Adam drew me back with a firm hand.

"For God's sake, listen to me!" said he, with more earnestness than he had yet shown. "If he sees you to-night the interview will be a short one. Give him time to get his senses!"

I obeyed perhaps with childish weakness, for he led me on at once toward the pavilion of Fortune, and bidding me to stand at the gate until he should return, he went to speak with her. Five minutes later I stood in her room for the last

time before my exile; and all the reality and the
bitterness of separation came upon me with such
overwhelming force as to draw tears from my eyes.

For I had looked at least to hear her voice
again, to feel once more, if for the last time,
the warmth of her lips upon my own, to be
nerved by her "God-speed," made strong in her
promises. But when I saw her then, in that
supreme moment of our lives, she lay upon the
couch in a trance—inanimate, a thing of marble,
voiceless, pallid even with the pallor of death.
Nor could any man have known greater agony
than this—to see one who was a mere child, whose
sweet, babyish face was half-hidden by her lovely
hair, held fast in the bonds of the twin brother
of death, and to know that she could hear, yet
could not answer; could see, yet was as one un-
seen; could suffer, yet must not weep; could
burn with the desire to lay her head upon the
heart of him who loved her, yet must not raise a
finger from her bed. Nay, as I knelt by her, and
kissed her again and again, and pressed my
cheeks to hers, and sought to call her back to
speech, I thought that this was the curse of God
upon me, and that never again should the cloud
be lifted from my life.

How I left the room I do not pretend to know. I remember that, after many minutes of walking, and while the blinding tears still choked my eyes, I found myself with Adam's arm through mine; and so we stood together, looking down into the vast well-like pit which I had first entered on the day of my coming to the Isle of Lights. Just as three months ago I had mounted from that gloomy chasm to the wondrous spectacle of the island, so now did I descend the lift to the sea-shore, and in descending shut from me that perfect home, its lights, its music, and its people.

At the foot of the lift one of the black, wasp-like boats awaited us. Silver Lincoln sat before the levers in the steel room which served for a cabin, and he greeted me with a kindly nod. Here, however, I found that Adam was to leave us. Until this time he had been my strength, my whole support; and to lose him was to be utterly alone. I tried to tell him this; but he had his reasons; and, giving me a hearty grip, he cried, "God guard you, old friend!" and so was gone from my sight. Before I could call after him the steel hatch was screwed upon the cabin roof, and we had plunged beneath the sea to the gate of the island.

Three months ago the passage of this tunnel had terrified me. Now I made it without fear. While the dark walls of rock were plainly visible under the glow of many lamps, and great fish butted at our windows, and the thought would come that we were for the time being as men buried, and might never rise again, the more potent emotions I suffered caused me to view the spectacle with equanimity. Nevertheless, the heat of the cabin was almost unbearable; the rush of ill-odoured air across my face seemed to suffocate me; the craving for light was not to be resisted.

When at last we rose to the surface of the sea, and the hatch slid back in its grooves, I came up out of the terrible cabin to take my farewell of the island. Away, near the encircling reefs of coral, the yacht *Wanderer* lay at anchor. In the distance, and toward the mountains where the prison was, a red light flashed upon the ramparts of the city. Presently the greater beacon, which stood upon the headland above us, poured its wave of tremulous rays upon the sleeping lagoon. In the flooding of the light I looked again to the mighty walls of iron rock, to the tremendous cliffs which stood around the count and his schemes, and shut him from the world. And it seemed to me that those looming barriers were now reared against me; that they mocked my hopes—that, henceforth, I might knock and no man should answer me; might cry out, and hear no word but the echo of my own voice; might search, but find no gate in that rampart of stone behind whose heights there lay such visions and in whose security men dreamed such dreams.

So was I carried from the Impregnable City, and as the yacht steamed out to sea and the lights were lost upon the horizon and my eyes looked upon the darkness of the greater ocean, there was upon my lips a prayer that the work might never fail because of the passions of man, or yield its might to the ignoble ambitions before which nations have perished and the children have lost their heritage.

CHAPTER XIX.

A VOICE FROM THE NIGHT.

I SAT in my study in London upon a sunless day in February, seven months after I had been carried from the Isle of Lights. In the gloomy street before my window men and women walked with quick steps through the wet and slush which the culminating winter. had bequeathed to us. A drizzle of rain fell from the low clouds which hung above the city. It was good to draw to the fireside, and to dream of other hours and other scenes.

Upon my table there lay a bundle of examination papers. They were the work of the students of Edinburgh University, to which I had been appointed examiner. My three months' absence from London had established my reputation. Though worthy Donald, my man, knew not whether I were alive or dead for many weeks after my disappearance,—until, in fact, I wrote to him and named my address as Valparaiso,—his canny instinct rose to the situation. He told my friends that I had been called to South America, to the home of a Chilian millionaire. The society papers were kind enough to spread the thing abroad; and I, who had known what it was to want a guinea, had now the income of a minister. So does fame tread upon the heels of advertisement.

Fame, indeed; but what of the life to which fame ministered? How was I the better for the plaudits of colleges, or the gold of patients? When did they help a weary heart or an unresting hope? I would have given them all for one hour with the woman I loved, one hour in the sunny gardens of the island, one hour when I might have touched Fortune's lips again. And seven long months had passed, and no word had been spoken, no message had crossed the seas, no sign been given unto me. Nay, there were moments when I started up in my bed to tell myself that all was a phantom of the air, a picture which my brain had painted, a shadow of the night; and I said, "Physician, minister to thyself!"

During the first weeks of my exile I had not ceased to plague myself with pretty fancies that the count would soon come to reason in the matter, and that Adam Monk would one day knock at my door, to carry me back to the home wherein all my thought of a future lay. Lincoln, when he had put me ashore at Southampton,— for they brought me straight to London,—had kept me up with this promise, and I had held to it with unsuspecting faith. But as the months went, and the vivid memory of many things grew dimmer, and only the face of Fortune was ever before my eyes, I began to say, "They have done with me," and to wrestle with the worst.

This conviction was stronger when, two months after my resumption of practice, I received a letter from the Bank of France, in which it was stated that the sum of ten thousands pounds had been put to my credit by their client, Count Andrea Jovanowitz. The sum was lavish to the point of absurdity; but thus were all the man's acts. I knew that here was my fee for three months' service upon the island, for that labour of love which had brought me to this surpassing grief. But I could not touch the money, and it lay where he had left it—an abiding memory of all that I had lost, yet lived on to win.

Toward the end of my seventh month of banish- ment, the earlier and more reckless schemes I had formed in my mind, and by which I told myself that I might come to the island again, began to give way to the settled and haunting melancholy of unconquerable despair.   Before that, there had been days when I had thought to fit out a yacht and go cruising for a year in the Pacific.   I abandoned the scheme only when I reminded myself that I had no sort of idea whether the count's haven were in the Northern Ocean or in the Southern, or, for the matter of that, any tangible notion of its bearings at all.   At other times, wild thoughts of getting Government help flashed upon my imagination; and I remember a night when I stood outside the Criterion Theatre, and seemed to hear again amid the roar of the traffic those words of treachery which Jacob Dyer had spoken to me upon the hillside.

What would the French president give for my information?   How if I published the whole affair in our English *Times?*   An island of refuge for political cutthroats! an asylum for cranks and fanatics—honest and otherwise!   A new Tolstoy preaching a new creed of universal amnesty.   A war against prisons; a system for the rescue of prisoners which in itself would astonish the world!   What a shaking up of courts there would

be if these things were told; what a bustle of
cabinets; and what a going and coming of warships! Yet to what would they come and go?
To the subjection of the city? Nay, I knew that
it could defy the world; and pride warmed my
veins at the assurance.

Thus will you see how wisely Adam spoke
when he said that they held in Fortune a hostage
for my silence. I would as soon have branded
myself thief or felon as have whispered to any
living man that devouring secret which I possessed. None the less did it weigh upon me like
a pall; none the less were all my works and my
achievements in London but barren and empty
honours. Often in the night I would cry out
aloud as though Fortune could hear me and
answer. I saw her childish face in every dream;
her eyes looked out at me alike from the darkness
and the light. Yet I remained without word or
sign; she let me suffer. It might be that she
had ceased to care!

This foreboding and restless speculation took
me from my work on that sombre February day
of which I write. Do what I would to read the
papers of youths anxious to qualify in *materia
medica*, I had no heart for the task. Day passed

to night, and still I sat in my armchair; darkness fell, and yet I forbade Donald to set me candles. Poor Donald! many were his sorrows, many his reproaches, in those months of my travail.

The hours passed, I say, and left me insensible to time. My thoughts were back to the island—to the lanterns and the music and the perfume of the gardens; to the room where I had left Fortune inanimate, motionless; to the thicket where last we had met. Upon the reddening screen of my fire, I saw the faces of the men I knew—of Adam, of Lincoln, even of the count himself; I lunged, in my fancy, to the bowels of the sea; I gained once more those rocky heights, and cried out that I was master of the world. Then the firelight died away, and I started up to reality, and to darkness.

Nay, not to darkness; for, as I moved in my chair, a chilling cold air seemed to fill my room. Though no light of nature was in the chamber, it seemed to my eyes to be filled with rays like the sparkle of diamonds; and, turning in my chair, I saw Fortune herself kneeling at my side.

She knelt, as I had often seen her kneel by the great couch in her own room—a long robe of white hiding her supple figure, her rich hair flow-

ing upon her shoulders, the curious clasp of
mother-of-pearl and gold shining upon her
breast. My first impulse was to take her in my
arms and to cover her lips with kisses, to tell her
that she had brought life to me, to speak the
hundred thoughts which come to lovers when
they meet; but—and this was the strangest thing
—I could find no word upon my tongue, could
not move a hand even to press her own, was held
silent in awe as one in the presence of the dead.
None the less was I sure that Fortune herself was
at my side, and that the sweet face I saw uplifted to mine was the face of all my dreams.

How long this vision lasted I may never know.
Though I was dumb, though my hand could not
so much as touch the hands stretched out to me,
nevertheless the cloud seemed lifted off my life
at her coming, and I was content to sit and watch
her eyes shining with all their fire of passion and
of love. For never did she seem to be more beautiful than when thus she appeared to me on that
night in which, at last, I was to awake from my
sleep of inaction, and scarce to rest again until I
held her, not as the spirit of my darkened room,
but as a thing of flesh and blood in the garden
of the sea.

The vision passed, indeed, but the message of it remained. There was in Fortune's eyes, while the apparition knelt before me, a whole world of pleading and of love. Though no word was spoken, though I was held to my chair as one from whose limbs power has gone, nevertheless did my soul seem to speak with hers, and, speaking, to hear voices of the night.

"Come to me!" was her cry, ringing in my ears like the cry of the wounded for succour. "Come to me, beloved!"

I heard the words a thousand times; heard them when the room was full of the light which she seemed to bring; heard them when the darkness fell, and I knew that she had left me; heard them when I stirred from my seat at last, to behold the fire burned low in the grate, and to feel a shiver of cold in every limb. And, hearing, I rose from my chair, and I vowed with myself that I would answer her cry, God helping me, and would not rest day or night until I had come to her home, to live with her or die with her, as it was written in the book of our unchangeable destinies.

CHAPTER XX.

I SAY that I made the vow with myself; yet scarce had I uttered it when the heroic folly of the resolve occurred to me. What more could I do to reach the Isle of Lights than I had done already? Whence was to come that phantom guide who would lay bare the secrets of the deep, and say: "Sail here, and sail there, and you shall find"? What scope was there for my new gotten energy? I could have laughed aloud at the irony of the thing as I stood in the darkness, and heard the clock strike six. And yet it seemed to me, despite the cold logic of reason, that a change had come upon me; that a new zeal had taken the place of the desponding lassitude to which I had been a victim for so many months; that Fortune had spoken a message, and that the echo of it would come to me again in words which would carry me to understanding and to action.

This may have been a mere impression, it may have been one of those strange inter-communica-

tions between minds in harmony, which science
is so little able to explain or even to recognise.
Be that as it may, the conviction was mine, and
I stood in the darkness by my window, and found
in it a strength and a freshness of heart which
had been foreign to me for many weeks. The
rain still fell in the street without; it no longer
depressed me. The lamps glowed mistily in the
fog; they failed to recall the loneliness and the
gloom of London. Nay, in my thoughts I was
back to the day when Adam had come to me in
this very house; to the hour when I heard a
newsboy crying of an outrage in the Café Mirabeau; to the yacht *Wanderer,* and the entrancing glades of the island. And, as though to
strengthen the mental picture, what should happen but that a newsboy came down the street
even while I stood by the window; and his words
were an echo of the words I had heard on that
never-to-be-forgotten night when first I had seen
Adam, and Donald had wished to set glasses for
him.

Arrest of an Anarchist—the boy styled it
"henerkist"—in Paris! That seemed to be the
burden of his cry. But anon, as he came near, I
caught the words, "Hawful revelashuns—Kefè

Mirabeau," and began to prick up my ears. Since I had returned to London no scrap of news concerning revolutionists and their meetings had failed to interest me. I was ever asking, as some new reformer stood in the dazzling light of public platforms, Will this man ultimately be the recipient of the count's bounty? Will he come to that perfect home in the South Seas from which I am so sorrowful an exile? The scantiest intelligence concerning the French prisoners at Noumea or upon the Isles de Salut was welcome to me. And now, remembering how the Italian, Marco Privli, who had been conveyed to the island with me in the *Wanderer*, was concerned in the dastardly business of the Café Mirabeau, the call of the newsboy set me itching with curiosity, and I threw open my window and sought his paper.

The room was in darkness, as I have said; but I remember that my hand was unsteady when I lit the lamp, and that for many minutes the lines upon the ill-printed news-sheet where blurred to my eyes. At last I came upon a small paragraph headed "Capture of an Anarchist," and I read it through—not once, but twenty times. When I put the paper down the room rocked before my eyes, and I held to my writing table for support.

Privli arrested at a café in Boulogne! The French Government in possession of intelligence which was nothing less than sensational! That was the whole of the news—to the reader of the street. How much it meant to me only those who have followed this narrative may know. A hundred confusing hypotheses rushed into my brain at once—a hundred fears, a hundred questions. How came Privli at Boulogne, unless he had escaped from the island? What were the revelations he had made? What would he say at this trial? How would his arrest affect the city and its people? Was it possible that he could guide the French Government, if a search for the count's haven were decided upon?

To none of these suggestions could I find answer; with none could I cope. It seemed, indeed, that my brain was on fire with the effort of thinking; and yet, above it all, and the one thing clear to me, was this—that here was the word of Fortune's message; here the intelligence which she brought; here the moment to wake from my stupor.

I must go to Paris—of that I was sure; for to Paris Privli had been taken. The more I thought upon it, the more was it plain to me that, unless the count knew of this Italian's arrest, I alone in Europe remained the friend of the island. That Privli would tell all he knew, if thereby he might save his neck, I did not for a moment doubt. He was a scoundrel, with a mind in the gutter, from the first. Common gratitude would never trouble him. The vital thing to learn was, had he brought with him to France any plan of the city? Did he carry in his mind any tangible idea of her situation in the Pacific? For if he did, I knew that the count's stronghold at last must prove itself, at last must face the warships of the Western world, and, facing them, must answer ay or no to the question of that impregnability which was the loudest boast of its people.

I must go to Paris—the determination became stronger every moment. It was then a quarter past six. I resolved to catch the eight o'clock mail, that I might be in the French capital early on the following morning; and since there was no time to dine—nor had I inclination to eat—I rang for Donald to bring me tea, consoling myself, as I looked at the student's papers which littered my table, that I could deal with some of them in the train.

"Donald," said I, when the honest fellow presented himself, "I am going to Paris; bring me tea and something to eat, and pack me a bag."

He looked me up and down, and shook his head.

"Sir," said he, "I'll not hold it from you—ye'd do better to gang to bed."

"Do I look ill, then?" I asked him.

"Save us!" cried he; "and dinna ye ken that ye're a' shaky like an aspen? Gang to Paris, but it's me that will be buryin' ye in that same place."

"Not so bad as that, Donald," replied I, though I imagine that I was no picture of health; "but hurry up, man, for there's not a great deal of time, and I'll get no dinner but what you give me."

"Do you bide long?" he asked, with his hand still on the door.

"Perhaps twenty-four hours—perhaps a month. I haven't thought about it. But I'll write you, and if I'm detained, Donald, we might find another Chilian millionaire, don't you think?"

"They're no so plentiful," said he, in his most doleful voice. And then he added, in the deep note of reproach, "Oh, sir, it's just wearin' out Providence to turn siller frae the door like this.

Gang to Paris, and a' the town deein' in yer par-
lour! Ay, but ye're no canny, man, at all."

He was still muttering "Gang to Paris, indeed!"
as he went down the passage; but he had packed
me a bag in ten minutes, and at the quarter past
seven I left Welbeck Street for Charing Cross.
The night was then intensely dark; thick and
clammy mists steamed upon the streets; London
was at her worst. Nor did I know, as I crossed
the river to the darkness of the open country,
that I should not look upon her lights again until
I had passed through the valley of the shadow of
death, and had heard the thunder of cannon upon
the silent seas of the island city.

CHAPTER XXI.

A PARLOIR IN THE MAZAS.

DAWN was rippling over the silent streets of Paris when my carriage left the Gare du Nord. A melancholy gray light came up out of the east, putting to shame such gas-jets as were yet burning; a few waiters lurked dismally about the doors of the cafés. But the greater city was asleep, and the ring of wheels upon the deserted pavements called echoes from the eaves of the older houses.

Though the passage had been a fair one, I had found it insupportably tedious. Later editions of the evening papers got at Charing Cross added little to the intelligence in the paragraph which had sent me from London. Marco Privli, an Italian, suspected to be one of the most active of the ultra-revolutionists, and the author of the almost-forgotten outrage of the Café Mirabeau, was indeed arrested; but it remained for me to learn if he were the man I had seen upon the island. Did my assumption prove false, I had come to Paris upon a fool's errand; did it prove true, the future was one I scarce dared to think upon. That it would be full of danger to all those I had learned to love was beyond question; that it might bring about the destruction—or the attempted destruction—of the city I foresaw all too clearly. But whatever was its moment, my own interest was not to be hid; and I thought, perhaps with selfish satisfaction, that the same revelations which should send French warships to the Pacific should carry me also to Fortune and to her home.

And thus it came about that, during my journey in the night, the one idea, "I must see Privli in prison," became a haunting one. From him alone could I learn immediately how far the count was compromised; how great were the possibilities of the island ceasing to be a refuge. And if this Privli proved to be a stranger to me, well, then, I stood where I had been twelve hours ago, but without my fears or the harassing contemplation of far reaching possibilities.

From the Gare du Nord I drove straight to the little Hôtel de Roche, on the Boulevard des Capucines. They knew me there; and, since any enquiry after the welfare of Anarchists was not likely to be without danger in Paris just then, I had security in the friendly *testamur* of the land-lord. Following the fashion of the city, although he was a German, six o'clock in the morning was his hour of rising; and, when I drove into the courtyard of the hotel, he came from his office to meet me.

"My dear Dr. Trevena," said he, with the strong accent of the Prussian, "what a pleasure! I hef not look to see you dis morning."

"I did not look to see you, either," said I. "Can I have my old room?"

"Hef him! why, who should hef him? I tell you that if de Prince of Cambridge was in him, he shall go out."

"That's very good of you. And now, before I get my coffee, tell me, in a word, is it possible for an Englishman to see a prisoner in the Mazas, and, if so, at what time?"

Had I fired a pistol at the host of the Hôtel de Roche, he could not have worn a look of greater astonishment.

"To see a brisoner in de Mazas! *Gott in Himmel!* what for you see him?"

"For very private reasons, my friend; but very good ones. If you can tell me how to manage this thing, I will be under lasting obligations to you."

He shook his head for so long a time that I feared an injury to his neck. At last he said:

"A friend of de doctor's?"

"Scarcely that; in fact, I might call him an enemy. Privli, the Anarchist."

"Privli, the Anarchist! See an Anarchist! *Mais, c'est impossible!* You bring de police here—de whole police."

"Nonsense, my dear Herr Meyer. I have come to help the police, providing this man is the man I believe him to be. If any of your friends can arrange the matter for me, I will give him fifty pounds."

The offer of money raised his spirits considerably.

"*Certainement*, to oblige Monsieur de Doctor; it is oder thing. And you are an oder man—I spik wid haste. But you hef learned de news? All Paris read him. De Government hef found out why de brisoner escape from ze Isles de Salut. They know where he go to; und I tink we sleep now wid no more smash und bang und blow-up in de air."

"You mean that they have traced the twelve prisoners who escaped two months ago?"

"Draced!   What is dat draced?"

"Found them—discovered them?"

"Ah, not so; but they vill, doctor; they shall hef found them soon.   All Paris make it fine talk; you read him in de journal."

He held out to me a copy of the *Figaro*, in which I read his news.   The report was headed with more lines than such a usually dignified print is in the habit of employing, but the pith of it was sufficiently amazing to justify the term "sensation."   For the *Figaro* stated that the Italian had confessed, and, in confessing, had made it plain beyond doubt that a conspiracy for the rescue of prisoners existed in the Pacific, and would receive the immediate attention of the Government.

The peril of the island was no longer to be questioned, then.   Privli had sought to save his neck, as I judged he would.   He had told the secret which presently, when it flamed abroad through Paris, would light a sensation the like to which Europe had not known for many years. The intelligence stirred every pulse in my body. It seemed that even while I stood I was losing

moments which belonged to the count and to his
people, was lagging when every nerve should be
strained in that friendship which they had a right
to claim from me.

"Herr Meyer," said I, when I put the *Figaro*
down, "I double that offer of mine. Get me to
the Mazas, and I will pay a hundred pounds."

He spread his hands abroad in amazement, and
said :

"One hundret pound to see ein Italian man
what hef blown peoples up?"

"Exactly, one hundred pounds. I am now
going to my room to have a bath. After that
you will find me at breakfast—coffee, and two
eggs *à la coque.*"

He remained stupid with astonishment, while I
entered the lift and went to my bedroom. What
he did in the meantime I have never learned ; but
I feel assured that my talk about Anarchists
frightened him out of his life, and that he walked
straight off to the Prefecture de Police. Be this
as it may, there was, when I returned from my
bath, a stranger sitting upon my bed, and for
a moment the man looked at me as critically
as a dealer at a horse. The situation was
embarrassing and unexpected, but I saw the

need of rising to it, and greeted the man most affably.

"I hope you speak English," said I.

"A little," he replied, with scarcely the trace of an accent.

"I presume you have come here to take me to the Mazas?" continued I.

"I have come here," said he, "to know why you want to go there?"

"What business should that be of yours?"

"Every business. I arrested the Italian you desire to see."

"You are a police officer, then?"

"Exactly, I am the second officer at the Prefecture."

"And your name?"

"My name is Fourcinier."

"Fourcinier?" said I, seeming to recognize the ring of it. "Fourcinier—there is a Fourcinier who teaches French at the University of London?"

"*Parbleu !* He is my father."

"And my patient," said I. "I am Dr. Irwin Trevena of Welbeck Street, London."

A more fortunate word than this never was. He rose up at the mention of my name, and deliberately kissed me upon both cheeks after the fashion of Frenchmen.

"A thousand pardons for my coldness, doctor," said he. "My father tells all Paris that you saved his life. That landlord of yours is an old fool. I will take an early opportunity of telling him so."

"There's no harm done, anyway," said I, gloating inwardly upon my luck; "and now, if you feel well disposed toward me, you can help me in this matter of the prison."

"Nothing will give me greater pleasure; but permit me to ask, what possible interest can you take in this Italian, who is a very low scoundrel indeed?"

"I take a strong interest in him. Your father may have told you that I was in South America during the summer. I met at Buenos Ayres an Italian, named Privli, who did me a great service. I am anxious to learn if the Privli of the Mazas is the Privli of Buenos Ayres? Is not that a rational thing?"

I was amazed, even while I spoke, at my capabilities in falsehood; but what I did then I would have repeated a thousand times if the city could have been helped by the words. And when the man answered me, I saw that I had convinced him.

"The best of reasons," he answered quickly, and I could see that he was thinking. "If you can assure us that the man was in Buenos Ayres last summer, we shall be glad of the news."

"When I see him," said I, "you shall have an ay or no in ten seconds. Meanwhile, at what time can we go to the prison?"

"With me, you can go at any time. And if it suits you, we will step round after *déjeûner.*"

"That fits in with my plans perfectly. I have ordered two eggs *à la coque,* and I expect they are ready in the coffee-room."

"Eggs *à la coque* in Paris! Oh, my dear doctor! You might as well order tea. Come with me and I'll show you how to breakfast. There's no such preface to investigation as a good meal."

I finished my dressing, feeling that it was a fine piece of fortune which put me in touch with this man. He, of course, remained in my company that he might snap up from my conversation useful facts about his prisoner; I went with him in the hope that I should glean information concerning the alleged "revelations" which would tell me

more particularly how things stood with the
island. This, however, was a poor hope, for he
had a cunning tongue, and what I got from him
was of the sparest. Only once during the superb
breakfast at the great café by the Opera House
did he broach the subject of Privli, and then in
the vaguest way.

"Your Italian," said he, "is a very plausible
rascal, and, I am inclined to think, a very cunning
one. At first I thought him a king of liars—but
he is not. What he has told us so far is the
truth."

"So I judged from the newspapers," said I.
"But is it really possible that he knows anything
of the so-called refuge for the men who showed
their heels to Cayenne and New Caledonia?"

He looked at me very closely, and passed from
the subject with a word.

"Possibly," said he; "but have a liqueur,
doctor, while I send for a fiacre."

With this he rose from the table, and I followed him to the carriage, which he directed to
the great prison for those awaiting trial, which
is nearby the Lyons railway. The hall of this
fine building is remarkable, I should judge, above
the hall of any prison in Europe; and there was

I left to inspect the altar of the rotunda with its Doric columns, and to read and reread the well-meant words upon the frieze beginning, "Gaudium erit in cœlo," while my new friend arranged for them to bring the prisoner from his cell in one of the six galleries to the *parloir*—the small room in which he could see his friends—upon our *etage*. Five minutes later they called me to the interview.

The system by which you talk to those lying in French prisons is much the same as our own. The visitor stands in a small cell; the prisoner is in a cell opposite to it, the two dens being heavily fenced by iron bars and divided by a passage, which a warder paces. The light in the Mazas did not appear to me to be particularly good, and it was not until my eyes had warmed to it that I could make out the face of the diminutive man who stood pressing his cheeks against the steel cage into which I peered. For some minutes, in fact, we remained staring at each other like animals in opposing dens, and for the life of me I could not answer the vital question— is this he whom I seek, or another of no concern to me? Presently, however, he spoke, and, although it was a greeting in a strange tongue,

the note of it told me beyond dispute that the
man I now beheld in a cell of the Mazas was the
Italian I had seen upon the deck of the
Wanderer—the Privli of the Isle of Lights—the
man I feared to meet, yet knew, from what I had
read, that I must meet. And so I confirmed
these biting fears which had not left me since I
opened that evening paper and read the fateful
news of the great capture.

As I have said, he was the first to speak, and
when he found that I could not answer his Italian,
he asked me in French:

"Who are you?"

"A friend," said I, speaking in English. "A
friend who met you upon the count's yacht in
the Pacific."

"Holy Virgin!" cried he at this, "it's the
doctor!"

"No one else," said I, signalling to him to
moderate his voice.

"And why do you come to see me?" he asked,
accepting the hint.

"To ascertain if I can be of any service to you,
and to ask how my friends are?"

He laughed satirically at this.

"To be of service to me. You!"

"Exactly. Tell me what I can do for you."

"You can throw me a cigarette."

I opened my case and tossed the contents into his cell; then I threw matches after them, and he began to smoke furiously—no one, to my surprise, saying him nay. But this I set down to the presence of Fourcinier, who stood in the passage during the whole of the interview, and had his ears very wide open, I make sure.

"Now," said I, when the Italian had come to the bars again, "how are your friends?"

"They were well when I saw them two months ago; but, my dear doctor, no one knows better than you that life is very uncertain. Next month they may be ill."

I read the meaning of his words without difficulty. He was thinking of his own treachery and its consequences, and I would have given a hundred pounds to have knocked him down upon the spot. Yet were there a thousand things I burned to learn of him, and I began to rack my brain if thereby I might find some method by which I could force him to speak of them, and yet in such a way that the warders listening might not be the better for that which was said.

"Well," said I, taking up the conversation

again slowly, "they are well cared for, though the climate of the Argentine is not the best for a man like our old friend. But what I want to know at the moment is, how can I help you? Have you any relations or people to whom I can be of service?"

This was no wise question, as he saw. No sooner had I uttered it than the man listening in the passage came a step nearer, and I observed his shadow cast faintly upon the stone pavement. He was drinking in our words, as I knew he would. Nor did the Italian take my offer in good part, but laughed a mocking laugh, and drew back his face from the bars of the cage.

"*Nom de Dieu!*" said he. "So you have come here for the address of my friends. And you think I will tell you?"

"I think it possible, though I quite understand your humour. If there is any relation of yours who has need of help, and does not mind the visit of the police, I will assist him, as a return for the service you did me in America."

I said this with all my voice, meaning that the others in the passage should hear every word of it. It lay upon me to talk then as though I had nothing to conceal or to learn; and I am convinced that I succeeded, for the shadow upon the pavement grew blurred again and was drawn back. As for Privli, he, I fancy, could make nothing of me, and he smoked quickly as a man thinking upon it. But he was evidently a rogue of some intelligence, and when he answered me, he, too, spoke with no curb upon his tongue.

"Doctor," said he, "if you have not come here to make a fool of me, you may send a hundred francs to my old sweetheart, Marie Berr, 25 Rue du Chemin de Fer, Boulogne—the house where they took me."

"I will send them," said I. "Is there nothing else I can do?"

Now, at this word, he began, I think, to see my drift; and certainly it was curious that the method by which I was able to ask him the one all-vital question should have been of his creation. Suddenly stepping back in his cell, he took a hand-kerchief from his pocket, and, while he made some ridiculous observation for the listener's ears, he began to signal to me in the flag-code used upon the island, a code which, as he must have known, I had amused myself by learning during my voyage in the *Wanderer*. With the slightest motion of his improvised flag to the right or the left, he spelled with amazing rapidity the words:

"What do you want to know?"

In a moment I had answered him with the question:

"Have the police a chart of the island?"

His reply electrified me. It was in one word:

"No!"

My whole opinion of the man—an ill opinion until that time—changed with his answer. He had endeavoured to save his neck, it is true; but he must have laughed in his sleeve as he did so. Without a plan, the French Government might as well have sought for the riches of the Incas as for the Isle of Lights. No better news could await me in Paris; and, as I prepared to leave his cell, I made known my gratitude to him.

"I hope you will come well out of this," said I, with my whole voice again. "I shall not forget to send a thousand francs to the address you have given me. If I can do anything more for you, let me know at the Hôtel de Roche. I shall be there for five or six days."

He gave me a nod of perfect comprehension, and I left him. Fourcinier was waiting for me in the rotunda, and he seemed inclined to accompany me to my hotel; but I got rid of him by the bold notion oi asking him to dine with me that night at seven o'clock, an invitation which he accepted greedily; and so I quitted the Mazas.

But I had got there news which I would not have exchanged for a handful of diamonds.

CHAPTER XXII.

THE DUC DE MARNE.

PARIS was echoing with the sensation of the hour when I returned to the boulevards. News-boys with morning editions of the evening papers ran wildly from kiosk to kiosk, telling of the new thing which had taken the city by the ears and led it to the cafés and to the market-place to dis-cuss the incomparable wonders. I found busy men talking in groups at the corner by the Opera House; the portico of the Grand Hôtel was thronged as upon a fête-day; the streets them-selves were alive with the story which I alone in all Paris could make whole and satisfying. And as I pushed my way among the loiterers, and laughed at the cries of the newsmen, and said to myself, "What if I added my tale to theirs?" it seemed to me that I was one man against a nation, one man fighting the battle of the city wherein my hopes lay, the battle of her whose love was my sustaining impulse.

It is impossible to tell of the uncontrollable

excitement which had been upon me since I left London.   I lived like a man carried upon a hurricane of surprise, swept as by the wind of destiny from idea to action, and action to idea, until the confusing images of men and things were blurred in my mind, and only the need of the hour was to be remembered or considered.   So it befell that my one thought when I left the prison was of the "No" which Privli had spoken, the "No" which meant so much to the count and to his people, the "No" which ensured for the hour the safety of the island.   For, without chart or plan, the discoveries which had been made were so many romances and fables, so much froth of gossippers powerless to help France or her government. What responsible man, I asked myself, would send warships to the Pacific with the order: "'Search until you find the prisoners that made good their escape from Noumea"? what commander would sail with the instruction: "We believe that a haven for prisoners exists; go you and discover it?"   I could have laughed aloud at the humour of the position; every newsboy's call was a new joy to me; every edition of the papers a source of fine merriment.

The island was safe for the day; that was not

to be disputed. But with this assurance to comfort me on the count's behalf, I had little to help me on my own. I was as far from seeing Fortune or her home as I had been a month ago. 'I had worked for many hours with my new energy, and yet lacked definite aim or plan. And when I thought of this—when I minded myself that I was without one friend in all Europe to give me a hand upon my way—then, indeed, even the good thing which the Italian had spoken was powerless to elate me, or even to occupy me long with satisfaction.

Without one friend! I spoke the words standing in the Boulevard des Capucines; and when a man, absorbed in the latest edition of *La France*, pushed against me, I looked up quickly, and saw that I was at the door of the Jockey Club. In a moment, by a flash of thought spanning weary months and carrying me swiftly back to a memorable scene upon the island, I recalled the name of the Duc de Marne—the duke who had written that first letter of warning to the city, who had spoken of the count in those abiding terms of love and reverence. I remembered that he had been a president of the Jockey Club; I felt sure that I could speak freely with him; I knew that his name stood high amid all the "influences" of Paris. And thirty seconds after I had recalled it, I was in the portico of the club asking for him.

A servant said that the ex-president was in Paris, but at his apartment in the Hôtel Windsor. Since the death of his wife he had ceased to occupy his great house by the Bois; and I congratulated myself upon this as I walked quickly to his hotel, and said that here surely was the second message Fortune had brought to me. Since I had thought to see her in my rooms success had dogged my steps. I almost prayed that it would follow me now to the apartment of the Duc de Marne. Nor did I hesitate when I came to the hotel to send up a card on which I had scribbled the words:

"COUNT ANDREA JOVANOWITZ."

The effect was amazing. Scarce had the servant left me when he returned, and invited me to go up with him. And hardly had I made up a sentence with which to open the interview, when I stood before a white-haired old man, who looked first at me and then at my card, and appeared as bewildered as I must have been. But his voice was hard when he spoke; and I had no doubt that a man of mind must be dealt with.

"Sir," said he quickly, "what is the meaning of this visit?"

"It is told in a sentence, Monsieur le Duc. I come here to save the life of a man dear to you— the Count Andrea Jovanowitz."

The room in which we were was a long one, heavily carpeted, and containing many books. The duke had risen from his writing-table at my coming; but now he deliberately walked the whole length of his apartment, stood a moment at the end of it to light a cigar, and then only made answer:

"Who are you?"

"I am Dr. Trevena of London, recently returned from the count's island home in the Pacific."

"Tell me your story," said he next, and with no less bluntness.

I told it him from the beginning, adding no theory or surmise—keeping straight upon the path of pure narrative. When I had done he took my hand in his; and I felt like a man who has been dragged from deep waters to the shelter of a sure haven.

"Doctor," cried he, "I could welcome no other man at this moment as I welcome you! I would give half my fortune to save Andrea——"

"But," exclaimed I, "there is no immediate danger?"

He shook his head.

"The danger is not only immediate—it is already active. Last night, at eleven o'clock, a full chart of Andrea's home reached Paris from London. It was sent to the Foreign Office there by an Englishman upon the island—one Jacob Dyer. Instructions for the despatch of cruisers were issued this morning at seven o'clock."

I said nothing—it was as though my last plank had been snatched from me.

"Yes," continued he, seeing my distress, "that is the worst thing that could have happened. But I had already made my plans before you came here—and the first part of them is the warning which must be conveyed to the Pacific."

"But," said I, "who is to guide you there?"

"That will we think of this afternoon," said he. "We have now two heads; they should be sufficient for the difficulty. But first we must eat. You have taken *déjeûner*—take a second, then, and call it lunch."

He slipped a fur coat over his brown velvet jacket, and descended with the light step of a man of twenty to the restaurant near. From the first I regarded him as a son regards a father. Helpless before, I was now made strong in his courage and his resource. And we had not been sitting at table ten minutes before he had laid his plans before me.

"I have thought it all out," said he, "and our course seems perfectly clear. The first thing to get is a copy of the chart now lying in the hands of the police. Fac-similes of that will be in many places. Some will be at the office of my friend the Minister of Marine—in the hands of him or of his secretary. We shall, therefore, call upon him at five o'clock, the hour he receives visitors. If it be possible, we shall get a view of the chart. We may even steal a copy of it; but we shall not come away until we know definitely where the count's haven is, and how it is to be reached."

I drank in his words greedily.

"And then?" I asked.

"Then? Why, then we shall trouble our heads to find some means of despatching you to the island."

It was all said with the utmost confidence, and

I found myself listening to him like a child. By and by, however, he began to question me closely as to the count's way of life—and more particularly he asked by what means he had got the prisoners out of the island by Cayenne. This I was able to tell him; and it surprised him not a little.

"He got the men off with one of his submarine boats," said I. "You read of an *émeute* upon the island some little while ago, and of others not so recent. They were all planned by our friend. The prisoners made a riot and ran for the shore, where the boats picked them up and then plunged beneath the waves. When the work was done the small craft steamed out to sea and were taken aboard the yacht."

"And do you really think," he asked, "that his place is impregnable?"

"That I cannot tell you. He makes the claim, and has confidence in it."

"Well, it is possible, if we do not get him off, that he will have to prove it before a month has passed. But we must prevent that folly."

I said that I, on my part, would risk my life and all that I had in the venture; and with this talk, and mutual suggestion, we remained until

dark began to fall upon the streets. Then we
walked to the hotel of the minister, upon the
Quai d'Orsay, and the duke sent up his card,
while I remained wondering if it were all true or
if I were dreaming again, as I had dreamed so
often in the months of my exile.

When we had waited in the ante-room for
some minutes, they told us that the minister was
not in,—a great disappointment, since he could
have done for us what no underling had dared,
—but that his secretary, M. Gondolcourt, would
see us at once; and, upon this, we mounted to a
large room on the first story. We had arranged,
as we walked, that when we were in the chamber
we were to use our wits in the attempt to secure
the chart, and the duke had promised to hold
the minister or his secretary in talk to give me
opportunity to make a copy, if it happened that
the document were in any way displayed. On
the latter point he had the most sublime confidence, a confidence which I could not share;
but he knew that an important paper like this
would be early in the hands of the Government,
and that, secrecy being in no wise necessary, it
would scarcely be hidden; but rather would be
under active discussion at the hour of our visit.

I had not been in the room of M. Gondolcourt five minutes when this far-fetched hypothesis was fully warranted. It was a small apartment, opening into a larger chamber; but it contained a great table littered with papers, and was lighted by a reading-lamp with three wicks. The secretary himself, a tall, clean-shaven man, received us with every courtesy; and the duke introduced me with a fine tale, which was worthy of his invention. When, however, I had made the necessary compliments, I had eyes for nothing but the table; and, at my very first survey of it, I was able to reckon up my companion's foresight. There, close to the secretary's hand, was a rough map on copying paper, a chart scrawled in black ink; the document, I did not doubt, for a grip of which I would have paid cheerfully a thousand pounds.

Children play a game wherein, if I remember rightly, they are either hot or cold as they approach or recede from the object which is hidden. I must have been hot and cold twenty times in the first ten minutes of that interview. While the duke talked ceaselessly, and I, perforce, must put in my word, no sight but of the edge of that chart could I get. Pretending

interest in this picture or that, taking up one
book and another, peering here and peering there,
I was yet as far from success as from the poles.
And all through it the secretary smiled, and
bowed, and paid me compliments; and no more
suspected my almost unbearable excitement than
he suspected the true object of our coming to
him. Nor did the duke extend to me a sign even
when it seemed to me that we had staked the
throw and had lost.

I say he did not extend to me a sign, but this
was in the first ten minutes of our talk. When
these were passed, he, of a sudden, turned to me
and spoke.

"Doctor," said he, "I have a word of the Jockey
Club's private business to speak to M. Gondolcourt. You are sufficiently my friend that I may
ask you to read the paper for three minutes
while we discuss it."

I told him that he need make me no excuses,
and took up a *Figaro* which was upon the table.
I had hoped that the two would disappear
entirely in the larger room which gave off
the secretary's office, but, while the duke endeavoured to draw the man into the room, the
other was content to stand in the opening of the

doors, and I was not one whit better off. The man could still observe my every movement. Had I gone round to that side of the table whereon the chart lay, it would have been to declare my intention as plainly as though I had spoken it. Nor could I get full view of the map, for it was half covered by a book, and nothing but the lower lines of it were visible.

It may be imagined that this situation was a difficult one for any man to face. A hundred schemes for getting the plan rushed into my mind, to be rejected immediately. There was no time for cool or reasoning thought. What was to be done must be done upon the moment. As I sat there, rustling the paper in my hands, I vowed that I would have the chart, even if I knocked down the secretary in the attempt. And then, at the height of my perplexity, the missing idea came to me, and scarce had it come when it was an action.

Perchance it was an ill thing to do; perchance I had justification in my need. I do not pretend to discuss the right or the wrong of it. Suffice it to say that I rose from my chair, and, making as though I would take a book from the table, I deliberately knocked over the lamp with the three wicks. The contrivance fell upon the floor with a crash; it extinguished itself in its fall, but poured its paraffin upon the carpet; and I, striking a match as if I would see to set it straight, dropped the flame into the running oil, and sprang back as a rush of fire leaped up almost to my face.

The confusion which followed upon the first burst of the flame was such as I had expected. Gondolcourt and the duke sprang into the room together and seized the heavy rugs upon the floor. I cried "Fire!" with all my lungs, and then besought them to save the papers—to which warning I added the practical example of filling my arms with the books and documents and rushing wildly to the staircase with them. But the first paper which I touched was the chart of the island; and no sooner was I out upon the landing than it went into my pocket. Meanwhile the room itself was full of servants and of men with buckets; and what with some crying that the hotel was to be burned, and others clamouring for the *pompiers*, the din and riot were indescribable.

At the height of the hubbub the duke joined me upon the landing. I made him a sign that I had succeeded, and he took me by the arm and hurried me from the palace. It was only when he had shut and locked the door of his own apartment in the Hôtel Windsor that he spoke.

"*Eh bien*, doctor," said he, "it was a bold stroke; but no damage is done."

"It was the only possible course," said I.

"And the chart?" he asked.

"Is there!" said I, and I spread it on the table before him.

For a long while we peered at this extraordinary document as though it had been the chart of a gold mine. Rough and ill-done and unornamented, it was the strangest plan man ever looked upon; yet a more complete one could not have been drawn. The bearings of the island, the soundings in the outer reefs, the place of anchorage, the approach to the harbour from three points, the great beacon, the flashing red and white lights at the southern cape, the stationary green and white lanterns on the northern heights of the island—these were laid down by a sailor's hand, and for a sailor's use. But, above all, the very clear and bold statement of the situation of the city—which was in longitude 120° 10', by latitude 41° 65' south—set all question of its utility at rest.

"Well," said the duke, when we had looked at it for a long while in silence, "I have not a grain of the seaman in me. I leave it for you to say. Is that paper sufficient to take you to my friend Andrea?"

"In the hands of a capable sailor, it is all sufficient," said I.

"Then," said he, "you leave France to-night."

"But——" cried I.

"In my yacht," he continued, "now lying at Bordeaux. She awaits my coming to set out for Monaco. She will go to the Pacific instead. She is of a thosuand tons rating, and has new engines. Unless the Government orders ships from Noumea by cable, you will arrive at your destination before Andrea is hopelessly cut off. Bring him to me in the yacht, and I will promise to settle the other affair for you. Are you willing to risk your life in the venture?"

"A thousand times. But what can I say in gratitude to you?"

"Say nothing; pack your bag! I must return to the Quai d'Orsay to make my excuses and yours. Your train for Bordeaux leaves at six-fifty."

"But," said I again, stammering out the most complete absurdity, "I have asked a man to dine——"

"Ask him twice when you return!" cried he, with a merry laugh. "Think of nothing now but our friend and his need. You have a great work before you; perform it with all your mind and heart, and God guard you!"

He would hear no more; and this was the first and the last time I saw him. But the memory of what he did for me is not to be clouded, and he is often in my thoughts. Never did any man find a better friend in such a day of need.

For it was by his help, and his help alone, that I came again to the Isle of Lights, and carried a message to the city in the hour of her sorest trial.

CHAPTER XXIII.

I KNOCK UPON THE DOOR.

THERE had been a misty rain all day, but it gave way toward the hour of sunset, and the whole of the west was painted in deepening bands of rich golden light. The shrill wind, which had troubled the yacht from the middle watch, fell to the balmiest breeze at two bells in the first "dog"; and now, when night came up out of the sea, there was scarce a ruffle upon the long swell shining like a mirror in the fall of the sun's light, darkened to infinitely delicate shades of green beneath the loose banks of cloud which rolled over the eastern heavens.

I stood upon the bridge of the yacht as the twilight deepened, and the ringing cry "Land ho!" which had just come to me from the fo'- castle, sounded like the note of some sweet bell in my ears. I had no eyes for the gentle seas of the Pacific, no eyes for the great golden mirror of waters whose immensity appals while it fas- cinates, no thought but for the dark line of cliffs rising like a little mound above the waters—there, miles away upon our starboard bow. For that little speck was the Isle of Lights, and by good hap we should drop anchor in its harbour before the dawn sprang up in the east. For many hours the duke's skipper and I had been upon the bridge with our glasses. He—a fine yachtsman, a man of Gosport, by name Jack Bannister —knew much of the history of the island and of its people. He had displayed a zeal in the passage which nothing could surpass; he had carried me from Bordeaux to this lonely sea in thirty-four days; and now he stood with me to ask the all-vital question: Have we lost or won? is our warning in time? do French ships already shut the city from the world and begin war upon its people?

We stood with our glasses while yet the light remained to us; and as the mountains beyond the city rose higher and higher above the waves, so did we put to each other the doubts which moved us to this unbearable excitement. For an hour past, the yacht had been steaming slowly between crags and barriers; for an hour we had heard the shouts of the men that cast the lead; and now the moment was at hand when we should learn all—for better or for worse, as it was to be written.

Until this time we had seen nothing of war-ships, either in the Pacific or nearer to Europe. Though we had swept the horizon with our glasses at every change of the watch we had found no company but that of sailing vessels bound for New Zealand, or steamers plying between London and Melbourne. And since we had made Cape Desire we were utterly alone; had not observed so much as a sail in all the days of passage. Nevertheless had we learned at Bor-deaux that the new first-class ironclad *La Gloire* had been despatched with sealed orders from Toulon, and that the fast cruiser *Atala* was leav-ing Cherbourg with a company of engineers and a considerable number of troops. And now we must learn if these had out-distanced us in the race; if they lay already in the harbour of the city; if other and unknown vessels had come before us, and had done the work which all France cried out for them to do.

The mountains of the islands, I say, became clearer to my view, the dark line of the barrier-reef more plain, as the sun set on this, perhaps, the supreme hour of my life. From my place

upon the bridge I could look over the rolling
sweep of sea; my spirits leaped up as the minutes
were numbered and no hulls of ships stood out
above the horizon.   One by one I gave greeting
to the landmarks I knew so well; to the great
headland with the beacon; to the hills above the
prison; to the vast precipices crowned by the
ramparts; to the channel of that strange gateway
beneath the rock.   And when, at last, I made
out the line of the harbour, and saw that one
ship alone lay anchored there, it was as though
the battle of my life had been fought and won.

Some of the exhilaration of my own thought
must have been shared by Jack Bannister.   For
an hour or more he had been cursing the island,
and particularly the narrow channels through
which he had navigated his yacht so warily; but
now, when he saw what I saw, he, of a sudden,
threw his hat upon the deck, and cried:

"May I be stretched if we're not first!"

"There's no doubt of that," said I.   "And a
hundred pounds to the crew that brought us!"

No sooner was the word spoken than the men
heard; and there went from deck to deck a cheer
which must have echoed down in the caverns of
the sea.   The most part of the hands were Eng-

lishmen; they had a vague notion that a "Frenchee" was to be outrun. When they learned of victory they were not to be controlled, and for many minutes they continued to bellow like beasts in a field. Yet they stood to their work, singing a lilting song of triumph with wholesome lungs, and, as the last notes of their song died upon the sea, the sun passed below the horizon.

With the falling of the light the skipper's burden was added to intolerably. We now stood in a narrow channel of the reef; the harbour lay away more than a mile from us; the night had come down with heavy darkness; the beacons of the headlands were not kindled. It was a place which might have set any man fearing, and I did not wonder at his prudence.

"Doctor," said he, "I'm thinking I must berth here, and put you ashore at daybreak. It's not exactly a pretty place to moor in, but the duke won't thank me to lose his ship, and you'll be no forrader, anyway."

The moments were precious, and the delay galled me. I thought that a way might be found by which I could reach the shore before the dawn, and this I told him.

"'The last time," said I, "we fell upon this place a gunshot brought us help. Fire a round now, and see if they have any answer."

He assented to this willingly, and presently the little brass gun upon our fore-deck flamed over the sea, and its report sent birds screaming from the heights. Scarce was the echo of it dead when the great beacon ashore spread a wave of glorious light upon the lagoon; and we began to look one upon the other as by the light of day. Never have I seen a crew so awed in a single moment. The hands stood in the sheen of the arc, which made all things golden, and their low murmur of astonishment was joined to cries of fear, and even of prayer. The engineers below hastened up to behold the unsurpassable spectacle. The ocean about us was as a carpet of silver upon which a myriad of jewels glistened; the lantern shone out above the city like an emblem of kingship, and men were hushed before it as before an unknown power.

When time had been given for the passing of this impression, I turned to the skipper and asked him a question.

"Now," said I, "have you light enough to make the harbour?"

He assented with a nod of the head, which he repeated many times, as though the thing stuck in his mind and he could make nothing of it.

Presently he said:

"Doctor, are there many of them up there?"

"A colony of six or seven hundred altogether," said I.

"Oh!" said he, still thinking. "And do they all expect to come on board this ship?"

I laughed at his fancy.

"It will be odd if you have the pleasure of seeing a man of them," said I. "The duke's idea that his friend will return quietly to France is a mere hallucination. He would never leave his home."

"Then what the devil are we here for?" he asked somewhat testily.

"To put me ashore!" cried I.

"And then?"

"To return to France, and tell your owner that we were in time to warn his friend."

"Well," said he, after a pause, in which he had condemned the eyes and limbs of a number of his men whose movements were not quick enough for him, "this is the queerest trip I ever made, by thunder! You commission me to pick up a bit of an island and an old lubber with a twist in his head, and—Go easy!—why, burn me! you run me on a colony—Stop her!—and—— I'll be laid out if they haven't got guns, too!"

A gun boomed over the sea from the ramparts of the cliffs as he spoke. We had come now within a cable's length of the harbour; and I could make men out upon the count's cargo-steamer—for that was the ship anchored in the offing—signalling by flashes to those behind the bastions of the high rock. The gunshot, I think, alarmed both our hands and their skipper, for he went on:

"Doctor, how many of us are going ashore with you?"

"A round number," said I; "or, to put it plainly, none of you. I don't suppose for a moment they will allow any stranger in there."

He looked at me with some surprise.

"Well," said he, "you know your men; and the duke made you free of this ship. But I wouldn't care for the job myself—that is to say, if I could get any other."

I thought that he was right; but I did not tell him so. It was a possible thing that, once I had passed the gateway of the island, I might never see him again. And, while I was thinking this, he continued:

"Will it be long before you put off again?"

"God knows!" cried I, declaring, perhaps, my foreboding in my voice.

"But you've those here that will stand by you if it comes to that," replied he; "and should a Frenchee's skull want cracking I've men down there that will do it while you wait."

It was the word of banter, but was not so to be taken. I make sure that every seaman on the ship would have come to my help had there been the least need of it; but I had no opportunity of saying this to him, for a boat had now been rowed to us from the harbour, and a man in the bows of it was hailing. He was my old friend Dennis O'Brien.

"Ahoy!" he shouted, with a cry that echoed far over the sea; "what ship?"

"*La Reine d'Or* from Bordeaux!" roared the skipper.

"And what will ye be wanting in these same parts?" asked the Irishman next.

"To come ashore with important news from Europe," said I, now standing at the very edge of the bridge.

"Howly saints, it's the docthor!" exclaimed

the man, and his fellows took up the cry and
repeated it.

"Tell your master," continued I, while their
surprise was still upon them, "that I come here
to save his life and the lives of his people."

He gave a great howl of wonder at this.

"Ye're a bold man, I'll be telling ye," cried he,
now pushing his boat away from us, "and I'll not
kape it from ye that ye'll do well to bide where
ye are. There's pills above, docthor, which is
mighty inconvenient to digest."

"Do you mean that we should bring to?"
roared I.

"The same," said he.

He rowed away with the word, and we dropped
anchor, being then some half a mile from the
headland. Ten minutes later, and after we had
observed him signalling once more to the ramparts, he was back again.

"Ahoy!" he cried.

"Ahoy!" roared I.

"Docthor," said he, "it's yerself that I'll be
having for company—yerself and no other."

I turned to the skipper and asked him to put
the ladder out.

"Mr. Bannister," said I, "you've done well by

me, and I'm grateful. You will make my business easier if you now weigh anchor and steam
for France."

"With a pretty tale for my master," said he.

"With the tale that I hold this course to be the
best," said I. "It must be plain to you that if
these people wish to quit this place, here is their
own ship ready to take them. Since they will
allow none of you ashore, you cannot help me by
cooling your heels here. I shall make it my
business to write to Europe and say what I think
of your work."

"Dr. Trevena," said he, for the thing was sudden and surprising to him, "I did not look for
this; and I'm the last man alive to turn my back
on a shipmate. Tell me, in plain words, do you
go ashore here of you own will and pleasure?"

"In plain words," replied I, "there is no shore
in the world I would so soon see as that of yonder
island."

"Then I make my mind easy," cried he; "but
with this by-word—I shall no more go to France
than to the moon. From here I steam south for
coal, which I'm wanting badly; but in one month
from this date I stand off this coast again to see
how you do. And here's my hand upon it."

We shook hands very heartily, and with the same farewell I took my leave of the crew, and stepped down the ladder to the boat awaiting me. The great light still poured its flood of rays upon us, and the whole scene—the dark headland, the silver field of the still lagoon, the men at the ship's side cheering, the white hull of the duke's yacht—is strong in my memory. With the echo of the men's farewell in my ears, I saw the last of the *Reine d'Or.* It was but a biscuit toss from the yacht to the steamer moored in the offing; and when we had made the passage, one of the small Nordenfelt boats was ready for us. The boom of a second gunshot rolled over the hills as, with Dennis O'Brien for skipper, I entered the little cabin of steel; and while the report still hung in the higher peaks, the great lantern went out, and we plunged below the seas to the wondrous forest-like paths of coral and the enchanting green lights of the city's gate.

Yet had I no fear of the voyage, for it carried me to the woman I loved; and I knew that I had come with a message which, perchance, might yet be life to those who were soon to wage the unequal war against the nations.

CHAPTER XXIV.

THE CITY WAKES.

THE muffled reverberations of the gong, rolling through the water, struck down to the cabin, after that which seemed to me an exceeding quick passage of the tunnel below the sea. When we came to the surface by the small quay upon the left bank of the lake, there was but one man standing to receive us. He had a lantern in his hand, and until he spoke I did not know him. I was still twenty yards from the landing-stage when I heard his voice; and my heart beat higher at the sound of it.

"Irwin!" said he.

"Adam!" said I—and that was all our greeting; but he held my hand for many minutes after I had come out of the boat, and I seemed to feel all that he would say.

When two men meet that have a weight of burning subjects upon which they would well talk, it happens often that they babel commonplaces for many minutes. I am not sure in this moment of overwhelming joy that I did not ask him how he did, and make observation upon the weather. Certain it is that for a spell we stood there, in the darkness of the chasm, he swinging his lantern nervously, I using words which had no possible concern with the momentous mission which had brought me. When at last I got control of my tongue the torrent of my speech was not to be restrained.

"Adam," said I, "you broke your word with me and left me all alone, and God knows what I have suffered."

He heard me very calmly, letting me run on in this wild way until I had done with it. Then he asked me:

"Am I master here, Irwin?"

I had shame of his reproach.

"Could I set his mind straight where it was warped?" he continued. "Man, as God is my witness, I've fought your battles until he will hear your name no longer. And now you come here like this!"

It was on my lips, and torturing me, to ask how Fortune did; but he anticipated my question.

"You'd like to know beforehand," said he,

"that somebody's been ailing since you left. You won't find her quite what she was."

"Adam," cried I, thinking the worst, "for God's sake, tell me all! Is she dead?"

"No," said he very slowly, "but it's been work to save her."

"Let me see her at once!" cried I, forgetting all else in this.

"See her!" cried he, and then, suddenly, he turned upon me with another question. "Irwin, tell me, how did you find your way here? I always said you would, but I'm curious to know."

"I found my way here," said I deliberately, "by a copy of the chart which Jacob Dyer sent to the British Foreign Office."

"Great God!" said he, and his lantern fell with a crash upon the pavement. But I did not spare him the tale.

"That chart," I continued, "was sent from London to Paris. It is now in the hands of the French Government, who have got Privli under lock and key in the Mazas. I am presuming that he escaped from here?"

For a while he did not answer me; he seemed almost in a stupor.

"Yes," said he, at last, "he escaped in the

yacht's longboat which we used to lend him to
fish in.   He and another, Vorofsky, the Russian,
got away in her after stabbing the man that
watched them; but the boat was found bottom
upward ten miles from here, and we thought he
was done with."

"Thirty-five days ago," said I, "he was in the
Mazas.   I saw him there, and I know that he has
confessed.   The first-class battleship *La Gloire*
and the cruiser *Atala* left for here the night I
sailed."

"And you came?"

"In the Duc de Marne's yacht; he behaved
nobly."

I have never seen a man so troubled.   For a
spell, after I had given him the story, he paced
the narrow quay, so confused and dazed that he
knew not what he did; but when I had spoken
to him again, he cried out of a sudden:

"O Irwin! help me to get my wits!"   And
with this his old coolness came back to him; and
taking me by the arm, he forced me into the lift.

The hour was then near to nine o'clock, and as
we came out upon the highroad at whose height
the lights in Fortune's pavilion were to be seen,
I found myself trembling like a woman.   Yet else-

where upon the island there was darkness where
lanterns had been of old time; silence where soft
harmonies had come up upon the breeze; no
sound of voices, no swell of merry laughter.
Only the twinkle of lamps upon the hillside, and
of a few in the great square before the Temple,
struck up the veil of gloom and of solitude.
Adam told me as we hurried along that they had
buried at the dawn one of the oldest of their
councillors, Felix Marno, exiled from France in
the year 1871; and for this cause was there the
night of mourning. I answered nothing—the
hour seemed a forecast of the days which were to
come; and at the door of the count's pavilion he
left me.

Though he was gone but a minute the waiting
space was like an epoch in my life. Not a hundred yards from the gate by which I stood was
Fortune's room. My troubled mind pictured her
lying as I had last seen her; living, yet as one
dead; seeing, yet worse than blind; hearing, yet
finding no words upon her lips. And in my pity
I yearned for her with my whole heart; yearned
to touch her lips, to press her cheeks to mine, to
speak with her, if it was to be for the last time.
Nor could I put from me altogether the strength

of a great hope, because I had come thus to the city with the tidings which I alone could carry; had made this effort for her and for her people.

Adam had gone but a minute, I say, and when he came back with a quick step he led me round by the garden gate to the study of the count; and, with no sort of formality, he opened the door, and I was again in the presence of the man whose very name had been a dread to me in my months of exile. He was dressed as I had first seen him, and he stood by his writing-table, a flush upon his face, his left hand busying itself with papers which he pretended to turn, his right hand lying across his chest. And, when he gave me greeting, it was with the slightest inclination of his head.

"I am informed," said he, in a very low voice, "that you come to us with very important intelligence. I thank you for your labour on our behalf. May I now hear of it?"

Standing where I was, like a man in the presence of a judge, I told him the story from the first. Twice while I spoke he paused to snuff one of the candles in the silver sticks. Once I saw his hand tighten upon the scroll of papers. But he showed no other emotion, though it was plain

that, during my speech, he had come up out of
his dreaming, and passed from the man of visions
to the man of acts. In a word, the habit of the
soldier had returned to him; and, when I had
done, no corporal ever stood up so proudly.

"Doctor," said he, "there is no common word
of thanks for services like these. This is not the
moment to speak of such things, though I have
them in my heart. You have come to us of your
own will in the hour of our necessity; you have
been our friend where no other friends could be
found for us; and now you shall stand or fall
with us in this night of trial which God has
willed."

He spoke the words, and touched a bell by his
side. An aide-de-camp appeared at the signal,
and he gave him commands in a firm voice.

"Let the 'boot and saddle' be sounded," cried
he, "and the great bell be rung. The women to
the hills; the men to the square!"

He touched another bell, and scarce was his
finger on the knob of it when a mighty report of
a gun roared over the mountains, and shook the
windows of his pavilion. And, with the echo of
the sound, he called for horses, and turned again
to us.

"My friend," said he, "I count upon you for the work.   Come with me!"

We found three horses waiting at his door, and though I, on my part, was chafing to hear a word of Fortune's name, I knew that the moment was not then, and I followed him down the path to the square.   Even while we rode the city was awakening.   Many lanterns began to flash upon the hillsides; countless arc lamps leaped into light.   There was the sound of horses galloping upon the roads; the murmur of women crying out to learn the news; the blare of bugles, the clash of arms; the sorrowful tolling of the bell in the cathedral tower.   Soon, upon the ramparts above, we could distinguish the forms of men who carried torches in their hands; soldiers, buckling on their swords, ran with us upon our way; there was a great company of men in the square when at last we came to it; a battalion of sturdy fellows whose white uniforms and gold lace shone with gems of light; a troop of horse already mounted and waiting for the word.

It was in the square that the others of the count's staff—De Rémy, the engineer; Coloron, the colonel of the cavalry; Malasac, in command of the heights, and half a dozen more—now joined him, and in this little group we stood; the light of many lanterns upon us, a vast crowd of excited men before us, the troops with paling faces, drawn up around. And when hurried counsel had been taken, the count addressed his people, and never was his voice more clear:

"Men of my city, men and friends," he cried, "the hour which the Almighty has appointed for our trial is upon us. Ships are at our gates. The moment has come when the governments of Europe will demand us to give up those for whose lives we have staked our good name and our honour. In this solemn moment I ask your love and your devotion—the devotion of your hearts, the devotion of your hands. Stand with me, and this work of yours shall never fall; be my right hand, and I will carry you to freedom and to victory. Fight the good fight in obedience and loyalty, and no harm shall come to you. For God and liberty, I call you to your arms!"

The very mountains gave back the cheers which followed upon his words; but in the succeeding hush there was to be heard over the lagoon without the echo of a great gun.

And every man, hearing, knew that the hour of battle was upon us.

CHAPTER XXV.

SHIPS OF THE NIGHT.

A LOW murmur of wonder, perhaps in a measure of dread, broke from the company while the echoes of the gun still rolled in the hills. The thunders of the report were like an answer from the world without to the brave confidence of the count and of his best men. Yet there were many, I may not doubt, whose courage shrivelled when the first ringing word of war was spoken so forcibly; many who would have sacrificed their fellows readily if thereby they might have saved their own skins. But these kept their counsel; and, with whispered exclamations and excited gesture, the throng dispersed to its work.

It was evident to me at this time that the defence of the city was not the gift of any chance or mere plan of the night. The order, the method, the readiness of it all spoke of long days of preparation, of schemes long since matured. There was bare need either of word or of command. The troops, animated by the count's appeal, went to their stations like men who have long waited for the welcome call. The cavalry disappeared at a canter, and spread itself abroad so that its hundred men were ultimately posted upon all the higher roads; the civilians, if such you might call them, made haste to get to the shelter of the hills; the iron shutters of the café were let down; the great Temple was shut—the plaintive tolling of the cathedral bell, the tramp of squadrons marching, alone came to us upon the breeze of the night.

For my own part, I had viewed all this as a man who knows not whether he has waked or yet lies in the pleasant bonds of sleep. I could find no longer either surprise or astonishment. And when the count and his staff turned their horses toward the ramparts upon the southern heights, and Adam called to me to follow, I went readily, and not wanting something of that fierce exhilaration which treads upon the heels of a summons to war.

"Adam," said I, as I forced my pony up to his, and so rode with him in the van of the little procession; "there's not to be sleep for any of us to-night, I'm thinking."

"Sleep!" cried he, in answer. "Who could sleep now?"

He spoke with all the excitement of one who has attained an ambition of old standing, and I could see that the gunshot had girt up his nerve, and that the desire to be up and doing was strong upon him. Indeed, it was work to get him to hear me, though I had much I would well have said to him.

"Tell me," cried I, after we had ridden some way in silence, "what will happen when they begin to fire shell."

He answered me with a little laugh.

"That depends upon the shell—and stay now, they are speaking for me!"

He pointed down to the street by the cathedral. A shell had sung over our heads with a low, moaning hiss as he spoke; and now a sudden flash of scarlet light, and a dull, deadly crash, followed in its path.

"Our friends from Toulon do not stand on ceremony," he went on. "They would have been wiser to have waited for the dawn, don't you think? But it's a strange game, and they must be taught how to play it."

"And they make no demands," said I, "pre-

sent no sort of ultimatum! It's a queer business
to come and knock down a man's house, with
never a word by way of explanation."

"Oh, but they have had their answer," replied
he, setting spurs to his pony in his impatience.
"We signalled it an hour ago from the headland.
Their cry is for the surrender of every man ashore
here; our reply is a flat refusal to treat with
them, or to deliver up the hair of a man's head."

"And that reply was given to them?"

"By the man in charge of our ship in the offing.
They seized her while we were waiting in the
square."

"How could you learn that?"

"From the wire which connects the headland
and the Temple. There is no point on this place
with which we can't communicate in ten seconds.
And this visit has been looked for these two years
and more. The answer we have just sent out is
a part of our constitution; there was no need to
discuss it."

"Well," said I, "that's all plain enough; but
where do you look to put the women when the
work quickens, as it will by and by?"

"The women lie already where the shells of ten
fleets could not harm them. My dear fellow, do

you take us all for children who play a game of
fairies? Have we worked for five years to build
up a citadel which the first rap might send tumbling upon our ears? Look yonder—that line of
light is your answer!"

It was said a little roughly, and this, perhaps,
he knew, for presently he spoke again, and with
better grace.

"Irwin," said he, "I'm the poorest idiot in the
two hemispheres to be out with this night. By
all that's holy, I believe I'm wearying to hear the
sing of a bullet! And, man, I always was an
impatient devil; but the whole thing is life to
me—just life!"

This was not to be doubted; but I had no ears
for his words. Looking up to the heights near
the great beacon, I was filled with wonder when
I beheld streams of light pouring from many a
loophole and many an ill-shaped casement; saw,
in fact, that the heart of the rock was, in a sense,
eaten out, so that a mighty cave, now lit up by
countless lamps, stood marked upon the amphitheatre of the hills. And to this wondrous shelter
of the mountain's heart there went a throng of
women, some with light step, some labouring with
fear, some indifferent, some weeping. Even at

our high place above them we could hear the lilt of their song, the wailing of their cries; almost could see their faces as the lamps by the roadway shone upon them, and the light from their hundred lanterns danced upon the stony path.

But we were now near to the ramparts, and, tethering our ponies at the guard-house by the road's end, we climbed the rough-hewn steps which led to the barbican. Nor shall I ever forget the picture which then lay spread before me on the glassy surface of the near lagoon. A far-reaching torrent of light had rushed upon the hither sea above which we stood at a height of two thousand feet. The whole harbour was clear to be viewed as though the moon's first rays were flooding upon it. Far away beyond the barriers of coral, the search-light of a warship shone out like a warning beacon. A second light from a vessel which had ventured near to our offing poured its whitening arc upon our sheer walls of rock in refulgent beauty, moved its golden round from point to point like some mighty lantern throwing pictures upon the fortifications of the city. The cry of many voices was borne up to us upon the wind: the inner lagoon swarmed with boats full of armed men, who rowed to and fro as though seeking creeks or more friendly harbour-age. As for our own steamer, that lay already in the hands of the besiegers. We could observe that men trod her decks. We seemed to hear officers bellowing commands; we watched the lowering of the boats from the davits; beheld the haste of attacking companies, all zealous for that task which they must have regarded so lightly—for that work which, I hazard, they looked to finish with the dawn.

This, then, was the spectacle spread out before our eyes when we came out upon the ramparts. But the silence of our own men, the determina-tion they wore upon their faces, their quick and methodical movments, were in fine contrast to the noisy zeal of the Frenchmen rowing there at such a vast depth below. The beacon on the headland no longer cast its light upon the lagoon; the turrets were in darkness save for those moments when the ship's lamps played upon them; the gunners received their orders in low words; the count and his staff watched silently the display of helpless force—all realised in that moment the immeasurable power of the city, the grandeur of her isolation, the supreme dignity of her restraint.

For, as yet, she had fired no shot, had vouch-
safed no answer to the clamour at her gates.
While shells had hurtled above her domes and
spires, while her harbour had been stormed and
her one steamer seized, she had been silent as a
city of the dead, voiceless, presenting no token
of life to the hastening ships which had gone to
the work so lightly. None the less was she prepared; none the less was her hand heavy when
the moment came for her to raise it.

My own place upon the ramparts was near to
that of the count. He addressed no words to
me, being absorbed in his work of observation;
but when from the bows of the nearer ship a shell
came crashing upon the rocks below us, he of a
sudden uttered a loud prayer, crying in a voice
which every man heard:

"Eternal Father, shine thy light upon us!"

A loud "Amen" was echoed by many, even by
the rougher gunners, and almost in that moment
it befell that we were observed by the crews of
the small boats below; for we heard a great
shouting, and could see some of them making for
the greater ships. Soon rifle-bullets began to
pepper the rocks below us; a few, but these were
rare, stuck the bastions or flattened themselves

upon the turrets. The distant warship joined
her fire to that of the riflemen, and the heights
trembled at her voice. A crashing shot struck
the headland some fifty feet below us, and hurled
tons of it into the lagoon. As the hunks rolled
down the cliffside, and fell with a great curdling
of foam into the sea, one of them hit upon a boat
which had been searching for a shore, and smashed
it into splinters, floating them up presently upon
the current and carrying them quickly to the
reefs. But of her twenty hands not one rose
from the tomb of the waters; there was no cry
to be heard, no swimmer to seek help of his fellows. The men had been struck from the roll of
life as by a visitation of God; they were the first
to die at the city's gates; the first of the strong
that fell before the might of the weak.

As the boat and her men were drawn down
below the placid lagoon, I looked up at the
count, and would have read his face. I saw that
it was stern and without evidence either of pity
or of triumph. But it was plain that he had
become the soldier again; and when he spoke to
me the fierce spirit which burned within him was
not altogether to be concealed.

"Doctor," said he, wheeling round of a sudden,

"what a spectacle of impotence! These men come here to kill their own. Do they look to shake these hills which have given battle to countless generations of the sea? Do they think that the splutter of a shell will wrench from me the lives I hold? Oh, immeasurable fatuity, that can neither sow nor reap in the field of the sweetening mercy, in the vineyards of the God that made us all!"

A soft and very beautiful expression was upon his face when he said this to me, and I knew that deep down in his heart there dwelt the consuming pride and belief in the city he had built. But I had no word worth the saying in answer to his appeal, and presently his mood changed.

"What business have you to be here when the bullets are flying?" he asked. "Why do you show yourself like this?"

"Indeed," said I, "it's a sight I would not miss for a pension. And, count, I must answer with a *tu quoque.* You of all men should first look to yourself."

A bullet, singing so close to us that I seemed to feel its warmth upon my face, gave a new note to his warning.

"My son," said he; and I had a great gladness,

for he had ever so spoken to me before, "there is
no bullet which shall cut me off from the fellow-
ship of Christ which I serve. I am the servant
of the Almighty, and to him shall my life be
given. But you—you are very dear to us. No
duty keeps you here."

"There is no place I would so well be in," said
I. And he was pleased at the word.

"Well," exclaimed he, "we must think about it
again when the dawn breaks. The danger will
quicken then; let them enjoy the follies of the
night, for many of them will never see another."

He spoke of the French seamen then swarming
in the harbour, which was dotted with their boats.

"You mean," said I, "that they will not attempt
the passage of the tunnel until we have the sun."

"They will never attempt that if they are sane
men," said he; "but they know not what they
do. Nay, indeed, they beat upon the eternal
rocks, and shall lay bare their own tombs. They
strike at the city of the Lord, and he shall answer
them with fire."

It was good to hear him with these pretty
metaphors in his mouth; and I watched by his
side long during the night—he standing motionless and silent when the bullets hailed and the

shells burst with flashes of exceeding brilliance above the island. Once, indeed, I offered him a cigar, and that he smoked with pleasure; but when, in the dark hour before the dawn, Adam came up to us with a silver flask of wine and a basket of food, he would touch nothing, or turn for a moment from the fascination of the scene. We, however, sitting under the shelter of the bastion, made our meal by the torches' light, the music of the rifles always in our ears, the sweetness of the night blowing upon our faces. And one by one the staff joined us, until the figure of the count alone stood prominent upon the heights of the ramparts.

For day, of a truth, we waited with the yearning of sick men. By the sun's light alone could we see how things stood in the outer bay; could number the ships, or judge of their designs. And every man who loosened his belt to sit in the shadow of the parapet had this in his head—that day would set him to his work again. For my own part, I watched the eastern sky with wearied eyes; looked often to the darkening fields of stars; listened for the morning gun in the sure hope that the dawn would hear the island's voice, would behold her awakening to the kingship

which she boasted. And when at last the
heavens opened to the herald of light, when from
the east the veil of darkness rolled up and the
gray mists winged across the sea, then, I say, my
heart beat fast with desire of the sun; my blood
ran warm in pride because the city should thus
speak for herself.

The first of the light scarce had come upon the
higher lands when the gun was heard upon our
own heights; and we leaped to our feet. At the
report of it the count cried, "Make ready!" and
a lusty cheer followed upon his words. From
sentinel to sentinel the echo went, until it ran
round our shores like a cordon of voices. The
island had spoken for the first time; but there
was steel in her voice; and I, with Adam, looking
eagerly over the sea to the rippling field, sown
already with the bodies of the dead, saw how
great a change the day had brought. The cruiser
which had cast her light upon us so persistently
during the watches of the night, now lay anchored
in our inner harbour, not a cable's length from
the shore; the greater battleship had been
brought through the narrows of the reef, and
was now steaming slowly toward the headland.
Two other ships lay beyond the outer barrier;

and the Russian shape of one was not to be de-
nied. But the Duc de Marne's yacht I could not
see; and I judged that she had made good of
the night and was on her voyage to the south.

"Adam," said I, when we had both looked long
at the new life that had come to our harbour,
"either they are madmen, or they know nothing
of your guns."

His answer was the offer of a cigar from his
case.

"Man," he said presently, "you're excited!"

"Indeed?" said I.

"You've taken the worst cigar in the bundle,"
he went on. "Do you remember, when Bismarck
wanted to learn what Von Moltke thought of
things at Gravelotte, he offered him his cigar-
case. Moltke picked the best weed in it, and
Bismarck went off happy. Not that this is
Gravelotte, or anything like it—not if there were
twenty more of them. The fact is, those fellows
don't believe for a moment that the business is
anything but a picnic. They were sent to a
pleasant island in the Pacific to capture some
prisoners; and here they are, just walking up, as
you see. Let us wish them the top of the morning before we have our coffee."

He pointed down to the harbour with the word, and I observed a new thing there. The warships had ceased for a spell to fire heavy shot; but the cruiser now put out a longboat, and, the sun's rim being above the horizon, I made out with my glasses that the boat held ten men, and that one of them wore the dress of a diver. The rowers drove the craft quickly toward the shore above the tunnel's mouth, and it was plain they were about to survey it. But I followed their progress with burning eyes; and, as for Adam, his fingers were about my arm with an iron grip.

"Look now," cried he, "how men may die! God help them!"

The boat had come within a biscuit-toss of the shore. Those of its hands which did not row sat about the diver, who was putting on his helmet; there was no sort of cunning shown, or daytime prudence—only the craft went on silently while we stood very still, and Adam's hand tightened and tightened upon my arm. When at last he released it, a word seemed to burst from his lips, and in that moment the count raised his hand, and the end came.

There were minutes—and, to my pent-up

imagination, long minutes—when the sea shivered
and seemed to rush headlong before the hidden
force which now struck it. As the mine burst the
cliffs trembled to their base; the waters of the
lagoon rose up in a snow-like column of foam and
spray; they divided in deep blue cavities; they
beat in rolling waves upon the black shores of the
harbour; they ran up the headlands like cascades
of silver. Far as the eye could see the ocean
answered to the shock; the spuming waves boiled
up; the still sheen of the water became a field of
churning and of whitening billows. From the
very depths the dull thunder—like the roar of a
thousand cannon—resounded; to the very depths
the sea was convulsed, was lashed into the fury
of a hurricane—all omnivorous and destroying.

As for the longboat which had rushed headlong to this trap, there may be no phrase found
to depict the fate of it. From my high place of
observation the craft seemed to be lifted, at the
first shock, high above the sea; then to be shattered into splinters so small that none of them
were to be distinguished upon the waters around.
In a word, I saw a boat and men, and then, still
looking upon the place, the boat and men had
vanished in the air, and there was nothing to be

seen but the cascade, which rose like a water-spout. One poor fellow, indeed, was hurled to so great a height above the lagoon that his body did not return to the sea which had cast him up, but fell upon a crag of the reef, where it lay, all exposed, and dreadfully torn. Of the rest not so much as a limb was to be discovered. The death which came out of the coral paths below had scattered them like fine dust before the breath of winter.

The island had spoken for the second time in very truth, and her voice had been terrible to hear. I had seen men die often, but death in this shape chilled me to the marrow. The strange silence which now fell, both upon the enemy and our men, was in true harmony with the scene of devastation. For a spell, it appeared that terror filled the Frenchmen below us. Such of their small boats as were still in the lagoon were rowed quickly to the cruiser; the greater warship began to signal with her flags; we could make out the hurry upon her decks, and the preparation for the new attack. And while we were yet debating it the count spoke again, and there was that in his voice which brooked no delay.

"Every man to shelter!" he cried; and then— he still standing there by the bastions, his eyes lit by the fever of the combat—he began to recite, as he was wont, one of the Psalms he loved:

"His trust shall compass thee with a shield: thou shalt not be afraid of the terror of the night.

"Of the arrow that flieth in the day; of the pestilence that walketh in darkness; of invasion, or of the noonday devil.

"A thousand shall fall at thy side and ten thousand at thy right hand; but it shall not come nigh thee."

Such a brotherhood of fine fanaticism and of a reckless, indomitable courage I have never known. While he stood there, alone and conspicuous upon the ramparts, we, fearing longer to disobey him, entered the steel tower below the gun; and from the narrow eye-holes of this we waited for the battleship as she swung round in the harbour, and, letting go her anchor, fired twice at us from her fore and aft barbettes. The first of the shots struck the bastions not fifty yards from our standing-place; and, carrying away many feet of the parapet, sent rock and stone hurling into the lagoon below. The second shell burst some ten feet above the turret beneath which we were; and, as the steel shell quivered to its core, and the splinters of the peak rained down, and the hills echoed the report, I thought to see the count fall almost at my feet, to have his body in my arms. But the flash, which for an instant showed a crimson light upon his face, passed; and still he stood unharmed. The God to whom he had cried had put armour about him—no bullet was cast that should strike him down.

With the booming of these great guns, and the fall of the rock from our headlands, the battle of the harbour creek culminated. From the fort above me the island gave rein to her voice again; the amphitheatre of sea and hill-land answered with a quiver of water and of earth, with reverberations which seemed to roll down to the ultimate depths of chasm and of ravine. I saw one curling tongue of flame shoot out over the abyss; I seemed to feel the ground quaking, the steel wall splitting; I heard a report which struck upon my ears as though to break in their drums; I looked upon the count, whose figure stood up in a well of fire—then the thick smoke came down upon the bastions, and the scene was hidden. Nor until minutes had passed could I observe the path of the shot; the desolation following in its wake—the tokens of our victory. But when the smoke-cloud was uplifted, when again I had the

lagoon spread like a map below me, then, I say,
the venturesome folly of the Frenchmen was no
longer to be questioned. For the shell had
struck the battleship low down upon her port bow
—and whatever it had come upon, whether one
of the torpedo tubes or a smaller magazine, it had
fired some mine, and had ripped up the great
ship as a fish is ripped with a knife. Listing
heavily to port—some of her men crowding upon
her hurricane deck; many throwing themselves
into the sea; many—as the glass told—lying
dead, or crawling to the forecastle with their
wounds—the vessel slowly settled upon an arm
of the reef, and then, cocking up her stern, she
gave to us a target which no gunner could miss.
A second shot knocked away her propellers and
her steering gear; a third burst open the shell
deep down below her engines; a fourth swept the
men from her aft decks like flies from a plate.
And now the rolling volumes of steam poured up
in enveloping clouds; a sheet of fire folded the
stricken hull in close embrace; the steel walls
split asunder; the whole vessel shrank as a
stricken thing. With a grinding upon the rocks
horrid to hear, with a second report when the
seas filled her, with the scream of men and the

roars of command, *La Gloire* rolled suddenly upon her side; and, turning as she went, sank swiftly to the coral depths.

The vessel sank, as I have written; the cries of dying men were hushed; the rushing waters closed above the scene of agony; the sun shone again upon the unruffled lagoon; but we, whose hearts than seemed to stand still in that terrible moment, found no word to greet the victory, no pæan of our triumph.

Silently, and with pale faces, we left the shelter of the steel house, and breathed again where the breeze blew fresh upon the ramparts; silently we watched the cruiser steaming from the harbour, nor asked why no shot followed her. The scene of death, and of death so pitiful, was still before our eyes; the screams of dying men was yet in our ears; the awe of the battle yet bound our tongues. And thus we stood until the fleeing ship was no more than a black speck beyond the reef; and from the city below us there came the sound of bells chiming in the cathedral tower, of women singing, of the joy of men.

But the face of the count was wet with tears; and no man ventured to speak with him as we came down from the ramparts.

CHAPTER XXVI.

I MEET WITH A GREAT WELCOME.

THE whole glory of the morning shone upon the island when we came down to the guard-house again. It was now ten o'clock of the day and the sun's heat fell unsparingly upon men worn with a night of fatigue and wakefulness. Yet even in that lull of battle, in the hour when those about me began to ask, what of to-morrow? what of the reckoning to come? there was no man among us that thought of sleep—none that had desire to go to his rest. Nay, the whole city resounding with its life; and the chiming of bells, the tramp of squadrons, the sweeter music of women's voices rose up to us in pleasant sounds like messages of the people's joy.

Upon the high road above the valley, when we had got our horses again, we could see for the first time something of the work which the shells had done. And it was surprising that such continuous firing had been accompanied by such a trifling ill. Here and there in the woods some winging shot had cut a path through avenue or thicket, and had left smouldering shrub or splintered trunks in its wake. A house was burning near the Temple; the flames which rose up from it waned dull and sickly looking in the sun's brighter radiance. A field of maize upon the hillside had been set alight and was now flaming merrily; but the most part of the shot had, as we learned, been fired high above the city, and had fallen impotently in the chasms of the uplands. Nor was the count's bungalow harmed; nor that of Fortune, which had been my chief concern, although I knew not whether she lay there, or had been carried to the shelter of the caves.

During the night of watching, I had been tempted often to speak to Adam of this thought which lay so sorely upon my mind; but the quick movement, the spell of the attack, the excitement and the danger had kept opportunity from me; and now that we rode together upon the wide grass track, I was in no better way. He, on his part, had but one notion in his head; could talk only of the scenes which had passed, of the future they must bring upon us. And when I observed how full of it all he was, I let him give rein to his tongue and babble on as he would.

"Irwin," said he, breaking into a new subject for the tenth time in ten minutes, "I am like a man who has just made a speech. Do you know that feeling?"

I admitted that I did.

"And," he went on, "it's natural, too. Here's a business which has been talked of, and thought of, and dreaded for five years and more—and now it's begun and we know the worst of it.'

"But do you?" I asked.

"Of course we do. It's as plain as that blazing house there. They can no more force the harbour gate than stop Niagara. And they won't try again."

It was surprising to me that he could take so narrow a view of it; but, like the others, he had no eyes to see beyond the city's walls, and laboured always under the spell of the common infatuation. And this I did not hesitate to tell him.

"That," said I, " is wild talk at the best. Do you suppose this night's work is the beginning and the end of it? And you can't forget that men have been killed. I doubt if there's anyone

among you, even the count himself, that ever
looked for such a turn. Yesterday, Europe may
have regarded you as a handful of cranks and
dreamers; to-morrow she must know that you
are dangerous, and will present her bill."

He laughed that rippling laugh of his which was
a joy to hear; then fell of a sudden to gravity.

"Well," said he, "I'll not hold it from you that
I wish their ship was floating, and the poor devils
with it. But for the rest, and what France thinks,
or what France does, I don't care a crack, and
that's all about it. We'll have to fight, that I
don't deny; but what was this place built for?
Not for a picnic party, surely? No, indeed; it
was built for the work it is doing, and might
have done any day these years past."

"And you have no fear of the aftermath?"

"Fear! Am I a woman, then?"

"Fear, I mean, of what must be when the
cruiser returns with a fleet of ships in her wake?"

"And what will they do?"

"They will shell you out to begin with."

"Indeed! but that's news to me."

"And after that, they will force the gate by
sheer weight of numbers."

It was a lesson to see the expression upon his

face when I said this. Nor did he attempt to reply to the supposition; but, offering me a cigarette, he turned about the subject again.

"Man," said he, "it's clear that you'll never be the hero of an epic. And I suppose I can't find fault with you for that. You were made to set men up; and it appears that I was made to knock them down, which is a beautiful dispensation of Providence. Meanwhile, I'd be glad to know that you're hungry. If someone would walk right along here with a fatted calf, as Silver has it, I fancy that I could kiss him on both cheeks."

"Talking of Silver Lincoln," said I, "reminds me that I miss him. He was not with you last night?"

"He is at Valparaiso with the yacht," said he, "and I shoud be sorry to put down his language when he misses this. There never was born a more reasonably fine swearer than Silver."

"Will he attempt to return, do you think?"

"If he sees his way. But he must have learned of this if he was in port a month ago; and I don't suppose he'll risk the ship. It's a piece of luck, too, when you come to figure it out; for if he had not sailed, the yacht would be matchwood by this time."

"They had the steamer, at any rate," said I.

"Which they may keep and be——" But there is no need to write all he said.

This talk had carried us along the hill road beneath the eastern headland; and now we found ourselves at the plateau before the strange caves wherein the women had taken refuge. There was a great concourse of people here to meet the count, and no sooner had we come up with him than he begged me to follow him to the hospital wherein the wounded lay. This I did readily; and so it was that I passed through the caverns in the heart of the peaks, and beheld with my own eyes that retreat which as yet I had seen only from the valley.

In some part these caves were of nature's making; in some part they had been blown out of the mountain's core. The greatest of them was a vast dome-shaped apartment, not unlike a mighty basilica with a ceiling of glittering rock, and walls which shone with a thousand hues of natural colour where the light fell. Though jagged spikes of stony crags rose up here and there in fantastic shapes from the floor, and dark passages opened into it like tunnels to an anthill, the atmosphere of the place was, nevertheless,

warm and dry; and at the far end of it a silvery
cascade of water fell into a chasm of the mountains, and so rushed downward toward the valley.
From many narrow casements, and particularly
from an aperture of nature's making, which stood
out like the eastern window of a church, the sun's
beams were focussed in funnel-shaped volumes
upon the glass-like pavements of this vault-like
chamber. And of such size and shape was it that
the least whisper of the voice struck upon its
dome, and was there sent circling back in tremulous and booming echoes which seemed to fathom
the depths of the hills.

Upon the floor of this cave many beds were
spread, and I observed that it was used for the
shelter of the women and the children, many of the
latter being now huddled together in the remoter
alcoves by the water, as though fearing still to
hear the thunder of the gunshots. We gave to
them what consolation we could, and so passed
through a dark aperture to a second cave, wherein
there lay ten men who had been struck down by
the fire of the night. Of these three were dead
when I came to them, and of the rest, a horseman,
who had been torn in the throat by a fragment of
shell, and a gunner, who had a rifle-bullet in his

lung, were past the mending. But I made haste
to do what I could for such as were to be saved,
and blamed myself not a little that I had delayed
my coming so long.

When the work was done, the count, who had
suffered much at this spectacle of acute suffering,
asked me to accompany him to his house, and I
rode with him through the thicket of the woods.
I judged that he was seeking opportunity for
talk with me; and so soon as we were alone he
confirmed that surmise.

"Doctor," said he, "we grow in your debt.
Your coming to us was an act of mercy, for which
I thank God!"

"Count Andrea," said I plainly, "there need
be no by-word between us. I came here because
I was bound to come. And let me speak the
whole of my mind, which is this: that I had no
fair treatment from you when you sent me to
Europe as you did."

For a spell he did not answer me, looking away
over the gardens, upon which the sun shone so
gloriously. Then he reined in his horse, and I
was face to face with him.

"What you charge me with I may not deny,"
said he. "There was no reason in what we did,

nor justice. But you asked much, doctor. And
I had looked to have her always at my side. I
have no other; without Fortune I am a very
lonely man!"

With such a note of pathos was it said, that
my heart bled for him.

"Was there need that you should be without
her?" asked I. "Surely you may speak a better
word for her than that?"

"Nay!" said he. "It is never the same when
the maid becomes the woman, and all the affections claim her. Husband, children—do not
these weaken the first ties of love, and so loose
them that often they drop away; and even the
recollection of them is not welcome. What place
had I, if she nursed a babe upon her knees?"

"The place," said I, "which no other may
occupy. And I will tell you, count, how poorly
you must think of me when you foresee the day
in which I could carry Fortune from her home,
and from him who has given her so great a care.
Such a day could never be!"

I spoke earnestly, seeking no fine words to
deck out my meaning.

"That would have been well said three months
ago, doctor," exclaimed he; "but now, when we

are cut off from humanity—and no man knows what the end may be, in this day of trial, when we are hunted like beasts, and are named for a scoff and a by-word—what think you now of the city as a home?"

"I think," said I, answering him with full knowledge of his question, "that there is no other home on the face of the earth which I could ever wish to make my own."

He stood a moment to weigh up this saying; then, without further speech, he rode from the wood, and presently he led me to the home park, and to the purlieus of the city. Nor had we gone very far before a grim evidence of the past night's work was before us, to divert our minds from the talk which had passed. For scarce were we twenty yards from the park gates when we saw, lying full in the road, the body of a man from whose side a great piece of flesh had been ripped by some fragment of shot. It was plain that the same shot had struck first the trunk of a mighty acacia tree, and so had twisted and strained it that the branches were bent over to cast a black shade upon the dead man's body. And not a hundred paces from this very spot the cottage of a keeper now stood up in a blackened ruin, the roof lifted clean from the walls, the main beams all black and charred, where the shell had fired them, the walls bulging and giving promise of collapse. But what was the more remarkable was the figure of the keeper himself, prominent there at the window, like the figure of a living man—the face placid, the eyes open, the hands upon the sill. Yet the poor fellow was stone-dead, though he bore no wounds upon his body! Even the dish of food by his side was unbroken and untouched by the fire.

This ugly spectacle, added to that of other houses splintered and riddled, and of the carrying of dead to the hills, brought the count to a state of grievous melancholy. The stimulant of activity was now wanting to him; he was the pure humanitarian once more.

"By death life is bought," said he to me almost at his own gate; "and by death comes victory. We may well weep for our children; but this night of darkness shall turn to a dawn of truth, and the new day shall be the day of mercy."

"May it come soon!" said I, at his prophecy.

"As it must. Of that I may not doubt. We cry no longer to ears that are deaf. Already our gospel is preached in all Europe. While men debate it, we shall stand impregnable above the seas; when they receive it, we shall open our gates to the world."

He gave up his horse with the words, and we stood together before the wicket of his garden. For a moment he seemed to hesitate; but then, laying his hand upon my shoulder with a gesture of love, he bade me to enter; and so turned abruptly to his own room. But I, opening the wicket and passing through the labyrinth of clinging plants and glowing orchids, came to the lawn, and found Fortune lying there upon a couch of wicker-work; and I seemed to live my whole life again when I held her to me, and could say no word because her lips had put a seal upon my own.

CHAPTER XXVII.

I GAIN ALL.

SHE had been sleeping; but, while I was yet some paces from her couch, she awoke with a little cry most pleasant to hear, and then stretched out her arms to me, and so took me in a sweet embrace. Yet while she lay all palpitating and flushed, with a dreamy ecstacy—as though my coming was a phantom of her dreams—I saw that she was but a shadow of herself, this fragile thing of warm flesh and blood, who had brought so much happiness into my life. And she lay, her great eyes all awakening with a hundred fires of light, her worn face wet with tears that gushed upon it, her exquisite hair spread upon the couch like silk of gold; and there were long moments before she could bring herself to think that she beheld me as I was, and not as a bewitching vision of her sleep. Nor was any word that I could say sufficient to convince her, until she had held me long against her heart, and had whispered my name again and again.

Moments such as these are not to be written down in the colder view of recollection. I could no more tell of our first whispered thoughts than recite a Rabelaisian catalogue of adjectives. But I remember that almost my earliest word was to chide her for being there in the gardens of the pavilion when she should have been up in the hills; and that to all my reproach she could but answer me with kisses.

"Dear love," she would say, "what harm was there, since you had left me? Oh, I had no thought of life—I did not care. It is all different now!"

"And you watched here the night through?" I asked, in amazement.

"I could not sleep—how could I? The whole city seemed lighted with fire. And while I walked here and saw the flames like stars in the hills, it was just as though you were at my side."

"Tell me, Fortune," said I, holding both her hands; "you have been ill since I left you?"

She looked up into my face with her tear-stained eyes, and made a brave effort to deceive me.

"I have suffered no pain," she pleaded.

"Pain of body, no; pain of mind, yes; I am sure of it."

She shook her head as though she would deny it; but presently she said:

"I have been lonely, dearest; they would not hear your name; but I have whispered it always; and at night, when I could not sleep, I used to speak to you, and fancy that I heard your voice."

I told her that I, too, had known such fancies, and then I gave her my story; and when she had heard me out, and knew that I had come to her at her father's wish, she could find no words for her joy, but must up and run to his room, where I saw her clinging to his knees, like a child that has been forgiven, and whose misery has been washed away in a freshet of happiness.

When she returned to me, she was so weak with her effort that she could scarce stand up; but I had my arm around her when the count came out to us, and so I held her while he spoke.

"My child," said he, "what God has willed, that I may not stand against. Open your heart to a love which has nothing of self in it, and think sometimes of an old man who has known many sorrows and few joys. Think of him because you will be in his memory always; and when he is alone, the recollection of the hours when you were all the world to him will be his abiding con-solation."

He turned away before she could say aught; and together we watched him mount his horse and ride slowly toward the western heights, whose broad grass slopes mounted men were pacing. Though the labour of the night had worn him, and the heat of the day was now at its zenith, he would take no rest of the truce, nor put off that zeal of watchfulness to which the city owed her early victory. But elsewhere the island seemed to sleep; a great silence was upon her woods; only the ring of sentries at the cliffs was awake to duty. But the count was not to be persuaded, and, with Coloron and De Rény, must now ride out to reconnoitre from the highlands of the west, and to begin anew the consideration of those schemes he had long since perfected.

We stood to watch him until his figure was lost in the first of the pine woods; and then, return-ing to the shelter of the bower of palms, Fortune called for my breakfast, and had a dainty little meal set out there upon the shaded lawn. I con-sented to the entertainment with the stipulation that she must eat and drink as I commanded her;

and, although this precept was not very faithfully obeyed, at the same time she so far suffered me to prescribe for her that I saw natural colour again in her cheeks, and began to battle with her exceeding weakness. It was then that I narrated to her the fuller episodes of the night. While the recital of the encounter held her amazed, she could in no way conceal her apprehension for the near future.

"Irwin," she said, and there was awe in her eyes, "did you hear them chiming the bells this morning, and the women singing? I heard them, and the sounds were like a knell."

And presently she went on:

"What do they sing for? Is it because we have brought death here? They cannot think that their victory is real. They must know that those outside will not rest until our homes are in ashes. Oh, they are blind—blind! It has all been an empty dream, and now it is floating away like a cloud."

"Indeed, sweetheart," said I, "it seems to me nothing of the sort. If your father can hold his position here long enough, he will bring public opinion to his side, and there will be compromise. The very fact that he can fight the ships of two

or three nations will win him European sympathy.
He is a noble man, and his own force of character
must weigh heavily in the balance."

"Yes, truly," cried she, and it was pretty to
listen to her childish philosophy; "he is all truth
and gentleness.   But how long will the others
stand with him when there is no city but the city
of the hills, no food but from the trees, no rest
nor sleep because of the dreadful sounds of men
dying, and the cry of the children who hunger?
I have thought of this—it is the horrid dream of
all my sleep!"

"Dear heart," said I, "your father has thought
of it too, be assured.   He tells me that he has
food for his people to last them three years.
Why should we trouble our heads asking what
will be when those years are gone?   Let us think
only of to-day, of the sun shining, of the flowers
blossoming, of our love."

She shook her head in a wise little way, looking for all the world like some pretty schoolgirl
stern in over-ripe philosophy.   And when we had
made the pleasant discovery that two could rest
very well, and without discomfort, upon her
couch, we fell to talking of simpler things.   In
which occupation the afternoon sped until I, full

of heavy fatigue, sank at last to a refreshing sleep; nor did I wake until the sun was hid behind the pine woods, and a delicious freshness of evening was upon the garden.

I had gone to my sleep with my head pillowed upon her arm, but when I awoke she was not by me, and the plantation was all dark save where the yellow and red light of lanterns danced among the boughs of the trees, and a bright aureola upon the grass marked the electric lamps in the study of the pavilion. I had begun to wonder what had become of Fortune, when I heard the count himself calling to me from his room; and to him I went, not a little angry that I had slept so long. He was then resting upon his couch, his heavy uniform still upon him; but I learned with satisfaction that he had slept, and after a word of commonplace, he entered upon the discussion of a subject which I had not looked for him to mention, neither then nor for many months.

"Doctor," said he, "what I have to say must be said briefly. There may be shell upon the city again before the dawn, for they have learned —as they must have learned—that our voice is from the south, and that we are impotent to the east and west where now their ships lie. In this strife to come, my own place is upon the heights, not at my daughter's side. But you I bid to stand with her, if that is the whole wish of your heart and your affections."

I heard him out, and the room seemed to reel about me. Clear as his speech is when now I set it down, it was to me then but a ripple of words, pleasing to the ear, yet not to be altogether understood. And I doubt not that I cut a pretty figure standing before him in the glaring light like a man who is dumb.

"If," he went on, not misunderstanding my silence, "it is your whole wish to remain here with us in this exile—an exile of months or of years, as destiny may write; if, of your free choice and will, you cut yourself off from your fellows, and would make yourself my son; then, I say, while now the time remains to me, be to her at once what you seek to be always—become her strong hand when she has most need of strength."

I told him that I had no other hope in life than thus to stand her friend; and my blood flowed warm in my veins as I began to imagine the happiness of his intention.

"Now that I have your word, doctor," said he, rising from his couch, and touching the bell at his side, "my own work is the lighter. You shall take Fortune to the shelter of my little pavilion by the Orange Road—it is over against the northern lantern—where no harm may come to you. There I will leave you, asking only your services for the sick and the dying. I have sent for one of the priests from the church, and he will be here at nine o'clock. There is time, therefore, for food and drink together—who knows, perhaps for the last time. But oh, my son! whatever God has willed for me, be to her I now give you what I have tried to be. Do not forget that she has no other life but in this, your friendship and your affection."

I answered him with all the gratitude I felt, and so, we sitting down together to the food they had brought, he went on to speak of what his wish would be if it befell that he should die while the city was yet girt about with ships. In this talk he pointed out the safes which held his papers and the directions for the carrying on of his work when he was gone; and to all his words I replied that I would act for him as for my own father. And so the hour sped; and when they came to tell us that the priest was ready, we went out to the little oratory in the garden; and, standing before the shrine whereon lights flickered in the night breeze—standing there with the sea wind fresh, and the island sleeping, and the perfume of the flowers coming to us on the light airs—they married me to Fortune, and crowned the chief hope of my life.

The scene was full of sweetness; nor will the memory of it ever be blotted from mind. Often, here in Lodon now, I see the tall figure of the priest, reddened in the guttering torches' flare; the altar shrine twined over with wild roses; the hard faces of the lantern bearers; the darkened garden, and the swinging lamps; the lawn upon which the golden aureola fell; the motionless figure of the count; the sweet vision of Fortune, whose brightened eyes were like diamonds of the night. I hear again her low words of promise, seem to feel her tears of gladness warm upon my cheek; have her trembling hand in mine as then I held it in that sacred hour.

When the priest had left the altar, Fortune, who had for ornament only a great clasp of diamonds upon the breast of her gown, was wrapped about in a mantle of white furs; and

when, very tenderly, she had kissed her father,
and for one wild minute he had seemed to cling
to her with pathetic love in his gesture, I lifted
her up upon my˚horse, and so carried her in my
own arms to the mountains. They had sent a
company of torch bearers out to the hill road with
us; but never once did she glance back to the
city below, nor to her father's house; only, laying
her cheek upon my neck, she held to me like a
frightened child, and was the fairer in her sweet
distress. It may have been that the hand of
melancholy, which ever touches all human gladness, was upon her as we rode; it may have been
that we both thought of a good friend and a noble
man whose heart would be wounded in our new-
found happiness. Nor did that hour pass without
a tender word for Adam Monk, and the ill which
unwillingly we did him.

At the thicket's end, high upon the mountain
pass, the torch bearers left us. Thenceforth we
rode upon a gentle slope of grass to the bungalow,
which lay sheltered by a jutting peak of rock, and
very pleasantly surrounded by garden and plantation. We had not come to the doors of it, however, when the landscape below us seemed of a
sudden to be lighted by jets of leaping fire, and

the hiss of shells was plainly to be heard above the fields.

For the French ships had made good of the night; and we heard their guns· begin to speak upon the western seas.

CHAPTER XXVIII.

JACOB DYER BEGS HIS BREAD.

THE first day of the fourth week after the beginning of the attack upon the city broke with a morning of cloud and fine rain; but before five o'clock of the afternoon the mists upon the mountain tops were scattered by a freshening north wind, and the sun began to shine most pleasantly upon the glades and thickets about my pavilion. Yet was I heavy of heart as I rode homeward from the hospital, and gloomy thoughts overtook me even while I remembered that Fortune was waiting for me in the garden of the house, as she was wont to do when my day's work was done.

An exceeding sweet and clear air had followed upon the storm of the forenoon; and the whole island was now very plainly to be seen, both in its beauty and the ruin which a month of siege had brought upon it. From the path, high upon the hillside, I could make out the burned and smouldering shells of houses, the blackened fields,

the deserted and desolate square, the great building of the Temple shattered at its eastern end,
until it stood up, as if in mockery, a thing of
gaping walls and tumbling beams; I could see
the white tents of the soldiers lying snug beneath
the headland; the figures of sentries upon the
cliffs; the purple crowns of the peaks above the
prison; the new-turned graves where our dead
lay sleeping. And even as I rode, the air was
alive with the music of the guns, with the crash
of rending timbers, and the whistle of the shells.

I say that I was heavy of heart that afternoon;
yet to·none of these sights and sounds do I
attribute the gloom of my mood. We had stood
for a month against the ships of three nations;
we had witnessed the coming of a second French
war-vessel and of a Russian ironclad; we had
watched our houses crumble to dust beneath the
unceasing fire; we had seen our crops burned and
our brave fellows struck down; and, withal, in the
hearts of those that led us there was no dismay.
These things must be. By death the victory
must come; by suffering should suffering be
undone. And through it all the city had stood
unshaken in her power, invincible, a citadel of the
seas, impregnable against the world. I alone,

perhaps, of all her citizens, asked how long; how long shall her reign continue, her might prevail?

The question may have been one of pure foreboding; it may have sprung up from those doubts and quakings to which the conduct of a few among my fellows had given birth. For in that month of siege I had seen men shot at the door of the great cave, had heard of arms thrown down and of orders mocked; more than all, had felt instinctively that sapping of men's courage which is the culminating weakness of defence. As the days passed, and we began to live upon the simplest food, upon salted meats and tasteless bread; when no wine was served, and our herds were left untouched, then, I say, there were those that whispered in little groups after the day's work was ended, even those that talked openly of compromise and of the possibilities of settlement. I alone foresaw the hour when these men might bring the castles of our hopes tumbling about our ears; might undo in one night a work built up to endure through centuries.

It was this thing that haunted my mind while I rode upon the bridle-track, and beheld at my own gate the pretty figure of Fortune as she waited for me. Not that there was any danger then to be expected; for until this time we had kept the strong grip of discipline upon the troops, and the personal force and zeal of the count had lost nothing of their strength. Men feared him as they would have feared an unknown power; his spirit breathed upon them with a courage which warmed them to fine deeds, or chilled them to dread. Wherever he stood, in that place walls of steel seemed to rise up about him; his barest word was worth a call to arms; his appeal was a trumpet-blast which hastened the pace of laggards and filled brave men as with devils. In his presence no doubts were spoken, no apprehensions named. He was the keystone of our arch, and even the weakest of us felt strong before his devotion and his love.

This far-reaching supremacy of the one mind was my chief hope at that time, as it had been during the month when, with Fortune's lips pressing often on my own, I had known happiness exceeding any other. This afternoon I was finding in it a new consolation as I watched the hammering of the shells upon the tottering streets below me, the path of flames, and the fall of masonry. Only at the gate of the wood which lies near by my pavilion was I called of a sudden to a new thought, and to the remembrance of a man whose very existence I had forgotten. I saw him standing in the shelter of the trees— haggard, worn, with flesh loose upon his bones, and eyes that looked out from deep-sunk sockets: Jacob Dyer, the rogue who had first betrayed us, who had sent to England that plan and chart of the city by which all our misfortune had come.

Never had fear so wrought upon a man. I judged at once that, so soon as he heard of my coming to the island, he had fled to the woods, and there had lain like a beast that is hunted with dogs. What he had suffered, what privation had done for him, was written upon his face, now whiter than a fainting woman's; upon his hands, all torn and bleeding; upon his nails, grown out like claws; upon his clothes, rent and dirt-stained. And his cringing, fawning attitude when he saw me, the palsy of fear upon him, the fever in his eyes, might have moved a strong heart to mercy.

"Oh, for the love of God! for pity's sake, doctor, give me a little bread!" he cried, and so stood shaking like a paralytic.

I reined in my horse to look at him, and saw that he walked in the company of death.

"Jacob Dyer," said I, "you are no man to be

seen talking with; but you appear to have been punished."

He made no direct answer to this, but continued to whine: "A little bread—for the love of God, a little bread!"

"Tell me," said I, troubled at the sight of him, "where did you hide yourself?"

"In the woods yonder: I have lain there three weeks in the cold and the wet. Oh! what I have suffered would draw tears from your eyes to hear."

It was plain that he had deserved to suffer, but this I did not tell him then; giving him, in place of reproach, my brandy flask, which he drained to the dregs.

"Now," said I, "come along to my house, and I will think what can be done with you."

"Is there anyone to see me?" he asked, peering nervously through the trees about my garden.

"No one who will interest himself in you," said I; and with that I offered him my saddle-strap, which he took.

"Doctor," cried he, "if they found me, they would shoot me like a dog! I have heard the troopers swear to do it when they rode by my hole."

"And they are men of their word," said I, finding no reason to give him comfort.

"Oh!" exclaimed he at that, "if only I was on an American ship!"

"But you are not; and if it's any consolation to you, there's no American ship in the harbour."

"Then I'm a dead man," said he; and his hand shook upon the strap he held.

We had now come to the garden gate, and I dismounted and ran to take little Fortune in my arms. Already she had seen the miserable man I had carried with me; and when she had touched my lips with hers, she broke away to fetch him food, setting a great hunk of beef before him, and a bottle of wine, which remained to us from that we had found in the pavilion on the night of our marriage. He, on his part, ate and drank so ravenously that the wonder was he did not choke; and when all the wine was done with, and what of the beef remained was not worth the weighing, he begged a pipe of tobacco of me and smoked to his great content.

During his hurried meal the problem he presented had troubled me not a little. That I could play the bold part and shelter him in my house was plainly out of the question. Even gentle Fortune, watching him at his food, had whispered to me that she hated him; and loathing of his treachery and ingratitude was not to be put aside. It was, therefore, to my satisfaction that he now proposed to go back to the woods; and I could not find it in me to dissuade him from his purpose.

"Doctor," said he, "it will be safer up yonder, don't you think? I can't forget that men will be coming to your house."

"Well," said I, "since you ask me, I think the woods are the best place for you."

"But you'll let me come down every day for food, eh? You won't forget me, eh? And your wife, there; she's too pretty to let a man starve. I'll be bound she'll give me something. I count upon you, doctor."

"For what?" I asked.

"For help when the Frenchmen come in. That'll be a great day for me; and I shan't forget my friends. I am not ungrateful. There's no warm and cold about Jacob Dyer. You've stood with me, and I'll stand with you. We'll cheat 'em yet, by the Lord Harry! There's not a man worth a guinea-pig among 'em—not a man!"

Fortune's pretty face flushed hot at his words; but to me they were as the wind. I knew the rascal, and when thus he stood up anew in the colours of a rogue, I had no surprise.

"Jacob Dyer," said I, "take yourself off, and don't let me see you again until you have civil words in your mouth."

"Oh, no offence—no offence at all!" he stammered. "I mean well; I'm a plain man, and speak what I think. Good-day, doctor; and good-day to the little lady. You won't forget me—eh, miss? I was a great man in London once—ah, that I was! There were many that would have taken my check for a hundred thousand, and glad to get it. You won't let me starve, doctor?"

With this apology, and having put the remainder of the beef and bread in his pocket, he went out of the gate. Fortune had then run into the house. I stood alone when he mounted the grassy hill which led up to the wood; but he was yet twenty paces from the copse when he gave a shrill cry, and turned about to run back to the garden. At the same moment three horsemen rode from the plantation, and no sooner did they catch sight of him than they put their ponies to

the gallop, and came flying over the grass in hot
pursuit. From my place at the garden gate I
could see the whole of the quickly passing scene—
the set faces of the riders, the agony of the running man. And I waited, as one waits for tragedy
in a theatre, for the end which nothing now could
avert.

Fifty yards from our garden, upon the open
grass, they struck him down. He had stood still
to stretch out his arms in supplication to me;
and the scream he uttered was ringing from
height to height when a trooper, bending over
from the saddle, put a pistol to his ear and blew
his brains out. I saw the body rocking upon its
heels during one long-drawn moment. I beheld
the arms drawn up convulsively, the quiver of
the flesh. Then Jacob Dyer dropped noiselessly
upon the grass, and the number of our dead was
added to by one.

But of all that perished in the siege none died
with more justice than this man, who had never
known an honest thought nor done an unselfish
action.

CHAPTER XXIX.

FROM THE WATCH-TOWERS OF THE WEST.

THE man fell; but the troopers rode on to my gate, calling to one another that the island was well rid of a rogue. I found that they had brought a letter to me from the count, in which I was asked to come up to the station upon the western heights at ten o'clock that evening. And to this simple request the chief of the three men added the news that an attack was looked for at midnight, or earlier, upon that side of the shore, where a break of the cliffs seemed to promise better hope of landing.

"Ay, it'll be sharp work, sir," said the man, who had not dismounted from his horse; "sharp work for them that makes it. Maybe you know the red light? It's where the old path from the shore was before we mined her. If they can lay their powder and bring rock down, they'll put men among us."

"Ay, like enough," chimed in a second, he who had just shot Dyer; "and give me men ashore, I say. This spit and spit agen do turn a man's stomach."

"Which is bare truth," said the third, for they were all three British seamen who had come in from the cargo steamer before she had been taken. "Hand to hand, Jack, and dead men to dance with."

"Ay, ay, Jack's my cut," cried the one who had first spoken. And then, turning to me, he said, as if in apology, "That's a tidy job out yonder, sir; and good news for the skipper. He was a bad 'un beyond compare, was Jacob Dyer."

They would have continued, as seamen will, to wag their tongues unsparingly had I not put an end to it with a word, and sent them about their business. But they were still mighty pleased with themselves at the work they had done; and as they went back to the woods they tied the body of the dead man to a saddle-strap with a length of rope they begged from my servant, and dragged it, all bent and broken, to the shelter of the thicket. And when they had disappeared among the trees I continued for a long time to hear their voices and the brutal jests to which their burden moved them.

Within the house Fortune waited for me with

such a dinner set upon the table as the scanty
allowance served to us daily would permit. Her
fine spirits supplied what was lacking to the feast;
and it was good to see her sparkling eyes and
flushed cheeks when, with an exemplary contempt
for custom, we sat very close to one another as
we ate, and my lips often touched her soft cheeks
and tumbling hair. At nine o'clock, when I rose
to call for my horse, she would not hear of letting
me ride alone, but must send for her pony and
dress herself to come up to the hills. And I had
no heart to leave her to the loneliness of the
pavilion, and consented to her coming.

It was near to half-past nine when at last we
set forth. I had a lantern hitched to my stirrup-
strap; in my belt were the revolvers without
which I had not lately ventured out. The night
was one of great darkness, for new clouds had
come over the sky at sunset, and there was no
moon. So black was it in the woods that I could
not see as much as the ears of my pony; and the
valley below was all hid from sight, save in those
moments when the unceasing shells lit up some
grove, or wood, or house with a flash of lurid fire.
Here and there upon our way we passed by small
companies of men hastening to the west, whence

the attack was to come. Herds of cattle, mad
with fury, bellowed in the fields below us, or ran
wild from plantation to plantation with strange
cries of pain and rage most mournful and terrify-
ing to hear. Upon the distant headlands rifles
were speaking fitfully; in one of the higher
woods we heard a horrid groaning as of a man
lying in the pains of death; but him we could not
find, though we searched long, and went on our
way with his moans in our ears. At the height
of the thicket, whence the lamps in the great
cave were to be seen, we came upon a party of
sappers with spades in their hands, and these,
working by the light of torches, were cutting
graves for the dead, or carrying bodies to the
holes which they had already dug.

From this point the road was straight and plain
to be seen. Volumes of light, streaming from the
loop-holes and the door of the distant cavern,
made a ready beacon; and when we had ridden a
little way we were at the camp, and found it
already busy with preparation for the assault to
come. Infantrymen were now falling in by companies: the thud of horses' hoofs was incessant
upon the grass; light guns came rolling up the
hillside; riflemen were upon every point of jut-

ting rock whence the sea below could be commanded. And, standing out prominent in the
throng, his white uniform flashing in the light, his
voice strong as the blare of a bugle, was Adam
Monk.

He saw us at once,—it was my first meeting
with him since I had taken Fortune in my arms
to the pavilion,—and now he ran up to me and
he held out both his hands, then dragged my
wife almost from her saddle that he might kiss
her. A prettier greeting never was from a man
who had lost so much by another's happiness;
and, wisely avoiding any talk of the days when he
had kept apart from us, he fell at once into a
pretence of his old humour.

"Well," said he, holding the bridle of Fortune's
horse, and looking at both of us with some curiosity, "this is a fine night to take an airing, I
must say."

"It is not good for man to be alone," cried she,
springing lightly from her saddle; and, when she
had let him kiss her as he had wished, she continued:

"And, Adam, if there's any shooting, I shall
follow you like a dog. Oh! do say that a bullet
won't come out the other side of you and kill me!"

"I'd say anything to please you, Fortune," replied he, as we tethered our ponies to one of the trees near by. And then he went on: "To-night's no play-time, let me tell you. They've mined the rock down there; and if it falls as they think it will they may get footing ashore."

"How will that help them?" asked I, looking down to the sea from a height of three hundred feet or more, and observing how curious it was that the low spurs of the mountains, here jutting out into the lagoon, so stood between us and any boats that might be below that we could scarce exchange a shot with them, or in any way harass their crews.

"It will help them," replied Adam, and there was a merry laugh on his face the while, "by landing them in that rocky pit yonder. There never was a more one-sided game than this played in all the world. It's just pitiable."

"And what are you going to do meanwhile?" I asked.

"I—I am going to squat by the fire here and make a beast of myself on dry bread and salt horse. It's astonishing what a succulent dish is a hunk of good beef if you sit down to it squarely—take the fat with the lean, as it were, and don't ask questions. You may look on at the banquet if you like, and think you're in Threadneedle Street."

"Adam," said I, "you're incurable."

"I wish the meat was," said he; and with that we all huddled round the fire, and he began his tasteless meal, not knowing, as he said, at what hour he would get his next bite or sup.

The scene was one to linger in the memory; nor do I think that I could forget it readily. The fire, bright in flame where the logs crackled and burned, crowned at its height with a cloud of sweet smelling smoke, cast deep yellow light upon the faces of the little group. Other fires, far and near, showed troops moving or horsemen at the gallop; beams of silvery radiance upon the sea lit up the warships preparing for their work; the crash of shells spoke of other vessels hammering at the eastern headlands. By the flickering lanterns' light we could see the bright steel of the guns, the sentries pacing, the rapid movements of the horsemen. Often, as we sat, some word of warning would be passed along the cliffs, and would carry from man to man as a winging message of voices. And upon the dis-

tant peaks the signals did not cease to flash: the
beacons were plainly to be seen.

It must have been near to midnight before
there was any sign from without of that which
these things foreboded. Adam, while he ate, had
told me that the engineers, both of the Russians
and the French, had been working to mine the
vulnerable face of the city, as they thought it,
for nearly fifteen days; and had given many
signs within the past four-and-twenty hours that
the moment for the assault had come. Formerly
there had been an open road to the shore at this
point, where the ridge of the mountains ran down
into the sea: and the lower cliffs, and seemingly
open way to the hills, must have held out no
slight prospect of success to those who had
learned already of what sort the count's power
was. Had these men known that a great chasm
lay between our heights and the shore of the sea;
that the old path had been blown away with
powder in the second year of the city's existence,
their undertaking had remained an idea. But of
this they had no intelligence; and now they were
to rush in where nothing but a miracle could
keep destruction from them.

Midnight had been chimed upon the bells of

the cathedral when they began their work.
Adam was lighting a second cigar, and I was
imitating him, when a rocket was fired from the
peak upon our southern promontory, and was
answered all along the coast by flashes of stars
and the crack of rifles. Running up to the high
point whence the whole of the near sea was to
be observed, we learned that a small boat full of
men had crept in under the shelter of the spur,
and there lay secure from bullets, though some
shots from our field pieces were discharged at
its crew, with what result we could not know.
Anon, however, the boat was pulled out to sea
again, and no sooner was it clear of the reef than
a storm of bullets from our riflemen followed its
passage, and the sharp cries of men struck were
an answer to their fire.

When the boat had passed into the darkness of
the further sea a strange silence reigned over our
fellows. It was plain to all that the mine had
now been fired; and as Adam raised his voice,
crying "Every man to the woods!" we ran down
from the cliffs, and lay flat in the thicket, waiting
for the discharge which must come. Ten seconds
we waited, and twenty; Fortune herself coming
for security to the shelter of my greatcoat; and,

then, as every man heard his own heart beating
and felt the twitch of his nerves, a vomit of flame
was belched over the sea, and the whole range of
hills seemed, to our strained imaginations, to rock
from their base.

For many minutes that roar of sound continued
to rush from the earth. The very sky was lit up
by the wings of the flame which enveloped the
spur of outstanding rock; the ear was stunned
by the terrible rending of the hills, by the crash
of boulders flying. All about us as we lay a
shower of stones rained down; the horses we had
tethered snapped the thongs that held them, and
galloped madly to the woods. Birds rose screaming above the trees; every lantern was put out;
the splash of the sea was like the fall of a mighty
cascade as the vast splinters of the cliff rolled
down; the western face of the island seemed
rent in twain.

The devastation passed when long minutes
were numbered, and we came up out of our hid-
ing-place, knowing that the moment for the
supreme attempt was upon us. The sea, hid in
darkness while the first boat had come in, was
now bright with the arcs of light which shone out
from the distant ships. We were now able to

discover what ill lay in the path of the mine; and it was surprising to me, even when I remembered the inconceivable force of the fire, to see the gaping chasms in the low wall of mountains, the great hunks of rocks which lay piled upon the beach, the thousand fragments of stone with which even the cliffs were littered. But more to be noticed than these were twenty small boats, now being rowed rapidly to the shore, their armed crews full, I may not doubt, of the hope that the next hour would see them hand to hand with us upon the heights.

At the first sight of the boats Adam left me—he running toward the chasm whereby the men should come up, I carrying Fortune to the tiny hut which had been put up for the shelter of our wounded. There were three of the troops then lying upon the straw mattresses of the hut, the poor fellows having been struck by fragments of the falling stone, and one so cut open by a splinter of rock that I had little hope of saving him. But Fortune's deft hands were quickly at work with the bandages; and, while I did what I could to stay the men's pain, the ceaseless crack of rifles and of field pieces without told of the crisis of the attack and of its progress. Often a wild cheer from our men assured me that Adam's confidence was justified. Often their silence or the very ferocity of their fire led me to fear that it was misplaced. And when, in great doubt at last, a new cry from them—neither of joy nor of dismay, but of exceeding wonder—came to me, I left the wounded to Fortune, and ran out impatiently to the watching-place upon the hill, that I might learn with my own eyes how near the danger stood to us.

At a stone's throw from the summit Adam called out to me, "For Heaven's sake, come quick!" His cry was taken up by a group of men about him, and another shout from them, added to that which was almost a moan, set me hurrying to be with them. And the sight I beheld when I came up to the place was such as the boldest might not wish to see, nor the weakest to turn from. In the pit of the chasm, some three hundred men were scrambling and climbing. A few of them had so far pulled themselves up the face of the precipice that they were within twenty feet of the top; others were no more than a half of the way; others, again, were at the foot of the spur. But when I saw them they were all standing still upon such foothold as they had got, and

their cries of pain and of fear were like the howling of wolves.

Out of the very rock which they had mined the
vengeance had come—swift, horrible, devouring.
For the same powder which had hurled the
boulders into the sea had given vent to the boiling
springs and flames of sulphur; and now great
tongues of fire shot from the face of the precipice;
volumes of steam burst out, stinking vapours filled
the air. Those of the doomed men that were
high upon the rocks dropped one by one, like flies
from a ceiling, as the fumes overcame them; those
that were in the direct path of the flames stood
screaming, as their flesh cracked and was
shrivelled; many ran to and fro imploring their
fellows to shoot them; the fire lighted the faces
of all as with the light of countless torches.

A. scene of death it was, indeed, revolting
beyond all scenes of death that I have known.
To those watching upon the cliff, it seemed that
the very caverns of the vast pit were filled with
fire and steam. From every cleft and crack of the
rocky bed, from the high face of the precipice,
even from the low spurs of the chain which
dipped into the sea, the red flames shot out and
curled their lapping tongues upon the white-hot

walls. Nor could the poor fellows who had been entrapped so pitifully turn back to their boats or look for any help from those that watched them in their agony. The sea herself bubbled up upon the shore as though some great furnace had been lit below her bed; a ridge of forked fire stood between the doomed and the beach; the hand of God alone could have stayed the holocaust.

How many of these unhappy men ever reached their ships again we never learned. It may be that no soul lived to tell the horrors to his fellows. With my own eyes I counted two hundred corpses, many of them burning long after death had done with them. I heard cries so agonizing that I shut my ears for very awe. And when these screams had died away, when, for any man's voice, there was silence once more upon the pit, the war of the flame was still to be heard, the splash of the boiling springs as they hissed upon the rock.

Day was breaking in the east when we turned at last from this terrible holocaust. So strangely had the whole episode come, so full of terror was it, that men left the hillside with blanched face, and went silently to their food and their sleep. They were as men waked from distressing dreams, carried by the wind of chance to a victory which none dared to boast, nor even to discuss. And I, well-knowing the moment of the night and the brighter promise of the dawn, could not shake from me that gloom of the spectacle, that feeling, not to be put aside, that I had suffered with the men who fell.

With which thought, I found the tent they had set apart for Fortune, and laid me down to a broken sleep that endured until the sun set.

CHAPTER XXX.

TRUCE OF THE STORM.

IT was near to the hour of six o'clock when
Fortune waked me from my restless slumber, she
fearing, as she said, that I must be added to the
number of her patients. But as the afternoon
drew on, a rising northeasterly gale began to
beat furiously upon the tent, and the heavy rain,
running from the hills, made little torrents of
muddy water upon the grassy floor beneath my
bed. It was then that my wife waked me, making all her pretty excuses for what she did.

As I opened my eyes and saw that hers were
looking upon me, I drew her near to me; but
when I kissed her forehead I found it to be all
wet with water from the tent above, and in the
same moment I heard the savage howling of the
wind and felt the quiver of the canvas as it tore
at the ropes.

"Sweetheart," said I, "we appear to have come
upon a flood. How long have you been watching me?"

She laughed merrily, while a fresh gush of water came from above.

"Would I count the minutes, Irwin? Oh, indeed, it was just a little time!"

"Has Adam been up here?"

"He came in an hour ago to take us down to the shelter. The hills are running water. It began at one o'clock, when I was by your side. But, you know, dearest, the thunder was just rest to you. That was the only time you slept without those dismal groans."

"At any rate, let us get out of this," said I. "Nature is a little too free with her water for a quiet family gathering. And what's more, she doesn't supply the towels. Are you very wet?"

"I drip," said she laconically; and with that we drew our cloaks around us and went out to the open grass of the plateau. Adam had left word that we were to join him at the shelter; but by this he did not indicate the great cave where the women were, but a little house reserved for the count, and lying a stone's throw from the larger cavern. This house, built some halfway down the valley, stood snug beneath the shelter of that same peak of the mountains whose hollow heart made such strange chambers of refuge for the community. But to ride to it then was out of the question, so powerful was the wind, so fierce the rain which beat down from the black veil of cloud hanging low over the island.

For the most part the camp, set up for the work of the night, was struck; a few tents for the guard, the hospital, and the store huts, alone stood against the triumphant north wind which swept over the face of the land, bending strong trees to the earth, howling as with the cry of drunken armies. All sound or sight of shell had ceased at this time in the city; not a light shone out against the intense darkness of the storm; no bugle tried a blast with it; no gun contested for echoes in the hills. Only the voice of the wind now rising with all the swelling force of a southern hurricane, now dying away with low sobs and moanings, reigned supreme upon the silence of the island.

As best we might against the violence of the storm, Fortune and I made our way to that which the count styled his hut. Oftentimes my whole strength could scarce hold her upon her feet. There were minutes when we must set our backs to the wind and stand with our heels digging into the grass; minutes more when we gasped for

breath and the rain cut our faces as though pellets
of glass beat upon them. And what with the
darkness of the road and the roughness of it, I
doubt that we had come to the hut at all but for
the men the count sent to seek us, and upon
whom we stumbled when we were yet some half
a mile from his door.

I found the hut to be a pleasant enough little
house, and mightily welcome after that bitter
walk down the valley. It was built almost
entirely within the core of the peak which contained the great shelter; but there was a fine
dining-room with windows giving a view upon the
whole city below; and many passages led to the
cave of the women and to the other chambers. I
saw that a glowing fire of logs was alight in the
first of the rooms when we came up; and in the
bedroom they had prepared for us a heap of dry
clothes had been spread before a blaze of wood
and coal. It was then that we began to laugh at
our experience; and, listening in that dry place
to the trumpeting of the storm and the beat of
the rain, we wondered that any human being
could have faced it on the hills.

When we were dressed, and Fortune had declared that nature and hailstones had combined

for the destruction of her curls, we passed from
our room to the larger chamber. I found the
count there, very wet, but smiling, as he stood
before the cheering blaze. With him were De
Rémy, the engineer, and Malasac, the commander
of the heights, bearing similar evidences of battle
with the hurricane. But all of them were in the
best of moods, and the excitement they wore was
not to be concealed. Indeed, as I came in, the
excellent Malasac, who was the noisiest man I
have ever met, had a bottle of wine in his hand,
and was talking with the volubility of a boy of
twenty.

"*Nom de Dieu*," he was saying, "let us wish
them *bon voyage*. *A bientôt*, count. As I live
the wind plays them out. *Ciel*, what music!"

"A dead march for some of them drummed
upon the hill tops," chimed in De Rémy. "My
anemometer marks a velocity of 65, with a
pressure of 20.8. If they weather that, their
hides are pachydermatous. I have never known
such wind, count, since the night we lost the
ten-inch gun."

"I remember it well," said the count; "the
night of the 10th of June, in the year 1889.
How you cried out when the gun went under!

There were devils in the air that night, De Rémy."

"Well," said I, coming forward, "I am not going to dispute the merits of your evening, count, but this particular occasion is hardly one for a picnic."

He turned round, when I spoke, to greet me with tokens of great affection; and, when he had kissed Fortune many times, he began to mention the night of terror which had passed.

"My heart is heavy that men should die like that," said he, "die with the grip of hell upon them. Yet how many must perish before the age of mercy and of peace shall be known to our children, or our children's children? What seas of blood have run from the countless thousands whose groans and tears have built up the shell of that we call civilisation? And if, by the death of these, we quicken humanity to the brotherhood we preach, is ours the reproach? Nay, indeed, though an army lay dead at my gates, they should remain shut until the voice of mercy opens them."

Fanatic as he was, for so the world has called him, it was not to be hidden from me that something of the simple passion of pure victory was now added to the finer emotions which were begotten of his creed. And this passion the others made no pretence to hide.

"Right or wrong," cried De Rémy, "it's plain that no ship of theirs will get to shelter in this, and I'm not humbug enough to say I'm sorry."

"Nor I," said Malasac. "I haven't slept for three days, nor eaten for twenty hours. Why should I complain, count, that I can eat and sleep?"

"You have no reason to complain, my son, for the dinner is served, I see."

"And there is soup!" exclaimed De Rémy. "*Diable!* What a beautiful thing is soup, when you must go wanting it!"

"This is no night for abstinence," said the count. "I would have every man fare as on a feast day."

"For my part," said Malasac, "I could roll a week of feasts into one blessed hour, and remain hungry at that. Destiny did not bring me into this world to fast."

We were all at table by this, and hardly had we begun to eat when Adam himself entered the room, water streaming from his hair and face, and the whole of him pitiably wet. He had come up from the barracks, where he had been looking after the welfare of the men, and he told us that the storm was then beyond anything he could remember.

"How I got up here I don't precisely know," said he. "I think I must have crawled. It's the sort of night when you regret that evolution deprived man of two legs and his claws."

"And you left the others well?" asked the count.

"They will be rationally drunk in an hour or less," said he. And then, remembering to whom he spoke, he explained, "That is to say, they will skirmish with the outposts of genteel hilarity about that time. They are merry souls, those men of ours—when you feed them."

"And why not?" said De Rémy. "After all, the first of human problems is summed up in the word beef; the second in the word beer. Civilisation is chiefly a history of light dishes and of glazing."

"While barbarism is a splendid ignorance of the utility of forks and aldermen," said I.

In this spirit of banter the dinner was eaten; but when cigars had been lighted and coffee was served, the count drew his chair near the fire, and with Fortune sitting curled up upon the floor by his knees, he spoke to us of the business of the morrow.

"It lies upon us, my friends," said he, "to see that good use is made of this truce which no work of ours has brought about. We shall know at daybreak what the sea has done for us. It may be that no ships will have lived through the night. But whatever it is, there can be no rest for masters or for men until amnesty is proclaimed."

"Which we may look for somewhere about the middle of the century," cried Adam, who never was an optimist before his master.

"I think otherwise," said the count. "It is my hope that sympathy will win for me what force can never win. The world is very ready to side with the weak if the weak can gain a hearing from it. And we, at least, have proved ourselves worthy of a hearing."

"I am trusting," said Malasac, now become serious, "that the voice of England will yet be heard. A beaten nation clings to arbitration— and for all that she has done to us, France is a beaten nation."

"Twice beaten," said the count, "and now

hurled back by the hand of Almighty God. What has she done; what is her achievement? She has left the bodies of her men in our harbours and on our hills; she has witnessed vengeance come up out of the mountains; she has shattered a few poor, pitiful buildings; she has battered down some tons of earth. And to-night the very wind writes her defeat—the storm mocks her."

"Which means," said Adam, striving for the practical, "that we shall see no more of her for three months. If news of this comes to Lincoln, he will certainly run in with the yacht."

"I should be glad to see him," exclaimed the count. "This is no scene for women or for children. And we're needing the cargo that he shipped."

"In twelve weeks," said De Rémy, "he could run through twice, and carry heavy shot the second venture."

" Trust Silver to wipe their eyes, though they had the devil for pilot," said Adam, " but the count's right about the women. They're the shadow on the way."

" Add the scum in the prison yonder, and you've named the whole of it," said Dé Remy. " Did you happen to hear, count, that seven of them went down last night? I saw a shell fall in among them when I was coming back from the point, and I waited while they took seven dead out. Oh, it's just hell in there now! There was froth on some of their lips when we fought our way in. No beasts' den could touch that hole."

"If I had a voice in it, I'd pistol them!" cried Adam. "It would be mercy, too. They are dying there like niggers in a sloop. It makes your heart bleed to see them."

"Yet what would you do?" said the count, who seemed always to shudder at any mention of the prison. "If they had deserved death, they had found it. Our necessity does not add to their crimes. It is not for us to judge because judgment would be convenient for us. We have no mandate to deal with them otherwise than we have dealt. What peril we suffer, they must suffer. We owe it to ourselves, to the men who count upon us, to the women who have put their lives in our hands."

He said much more to the same end, declaring that he would have no mad work done, nor any departure from that which had been laid down; and from this, since the subject was not to his

taste, he went on to speak of the work which
must be done if the morrow found the near sea
wanting ships, of the crops that must be got in,
of the tunnel which must be cleared, and the
ramparts which must be built up. He spoke, too,
of the possibility of building pens for the cattle
in some chasm of the hills, where they might be
hid from the shot ; of the prospect of Lincoln's
coming ; but chiefly of the hope of getting the
women away to Valparaiso, and then of setting
up so sturdy a defence that siege might do what
it would.

In this making of plan and counter-plan the
night of storm passed. Though the wind howled
without, and the rain beat as with hail of shot,
and torrents of water rushed down the hillside,
there was warmth and dryness by the great fire of
logs ; and even in the women's cave, which we
visited before the bugle sounded " lights out,"
the comfort was very wonderful.

From a little gallery in the wall of the great
cavern, to which we had access by a passage
from the count's pavilion, we looked upon a
sight as strange as any I have seen. In all the
corners of that vast and natural basilica huge
fires were burning. The electric light, shining

down chiefly from arc-lamps, showed us the women playing, singing, feasting ; little children were sleeping in many a rough-shaped cot ; music was heard from harp or mandolin ; the cascade of water falling from the rock shone like a fount of dazzling gems ; the depending stalactites were as spears of silver.

The terror of those hours when shell fell upon the city had passed like a dream ; the triumph of the day was not to be resisted. None sought to turn from the carnival of the night, when the island had shaken off her foes, and stood up again unharmed by the nations that had challenged her.

Joy of this triumph had, for a truth, seized upon the people like a pestilence. From the barracks at the hill's foot snatches of roaring song floated up to us ; sentries on the heights were huddling near to sheltered beacons ; the bells of the cathedral strove against the wind to peal a note of gladness ; wine flowed like water, men had but one word to speak, and that a word of victory. Of the morrow, or of the morrow again, none paused to think. The spell of the present was too potent, the new freedom all-conquering.

So far as my own share in this wild business
went, I spent the night going with Adam from
cave to cave and camp to camp. When at last
I returned to my room, Fortune was in a deep
sleep ; but the troops were still making merry in
the houses below, and there was no silence save
in the chamber of the women.

CHAPTER XXXI.

I WAKE TO STRANGE DREAMS.

THERE is nothing more curious in all the vagaries of Sleep than the way in which he coquettes with us when we have most need of him. I am acquainted with no greater provocation of the night than that of waking from an apparently unbroken slumber of hours to find it but a doze of minutes. The mind resents the fraud played upon it; the brain can scarce be coaxed to rest again until dawn comes; and all the while one thinks to see the aggravating god himself sitting at the bed's foot with a leer upon his face, and the down-turned torch in his hand.

Though I know no cause to which I may set it down, for I have no pretence to any foresight beyond that of my fellow-men, sleep came to me fitfully on that night of storm and hurricane. And the want of it was the less to be explained since the fatigue, both of excitement and of labour, was still strong upon me. Yet, do what I would, I could catch no doze from which I did not wake when ten minutes had passed, find no position which was not unbearable when the new quarter was chimed upon the clock. And stranger still was it that every doze would seem to me like a sleep of hours, every moment of oblivion a period of satisfying rest.

It must have wanted yet an hour to dawn, when a series of these fitful wakings drove me from my bed to the camp-chair in the room, and then to the narrow window, whence a great part of the city below was to be observed. Fortune herself lay in the sweetest of sleeps ; her face was the face of a joyous child ; it was plain that she dreamed pleasantly, and I feared to wake her, and watched for a while the sleeping island through the rain-stained glass. But so fine was the prospect, so magnificently did the whole land stand out in the soft rays of the moonlight, that anon I dressed myself and sought the fresher air of the open valley itself.

It was a little to my surprise that the storm had passed so suddenly; but this was my first experience of a true Pacific hurricane, of its strength, and of that delicious freshness it leaves in its path. Never have I known a night so bracing or

so sweet as this one of which I write. Through a
break in the distant peaks the full moon, set as a
great lantern in the heavens, shone with refulgent,
dreamy rays. Its rich flood of yellow light fell
upon the rounded hills and gave them majesty of
their loneliness ; it cast lengthening shadows and
shapes as of black rivers running upon the grass ;
it illumined the spires of the mountains and cut
windows of silver in them where the feldspar or
the jasper grained the duller rock. In the lower
valleys, where the beams fell soft upon the lawns
of the park, and the cattle were still herding in
the shelter of the trees, the splashing cascades
were turned to falls of jewels, the streams took
the colour of amethyst or sapphire, the chasms
of the passes showed walls all glowing as with
tracery of gold and precious gems. And over all
was an entrancing stillness ; the song of night
birds in the woods and the lowing of the kine
were like dream-music to the ear.

With this perfect peace and beauty of the night
as its legacy, the storm had passed ; yet in some
of the higher gorges, and particularly in that
place of the hills above the prison, was there left
striking evidence of its activity. I had never seen
the boiling springs cast spray so high, nor the

flames of sulphur, which burst up from the crevices of the headland, so blue and fierce. And to
these signs ever and anon would be added a
strange tremour of sound seeming to come up from
the very bowels of the earth. At one time I
feared that earthquake would succeed to hurricane, and was half tempted to wake the others ;
but the thunderings passed with no quivering of
the ground, and the fascinations of the night
turned me quickly to other thoughts. I began
to remember how strange it was that I should be
standing there, cut off as by death from all those
pursuits and circumstances which once had been
for me the hope and strength of my life. I recalled the forebodings of the worthy Donald
when I had left him in Welbeck Street ; I thought
on the fever of action which had possessed me in
Paris ; I reminded myself that I had become the
servant of a fanatic upon whom Europe must
soon lay her hands to crush him ; I told myself
that by no process of reasoning could I make
logic of my sacrifice ; I tried to look to the future
to ask, Where shall I be when a month has past—
in what state, in whose company ? At one moment foreboding, in the next hoping, because of
the example and the heroic personality of him I

served, I turned the problem over and over in my mind; nursed it, petted it, enjoyed it most when to its perplexities was added the memory of my child-wife sleeping within there so sweetly; the memory of her at whose call I had come to this exile, whose love had been life to me since the hour I had seen her in the pavilion of the gardens.

The pursuit of these perplexities—an idle pursuit, but one worthy of a night dream-begetting and all still—carried me from the count's house over the grassy plateau which lay between the hill land and the lower slope of the valley. And sauntering thus, with my pipe for company, I came at last to a little gate which led to the paddocks where the horses of the cavalry grazed. From this place I could see the barracks wherein the greater number of the troops were quartered, and I observed that the riot of the early night had now given place to sleep and solitude. A single sentry paced before the iron gates of the low building; not a light shone from its windows, not a soul walked in the moonlit streets of the city, whose shattered houses stood up like the ruined tombs of ill-remembered dead. Nor elsewhere upon the distant cliffs was the customary guard to be seen. Here and there a single horse-

man paced the heights; the glimmer of ebbing
fires told of men watching and of stations kept, but
that cordon of troops which the siege had called
for was no longer a necessity. Men, wearied with
long weeks of duty, had gone down to the rest
they had earned so well; the truce of the storm
had sapped the zeal of doubt and of combat; all
looked to sleep, and to sleep had the most part of
the honest fellows come.

When I had come to the little gate of the pad-
dock, and had sat there smoking for the best part
of an hour, my heavy cloak protecting me somewhat from the night, I began to think that folly
had drawn me from my bed. Sleep, which
played with me in the house, now began to cry a
truce; I found myself nodding, and was held
back from complete forgetfulness at last only by
the scamper of a herd of deer which, for some
cause I could not indicate, came flying up the
hillside, and did not cease to gallop madly until
they had got the shelter of the higher woods. I
thought it strange that the herd should run thus
when the night was without voice or sound; but
while I was still thinking upon it, there came
from one of the hills to the east of me a sharp,
shrill cry, like the cry of a man taken suddenly

in the grip of death. So weird was this sound,
so long sustained, and so pitiful, that it called me
in a moment to complete wakefulness; and, conscious of a fear which I could in no way explain,
I jumped from the gate and ran up the hill again
to see if there was any sign upon the higher
land either of friend or of enemy. But when
I came again upon the plateau the whole island
lay in the sleep which the calm had given to
her. I could no longer see a single horseman;
the watch-fires had died down until they had
become heaps of glowing embers; the sentry
before the barracks had found warmth in his
box; I was alone to ask, What means the
cry?

The assurance of this continuing sleep recalled
me to some calmness. I began to say that I had
dreamed the thing. The panic of the deer had
brought me to hear in fancy the sob of a human
voice. And I should have gone back to my bed
very contented if, and this just as I was at the door
of the house, I had not heard a second cry; not
as the first, but as of one man hailing to another.
The new voice came from the lower spur of hill
not a quarter of a mile from the count's door.
Scarce was it raised when upon the grass of the

park I seemed to hear the tread of many men; a low, buzzing hum of voices floated upon the air; then, to my burning imagination, the whole city seemed to leap into life, the woods to be peopled, the valleys to be full of the whispers of an advancing enemy. And no longer doubting, but sure of the presence of some sudden and momentous peril, I burst into the house, and in a moment was at Adam's side.

"Adam!" cried I, "for God's sake, wake up; the park is full of men!"

With a start he roused himself from his sleep. This was the first night since the attack began that he had thrown off his clothes; and now fatigue lay heavy upon him.

"Who is it? Who speaks?" he asked when he had rubbed his eyes.

"There has been a man stabbed on the hills. I heard his cry," said I. "There is the tramp of a hundred men in the park. Come and hear for yourself."

He was wide awake now and busy with his things.

"Are you sure it isn't a drunken brawl?" he asked as he pulled on his boots.

I went to tell him that I was sure; but, before

I had said a word, there was a trooper at the door, crying:

" For the love of God, captain, dress yourself! The tunnel is down, and the prisoners are out!"

The man was splashed from spur to cap with clinging mud; there was dirt upon his face; blood ran from his cheek, which had been laid open by some blow. The words that he spoke came from him with stuttering efforts; and so great was the excitement under which he laboured that he would listen to no questions of ours, but must go on with his news.

"It was an hour ago; I was patrolling the long valley, when they hailed me from the white-house station. There are four dead there now, and more dying. They cut the colonel down at the old watch gate, and are now swarming into the barracks. You can hear them yourself. Oh, my God, what things to see!"

Adam finished his dressing and buckled on his sword. He made no display of haste or panic; but when the man had spoken, he said to him:

" They came out by the great gate; then where was the guard?"

" Ay, where was the guard?" answered the other, repeating the question in his exceeding fear. " But there was wine served last night, you may know, captain. Oh, truly, we all sleep like dogs while they are cutting throats. But I know nothing; I'm a hill man, and did not see."

"Exactly; we must see for ourselves," cried Adam, and with that word we all three went out to the passage, and ran from room to room crying out to the others. But my way lay to Fortune's side, and so lightly did she sleep that a press of my hand waked her.

"Sweetheart," said I, "there's bad news from below; dress yourself and put your cloak on."

She was still full of sleep; and the din of a great gong struck in the chamber of the women did not help her to understanding. But she was no subject for alarms, and when she had waited a moment to watch me load my pistol she obeyed me.

"Irwin," said she, speaking only when she was quite dressed, "why are they waking the women?"

"The prisoners are out, Fortune!"

"Oh, Heaven help us!" said she, and there was great fear in her voice.

"So far as I can learn," said I, " the shells and

the storm together brought down a part of the wall, and the men got free. They are now fighting in the barracks and burning the city."

She came trembling to my side and held close to me, while from the window we beheld a great red glow in the sky and saw flames licking the walls of the nearer houses. The new light fell upon the figures of many men running to and fro from the quarters of the troops, some dragging bodies by the heels, some bearing arms, all shouting and halloaing very wildly. And to this spectacle there was now added the screams of the women in the great cave, the clanking of arms upon the stone of the passage, the rattle of musketry from a hundred places in the higher woods and the outskirts of the park.

When we had stood a moment at our window, looking upon the terror, Adam called to us to come out to him, and then it was that Fortune raised her lips to mine and kissed me very sweetly.

"Irwin, dear husband," said she, "I cannot ask you to stay; may God bring you back to me!"

For answer, I took her to my arms, and held her there, and when I had kissed her many times we went out to the others, who were all together upon the knoll of grass before the door. Some forty men had now come running in, many of them from the watching-places on the hills, a few from the barracks, a few from the city; and each had his own tale to tell. But the majority of them bore no arms, and such rifles as we had in the house were gone already to the servants.

The noise and incoherent talk, the cries for lights and for weapons, the commanding and countermanding to be heard at the door of the house, helped the confusion of a gathering which was confusing beyond experience. While many ran hither and thither seeking some weapons for their defence, others bawled that we should hold the caves; others, again, that we should get the women to the hills. Everywhere an uncontrollable panic prevailed; mad terror was the only impulse. The women themselves, waked from their sleep to these horrid sights and sounds, had ears neither for counsel nor for consolation. Some of them snatched up their children and fled sobbing to the heights; others crouched by the fires in the cave and cried out for us to kill them; some prayed hysterically; a few were silent for very despair. And in the midst of the hubbub three more troopers came riding in with the news that all the more dissolute rogues, but chiefly the men who had worked in the mines and the leaders of the discontent during the month of siege, had joined themselves to the prisoners, and were burning and slaying in the city and the camp.

Until this time I had heard no word from the count, who stood in our midst like one in a stupor. But at the tidings that many of his own were turned against him he seemed to wake, and he began to call men to themselves.

"Men," said he, "you hear what has been said, Will you stand to die like sheep, you and the women who look to you, or will you strike a blow for God and the work?"

They answered him that they would stand, and many who before were wild with their fears now came round to him like children, depending upon his word.

"Then prove yourselves," said he, "and the Lord have mercy upon us all! Let those who have guns hold the platform of the great room; the others will form a second line before the women while we get them through. Captain Adam, I look to you; gentlemen, I am counting upon your devotion."

It was wonderful to see how the courage of the one man was spread about at this speech, so that presently the whole forty had shared it. And never was there sorer need of cool heads and quick hands. Even while we stood upon the hill, and I, for my part, thought only of keeping Fortune at my side, the scene of devastation in the city below had become nothing less than a massacre and a sack.

By the flaming light of burning houses we could see the devils at their work; some running with torches to fire the buildings, some pursuing wretched creatures waked from their sleep by the touch of knives at their throats; some slashing and maiming the bodies of the dead; some broaching casks of liquor, which ran flaring in the gutters. To the sound of crashing timbers and bursting windows there was added the rattle of muskets, the piteous cries for mercy, the shrill notes of the women, the clamorous shouting of the men.

The city burned almost from end to end. You could see every tree of the woods above; the near park was lit by the red light until its very lake seemed to be a lake of blood. And when at last the leaping fire took hold upon the cathedral, and burst from its roof and the windows of the belfry, the downfall culminated—the bloody chaos was at its height.

I say that we watched these things, but none the less was our own work pursued. While the din of the riot rose up in the city below, and the streets ran with blood, and the buildings tottered, and men were drunk with slaughter and debauch, we on our part were quieting the women, and distributing such arms as we had. And I could not help but remember what a surpassing misfortune it was that the night of truce had sent a majority of the honest fellows to their homes again, had taken from the refuge so many of the women wearying for air and freedom. All these, I could not doubt, had gone down to death, or that which was worse than death, with no blow struck for them; we, at least, could give our lives for those who looked to us. Nor do I think that any man, waiting there with mind benumbed and aching heart, believed that he would know another day—nay, perhaps another hour.

For myself, I cannot tell what an agony of grief and apprehension filled my mind. Had I stood alone, I might well have trembled at the thought of what must be ; but with my child-wife there at my side, with her cold hand in mine, and her white face to reproach me, it seemed indeed that some curse was on my life. And the bitterness was greater when I remembered that I had lived to possess her, had learned the whole sweetness of her love.

This, of a truth, was my thought; and had it not been for the consummation of our need, I know not that I could have borne with it. But while it was pressing most bitterly upon me the crisis of the attack came, and all reflection, save that begotten of the moment, passed. And this time we had drawn up in the cave such lines of defence as we could make, and what preparation was possible that we had completed. I saw with some surprise that the women had been carried to a higher platform of the rock which jutted out upon the left hand of the cascade; and huddled there were thirty or forty of them, with many little children. But the movement, as I soon learned, was but a stage in their journey, for they began to disappear one by one down a narrow vault-like tunnel, which opened behind the platform of the rock; and before the devils of the city had come up to us, there were not ten of them remaining in the open. For the rest, the

men waited in a double ring upon the outer edge
of the platform, making no pretence to defend the
doors, but only seeking to cover the retreat of the
helpless creatures who moaned and cried behind
them, nor would listen to any words of comfort.

That the door should not be the rallying place
astonished me at the first; but the caves had not
been built up against any enemy from within,
but only as a refuge from the shot and shell of
a besieging force. The gates themselves were
light and easily to be broken; there were loop-
holes of size where the chamber did not face the
sea, other passages by which attack could here be
concentrated. Any attempt to hold ground at
the door was not to be thought of with so poor a
force; and it soon became plain that, if we could
keep the platform for ten minutes, all the women
might be be got to that place of shelter to which,
as it appeared, they were being conducted. And
with this knowledge giving me some little hope, I
waited while the shouts of the advancing hordes
gathered strength and ferocity, and their cries of
triumph became more deafening and unmistakable.

We had reached the platform by a short wooden
ladder, which, when at last Adam and the count

came to us, we drew up. The light had now been
turned off, so that the great cave was all dark,
save where the glow of embers reddening cast
faint rays upon the walls of rock and the glistening crystals of the dome. And in plain contrast
to the hoots of the crew without, our men shut
their lips and said no word, only lying with the
barrels of their rifles out beyond the edge of the
dais, and their swords at the side of them. My
own place was immediately behind that of Adam,
he having the station next to the count; but
Fortune, who had refused to hear any talk of
going away with the women, was curled up at my
feet—and a pressure of her hand, often repeated,
was the news I had of her.

The first note of the attack was just such a one
as we had looked for. During many minutes we
had heard the cries and oaths of the maddened
crew come nearer; then a silence fell, to be
broken immediately by a showering of blows
upon the gate, and loud demands and threats.
To these we answered no word; not a man
moved; there was not the clang of a single rifle
barrel; even the women passing to the inner
cave stood still. And at the height of the stillness, one of those without spoke.

"Count," cried the voice, "belike you aint recognising me, count; my respects to you, sir, I'm coming in to cheer you up, you white-livered old swine!"

A second appeal, and some filthy oaths in French, drew no more response from us; and at this the first man spoke again:

"You, count, are you going to bail up, or am I coming in to fetch you?"

"Fetch the old lubber out," chimed in a second, "and don't waste no words, Jack."

At this they beat loud upon the door again, and hammered it so that it rattled on its hinges; but one, more suggestive than the others, now cried out:

"Go aloft to the window; maybe the game's missing."

We heard them pause a moment, and then there was the sound of one man helping another, and presently the cry of a voice high up at an arbalestena upon the left side of the door.

"Hand up a light, Jack; it's as dark as hell!"

"Can you see, Bill?"

"Strike me blind, I can't see myself."

They now gave the man a torch, and he poked it through the hole; but hardly had he raised it when Adam at my side clapped his rifle to his shoulder; and at the crack of it the man rolled headlong to the ground. A whole volley of tremendous oaths went with him; and from that moment there were no other calls for parley or admittance.

The rogues themselves forgot any longer to blaspheme and curse; but falling to their work in earnest, they began to hurl themselves upon the door, or to clamber to the loopholes or casements; where, seated astride the rough-hewn rock, and wisely discarding any light or torch, they poured volley after volley in upon us. And grimly, silently, earnestly we answered their fire wherever and whenever a flash of a musket showed for a moment the face of the man who bore it.

For some time this interchange of shot was fitful. The door of the cavern proved to be stouter than any of us had thought; it did not break even when they carried up some ill-fashioned ram and beat it savagely. Nor did any of their fellows bethink them at first of forcing the lighter gates of the other passages, but continued about the chief entrance, working savagely to break it down, or pulling themselves up to the lower casements, whence they poured their shot in upon us.

And while they did this we could but lie and wait, numbering with beating hearts the women that were passed into the tunnel, praying very fervently that our own turn would not long be delayed.

"Eight, seven, six! For God's sake hurry, men !"

The words came from Adam in one of those fitful moments of truce which must be known in any such encounter as this. But six of the women and Fortune remained upon the rock. If we could hold on for some minutes it was my hope that whatever shelter had been prepared would be gained by us. This I knew was Fortune's thought, for now she sat up watching what was done, where before she had rested her head upon her arms as though she would see nothing of the death around her. And even while she was telling me to hope, they cried that two more of the women had passed; and our own men for the first time sent up a ringing cheer of defiance, which echoed up in the very vault of the cavern.

It is not possible to conceive a grimmer picture than that which the great cave then presented to our eyes. Upon the platform the flash of the rifles showed the little ring of men, broken here and there where some poor fellow had rolled dead upon his side or lay groaning with the pain of his wound. The dying fires of logs cast fitful beams upon the walls shot with quartz and jasper and fantastic crystals ; the cascade splashed and foamed with unceasing music ; the singing of the balls was like the whistling of winds, the sharp cries when men were struck rang out discordantly ; the clamour of the throng became minute by minute more dreadful to hear, more fierce, more uncontrollable.

" Oh, for the love of God, be quick with it ! "

The count spoke now, and but one woman remained. I turned to Fortune and bade her go with them, but she did not answer me ; only she clung like some terrified thing to my arms and nestled her head upon my shoulder. And the count when he saw her was of her mind.

" The child is right," he cried ; " her place is here."

He said the thing, and in the same instant Adam cried :

" The women are through ; let the rest fall back in close order."

We heard this order as men to whom a new

span of life has been given. One tremendous
cheer scattered echoes through the caves; then
the old silence fell upon us, and forming up, as
one by one the rear rank passed to the darkness of the rock hole, we waited to know what
was the meaning of the sudden hush of voices
without. For a hush it was, coming of a change
of plan, I made sure; and this was justified when,
it might be after a truce of five minutes, we were
all conscious, though we could not see them, that
men actually moved within the chamber.

They came silently, leaping from cover to
cover among the uprising stalagmites; and when
they had kept their breath until they were almost
at our feet, they blazed, with such guns as they
had, a full volley at us. Ill as the light was and
poor their shooting, nevertheless some sharp cries
of pain were wrung from our men; and an Italian
near to me fell back dead upon the floor, grip-
ping my flesh in his agony so that he cut it with
his nails. I had not thrown his body off my legs
when the great gates were opened from within,
and the howling mob, which had gathered anger
from its waiting, came headlong at us, crying,
some that the women should first be seized, some
that we should be dragged out to the open, some

that lights should be got. And from that word the whole fury of the fight befel.

How it was, or whose doing, I cannot say, but as the cave was filled with the horrid cries of this band, drunk with the foulest desires and mad for slaughter, Fortune was dragged backward from my arms by the strong hand of an unknown friend. The wisdom of the deed was no longer to be doubted. The pit was becoming a shambles full of woful sights and sounds. There was need of every man's blade and every man's strength. She had been taken to the shelter, I knew, and my thoughts were all of thankfulness. No longer harassed by the need of looking to her, I pressed close to Adam, and, shoulder to shoulder, man cheering man, we met them as they came.

Had there been any discipline among them, had they rushed upon us in any good order—and more than this, had they possessed any considerable quantity of ammunition—our shrift had been short. But the magazine they had not broached, and such cartridges as they had found came out of the pouches of the soldiers. Of these the most part had been shot away in the massacre below, and now, when the rogues rushed

upon us, they must fall to with any small arms
they had got.   Looking down below me, as
the first gray of the dawn-light came streaming
through the eastern window, I beheld the savage
faces of rugged men raising bayonets torn from
the troopers, or short swords taken from the barracks, or even common knives and sticks picked
up in the houses they had sacked.   And with
these they slashed and cut and stabbed at us
above, now trying to clamber, man upon the
shoulders of man, now roaring in their fury when
our blades pricked them, now beseeching their
fellows behind that they should not fire, but only
help them up upon the platform.

On our side the square we presented was a
sight to warm the heart.   But above all, and
never to be forgotten, notwithstanding the fine
swordsmanship of the count, who was near to
being the best man among us, was the work of
Adam, who stood there reaping the human crop
before him like one who cuts down long grass
with a scythe.   Never have I seen a sword thrust
with such lightning passes; never seen a com-
rade who so bore himself.   Man by man he
cut them down; man by man he spitted them,
now through the throat, now through the heart.

Blows rained upon him, the air was bright with
the flashing of the knives, rare bullets sang above
his head, there was blood upon his cheek—yet
still he stood to cheer us with his word, to cry to
us to hold on, to breathe upon us the spirit of his
own magnificent courage. And the mob fell
back at last in awe before him, and one ruffian
alone stood to that flashing blade.

This man I knew. He was the yellow-haired
ringleader I had met in the prison, and when I
saw him now he was no less dreadful to look
upon—a man of gigantic size, rags upon his back,
scars upon his face, sweat dropping from his forehead, his eyes outstanding. When he saw Adam
waiting for him, and the count at his side, he
cried out with ferocious joy, raising a great sword
and swinging it in the air with ugly blows that
would have hacked iron bars or severed beams.
But they fell upon Adam's blade like the beat
of a child's stick; he turned them with infinite
skill, he mocked the striker with that merry
voice of his.

" Jack Roberts !" cried he, while blade clashed
upon blade, and sparks flew from their steel, "a
merry evening to you, Jack ! Shall I spoil your
beauty, or will you have it in the throat ?'

The huge fellow made no answer, but spat upon him, and so, taking a backward step, he swung himself round to strike a mighty blow. While he turned, showing us the flesh beneath his arms, wherefrom his clothes had fallen, Adam's sword flashed again and quivered as the blow went home. The man fell stone dead, struck three inches below the arm-pit and pierced to his heart.

"Good-night to you, Jack Roberts!" was all that Adam said when the body rolled upon the stone; but to us he cried:

"Let every man that can charge a pistol fall back; swordsmen to the front. Hold your fire, men, until I ask it."

When the leader fell the mob halted; but at these words they came rushing on again with a new zeal; and I, who had attempted to obey the word, found myself jammed in with the others, fighting and slashing for my very life. My pistols had long been empty; I could but use one of them for a club, and defend myself, as might be, with the short-bladed knife I had taken from the armoury. As for the others of our men, not a few of them had come to use their rifles by the barrels, aiming crashing blows upon the skulls of the throng below, caring nothing for the cuts they received, for the bullets that still sang in the cavern.

Daylight was now streaming into the chamber from every loophole; there was even sun, when we formed together—the ten who remained upon the platform—to meet that last great rush, to know that success even for minutes might bring life to us. With louder howls of fury, the mob came on, cursing us, beating at us with their fists, filling the air with the shriek of oaths. There never was such a sight of angry faces, of men possessed of devils, of gaping wounds and flesh ripped, of hands stained with blood, of heads laid open. Again and again, as I struck some up-turned face and heard the bones of it crack, as I dug my knife into the bodies of those who pressed upon me, I thought the end was then; that they must engulph us to tear us limb from limb as they had promised to do. But still we held them; still the voices of Adam and the count encouraged us, and there remained but five before the door of the hole.

It was at the supreme moment that the call for those who were behind to load their pistols was explained. Adam had seemed to forget it; but now, of a sudden, he made a supreme effort, cutting the men down like nettles. Then we heard his word, and all dropped upon their knees.

"Now!"

A great flame of the shot rushed out from the tunnel at his call, and, of the ruffians near, six fell dead. In the same moment the count drew me into the passage, and the secret of it was revealed to me. It was a hole above a trapdoor, and in a room twenty feet below there was a torch held to show us the iron ladder down which we must pass. And to this the count helped me, while for one terrible minute Adam held the door alone.

Though I might live ten lives, I could never learn to write of that man's work, of his unsurpassable courage, his strength, his cleverness. I know only that when I had stood a minute at the ladder's foot, listening to the clamour and the outcry above, he came to the trap, and with incredible quickness he swung himself upon the rungs and drew down the door. A hundred blows beat upon it even as it shut,—there was a man's hand crushed in its fall,—but for precious moments we had put a barrier behind us, and he, to whom we owed it, now stood with us, blood running from his head, his hands cut, sweat thick upon his forehead, his face all grimed and blackened with his labour.

"O Adam!" said I, "God be thanked for this! Have they hurt you, Adam?"

He turned round and gave me his hand; but his meeting with the man he had served so well was another thing, and for a minute they held to each other like women in a tender greeting. Then he snatched the torch from the hands of the bearer, and lurching, nay, almost staggering down the passage, he bade me follow him. But with every step that he took blood dripped from his clothes, and the blows upon the trap at the ladder's head promised every moment to burst it.

We went down the passage, I say, and it was then that I began to understand why it had been necessary for us to hold the platform until the women had passed. The trap itself was the flimsiest thing; in the narrow way of that steep and winding tunnel, with a floor of slime and sharp rocks to trip upon, we could not have held an enemy for an hour. And above this, when we had walked, crouching down and often stumbling, for the sixth of a mile, we came out upon a chasm which made clear to me in a moment the whole strength of the position.

The gulf was as black as night save where our torches, one upon either bank, cast a glow upon its roof and to its depths. Down a hundred feet below us there ran the little river, dark and foaming, which was the cascade in the cavern above; across the abyss, in whose walls there were now the bright lights of crystals and strange minerals shining, the rudest bridge of ropes was strung. A belt of cloth running upon a block, a cable stretched taut—these were the contrivances by which the women had passed; by which we must make good our place against the rogues, whose shouts we heard in the tunnel even while the first of our five remaining was drawing himself across the chasm.

The first to cross was the man upon the hither side who held aloft the torch. Adam took it from his hand, and we watched him while he swung above the depths like a sailor upon the futtock shrouds of a ship. It was a dizzy thing to see, a transit to make the heart stand; one light rope held up the man from eternity; below him the Styx-like river foamed and hissed with the black spray and sucking rapids of the sharp rocks. And through it all we heard the distant howling of the mob, the echo of their voices muffled in the tunnel.

Another man passed and three of us stood upon the brink when they sent the belt back. Adam's need was the greatest, but again he would not hear of it.

" Count," said he, " you are next."

" By what right, Adam ? "

" By every right ; we shall go the faster for knowing you are safe. Hark to that ! they are through the trap."

A louder sound of voices, no longer indistinct, but very plainly audible, now came down to us. It was not to be doubted that the men had burst the door, and were feeling their way along the passage.

" Count," said I, " if they are to be held, it must be by young hands. For the love of God, go over ! "

He hesitated no more, and, for the matter of that, he was like a man who dreamed, then, and until the end of it. During a spell that seemed one of hours, I looked upon him, while he swung over the abyss, the torchlight strong upon his remarkable face : and I remember that of all my fears, this was the greatest, that I should see him no more. Yet, although the rope quivered and swayed until the brain reeled at the sight of it,

they pulled him to the brink, and, in the same
moment that the belt came back to me, the first
of the mob appeared, and grappled with Adam.
For one dreadful instant the two were locked
together like wrestlers in close embrace; then
the man's breath rattled in his throat, and his
body went hurling down to the jagged crags
below.

By this time I had the belt about my body;
but so great was Adam's peril that I hallooed to
those on the other bank not to pull me over.
Three more of the rogues had now crept out of
the tunnel, and were closing upon us; there were
others yet in the passage trying to force their
way to the brink. So narrow was the ledge of
rock upon which we stood, so dark the place,
that, although I had got cartridges in my pistol,
I dared not to fire, and must hack blindly with
my knife. And all through it I felt that they
were forcing Adam to the gulf, that it could be
only a matter of moments before he was thrust
down to the horrid death below. Never, I think,
in my life, has death come so near to me. Even
now, when many months have passed, it is my
fear to dream of that dim-lighted cavern, with its
swirling river at its depths, and devils crying out

upon its brink, and the red glow of one torch touching all things as with the dye of blood. Again I have Adam forced back upon my arms ; I hear the sound of his blows ; I watch the man fall before him ; I strike with all my strength, and groans and oaths and dreadful threats are hurled back upon me. Again I tremble at the play of chance by which we were snatched from the peril. I watch that holocaust of men done to death by the fury of their fellows.

For thus it was in our awaking, and thus it is in my dream. Adam, as I have written, was forced back into my arms by the press of men, who, knowing nothing of the chasm or its bridge, pushed out upon the ledge in such numbers that they began to fight with their fellows for sheer foothold. And now shouting, some that they should get back, some to cut us down, they began to tumble to the abyss, or to hang upon its brink, while the rocks cut their hands, and we struck them off with our blows, or they were shot by our fellows upon the other shore. Such a terrible sight of men hurled suddenly to the infinite darkness, of men drawing back from the pit as from the gates of hell itself, of rogues turned upon rogues, was never seen ; and at the very height of it I heard Adam's voice again, and new strength came to me at his cry.

"Irwin," said he, and he had little breath for words, since he was then striking at a great fellow who held to him, so pressing us both toward the gulf, "cut me free of this man!"

I saw then that he was locked in the fellow's arms like one hugged by an octopus. So great was the man's strength that we all three toppled upon the brink of the chasm, and, save for my own hold of the rope, we had gone over. But the belt was still round my waist; I held to the cable itself with my left hand, and, making a supreme effort to keep Adam upon the ledge with my knees, I struck over his shoulder at the fellow who held him. Twice I struck, and thrice, and at the third blow the grip of the man's arms relaxed slowly. He dropped upon his knees, then he fell headlong, and you could hear the crack of his bones as he struck upon the rocks below. But Adam rolled backward into my arms; and, by the very force of reaction, he swung me out over the abyss, and our fellows upon the other bank began to haul away.

I say that I had him in my arms; but it is not to be thought that I could long have held him there swaying and rolling above that terrible chasm. Nay, the belt was already cutting into my flesh and the blood surging to my head when he grasped the rope above us, and so began to pass hand over hand to the other shore. At this sight the mob we had left were near to raving with their fury, some hacking at the cable with their knives, some throwing lumps of rock and great stones at us; while our own fellows cried out for us to go back, since the rope would surely break. And this was the most dreadful word of any spoken:

"Oh, for God's sake, the rope is giving! Back, back!"

So they cried, ceasing to haul, in their panic, and minutes seemed to pass while we hung there, beseeching them to help us, looking up to the savage faces upon the nearer brink, shuddering when our eyes fell upon the black gutter of water and rock beneath. And every blow that fell upon the cable was like a blow struck upon our own bodies.

"Adam," said I, when at last I felt the belt moving again, "do you think we can hold?"

He turned to me with a face very white and

worn, and even bloody; and a great tenderness
for me in his eyes.

"It will hold for one," said he, speaking with a
calmness I could not misread.

"God forbid!" said I. "We have stood
together all through. O Adam, not that!"

I saw what he would do; and even while he
let go with both his hands—we being then no
more than two feet from the brink—I had
gripped his wrist; and I held to it while in the
same moment the rope snapped, and we swung
together beneath the bank upon which our own
men stood. So great was the force with which
he struck against the rock—for he was below
me—that the blow stunned him; and I saw that
his head lay upon his shoulder, and that his eyes
were closed. But I hallooed with all my voice to
those above to haul us up; and inch by inch, and
foot by foot, through that which seemed an
eternity, they pulled us to the ledge.

What agony man may suffer and live I knew
then for the first time. It were as though the
weight I held would wrench my arm from its
socket. Drawn over by the burden, I seemed to
swing head downward above the chasm. The
rush of blood in my ears was like the surging of

cataracts; the horror of death in that pit beyond any horror conceivable. A great sickness came over me, a giddiness which made all the walls to move, and brought to my distorted vision a multitude of faces, a wheel of torches. All the cries were now deadened to me. My one wish was to know if I should lose my consciousness before I struck upon the spikes below; if my body would ever come out of that place, so full of darkness and foul airs. And from this thought I passed to another—to that of my child-wife; of the island above me as I had first known it: of its glorious pastures and wooded hills and unperishing flowers. The new dream was almost a sweet one. I began to wish that it might last; the sense of fear left me; there were even sweet breezes blowing upon my face. I heard one speaking to me, and I had the fancy that the voice was the voice of Silver Lincoln.

.   .   .   .   .

When I came to my senses I lay upon a lounge on a ship's deck, and Fortune held both my hands. By her side there stood no other than Lincoln himself, and he was now looking down upon me with a smile of infinite satisfaction.

"Well," said he, "I guess you're mending."

I raised myself upon the couch to stare about me; then I knew that I was on the *Wanderer*. And, anticipating all that I would ask him, Lincoln began to speak.

"Yes," said he, "barring that tattoo on your thigh, you don't seem to want much patching. I reckon Adam's worse. He hasn't spoken yet."

"He is alive, then!" said I. "Thank God for that!"

"Yes," said he, "you may put me down in that lot. But he was just about a thumb's breath from the other thing when I came up."

"Then it was your voice that I heard?"

"I guess so. And it was a loop of my rope which hitched the old chap up just when you were finding the baggage too much for you. Lucky, too, for there wasn't a shoot left in the party."

"Silver," said I, "it's all Greek to me. How did you come up, and how did I come aboard here?"

He sat upon the bulwarks to tell me, while I kept my wife's hands close, fearing that my dream still cheated me.

"It was this way," said he; "I've been lying

off here a week, hoping to see the Frenchmen
weigh and cut it. When it blew hell, three
nights ago, I knew they'd run for the open sea,
and so they did; but I got into the eastern
harbour—which they never surveyed—and I rode
the gale out there. At the fall of the wind I
began to look for news of you; but the tunnel
was just right full of splinters, and I reckoned it
up that you'd come out by the safety-valve. It
was that which brought me under the western
light about the time you were holding a meeting
up yonder."

"So the tunnel led down to the sea?"

"Exactly, though there weren't six men that
knew of it. It comes out upon a little bit of
footing-room, under the western light, fifty feet
above high-water mark. The mischief of it was
that, when they hauled the women out, and we
shot up a rope, the gear fouled. Barring that
another chap was alongside me, with a spry little
French yacht party,—by the name of Jack Bannister,—we'd never have done it. But he got his
gear up at the second go, and I wasn't long
going up after it. Guess I found you occupied."

There had been a great heaviness in my head
while he had spoken; but now the sea air was

reviving me, and things came clearer to my view. It is true that I had pain in my thigh from a cut I had got in the scuffle, but this they had bandaged, and I could sit up to look over the sea. And my astonishment was very great when I saw that we had run to the open, and that the Isle of Lights, whose headlands were still wreathed with the smoke of burning houses, was no more than a rocky pillar of the horizon.

"Silver," said I, "we leave everything, then?"

"I guess we've no choice," said he. "Look yonder."

He pointed away to the west, where the Pacific was aflame with the gold-red sunlight; and I saw, low upon the horizon, the hulls of three warships.

"You may reckon it up that we don't show our heels for choice. I guess they weathered the gale, and are now coming back to hold a swarry."

He said it carelessly, but little Fortune winced at his words.

"Dearest wife," said I, "how does your father bear this?"

"God help him!" cried she, and my face

was all wet with her tears; "he has no home now."

I did not answer her. It was plain that the day of the count's dream had passed, and that he must awake to unending night.

. . . . .

The flight of the *Wanderer* was not unobserved by the French and Russian ships that came again to the island at the moment of her departure. One of their cruisers set to the pursuit, and held it for twenty hours. We lost her upon the second day, always having the heels of her, and then shaped our course boldly for Cape Desire, and after that for Rio. It was here that we put ashore the forty-five souls, men, women, and children, we had brought out of the city with us, paying their passages to Europe, and looking to a future provision for them. Here, too, that we read in the French newspapers of the ultimate sack of the island, and of our own deaths—for so the journals would have it. I remember the hour well, for it was that in which I first knew that Adam would live; and all else was as nothing to this—this life given to me, this new day for one of the noblest men that ever breathed God's air.

As the French press, nay, the press of all Europe, wrote of it, we had perished in the City. I read the words to the count, and when he had heard them he said:

"My son," said he, "we will go to Europe to tell them that we live."

And that was all he said.

CHAPTER XXXII.

"MINE IS THE NIGHT WITH ALL HER STARS."

THE breeze was very sweet and fresh as the sun set behind the hills of Henley. There was a musical ripple upon the dark waters of the river; a lap of the little waves against the dog-eared lilies, most pleasant to hear. And when the deep red light struck upon the brown-red leaves of the higher woods to deck them out in a hundred tints of September's making, and the soft wind brought the perfume of roses in its breath, and the scattering buds of the later flowers went scudding over the stream—then could I echo the count's words, "I have come home again"; and sit down contented to my rest.

I had taken this little house, at the foot of the greater woods near Shiplake, immediately upon the return of the *Wanderer* to London. We had made a good passage, but the intensity of the strife through which we had passed had left its

mark upon us all. At one time I had thought
that the count would not live to realize the loss
of his city and of the men who had given their
lives for him and for his hopes ; but Fortune had
tended him with all her depth of love, and while
he did not awake from his stupor for some weeks
after the fall of the island, nevertheless his
strength of body came back to him under the
stimulating influence of the sea ; and so I got
him to the Thames—and in the shadow of the
hills we rested.

On my part, I had given many days of those
quiet weeks to the completion of this narrative
which I have written under such strange circumstances, and in so many moods. The inspiration
of the sparkling river, the silence of the woods
and of the dark and leaf-strewn paths, the gentle
encouragement of my child-wife—in these was
my opportunity to complete a story which the
count himself no longer forbade, and all my more
active impulse urged me to complete. For the
justification of one man and of his friends, for
a memorial of those who died in the service of
their fellows, for an abiding history of a city of
cities, the work must be done. And now the last
days of September were upon us ; and still the

count held back from me the facts I sought ; and his lips were shut when he spoke of the home he had left and of the people who had betrayed him.

On this autumn afternoon I had carried my manuscript to the bank of the river, and there had spread it upon a wicker table in the hope that the warming sunshine would help me to a little work. Fortune, in a pretty gown of white, lay upon the perfect lawn at my feet, her mandolin in her hands, her head resting against my knees. Her father, wrapped about with rugs, was half dozing in a great armchair which we had dragged to the stream's edge, and there placed so that he could watch the sun upon the golden woods and the rippling waters of the islands. The passing of a rushing launch, the occasional splash of oars, the drip of a punt-pole, the cry of a bird—these were the jarring notes upon the music of the river ; that harmony of gentle whispers in which the mind may be lulled to the perfect rest and the body to unfailing ease.

Helped by my environment, I had written some lines of the narrative when the count moved in his chair and spoke to me, pointing with his finger to a letter which lay upon the grass.

" Read me that again," said he suddenly ; and I put down my pen to obey him.

It was a letter from Adam, dated the 1st of September and sent from Archangel. He had sailed to the North to leave his wounds in the ice, as he said ; and he told us cheerily that the Arctic breezes were making a new man of him. Of his own case, however, he spoke but briefly, going on rather to ask how we did, and particularly to inquire in what mood the count was. But in this matter, I prefer that he should speak for himself.

" You are all in my thoughts, Irwin, you and your dear wife, and him we love. May God's blessing be upon him now, and the good words of his fellow-men be with him. We dreamed a dream together, and we awoke from the sleep together. Perchance the day will come when that dream will return to us. May no discordant note of selfish ambition be in our ears when we sleep again. And who can say that upon the ashes of our city there shall not be built a temple of mercy and of might in which many may profess the faith which is in us. Of these things, I scarce dare to think now. But some day soon we shall all speak of them, it may be in a new home of the Master. And until that time, let your letters help a poor devil who is in exile and homeless, and wearying for a sight of all your faces."

In a postcriptum he added the hope that the "tattoo," for so he spoke of it, meaning the cut upon my thigh, was better; and he reproached me for giving him such small news of Fortune and of our happiness. Yet this I had no heart to do; and I doubt not that he knew my reasons.

When I had read the letter, the count sank back in his chair and seemed to be buried in profound reflection. Many minutes passed before he spoke; but when he did so, I felt that at last he was about to take me into his confidence and I listened with ready ears.

" No," said he, and with great deliberation, " we shall never know that sleep again until we rest in the embrace of death. We leave the ashes of a city—let them lie until the wind scatters them as the wind of evil scattered our hopes. Humanity to-day is too young for the message of mercy. It must have its contrasts of misery and joy, of splendour and of squalor. Fifty, nay perhaps twenty, years hence men shall arise to take up the work which I have left. But I must live alone as God wills. May he keep my heart from bitterness!"

There was a ring of such pathos in his voice that I was moved to a great pity for him; and Fortune, putting her arms about his neck, told him that he was not alone, nor ever would be while life remained to us.

He had been sunk in depression all that day, and, indeed, that was his mood since he had read of the final dispersal of his people, some of whom had been carried by warships to France, others set down in neighboring islands, many taken again to the Iles du Salut and to Siberia. For the most part, no quarter had been given by the Russians to their prisoners. We had learned that, when the troops came ultimately to the citadel (being brought in by our own ruffians, who had no knowledge how to maintain themselves, since in their madness they had burned and destroyed the stores) no less than fifty of the honest fellows who had escaped the massacre were cut down. The remembrance of the death of these men was not to be borne patiently by the count, it cut him as though he himself had contributed to their end. And to drag him from any such reflection I began to speak of what might have been, of the power of the city that lay in ashes—even of the building of it and of his discovery of the island. At this, some of the old pride was stirred in him, and he answered me with much warmth.

"You are writing" said he, pointing to my manuscript, "of me and of my work. Let the world know that it is finished; let them know also why it was begun."

I took my pen in my hand, assured now that I should have something of his story. When he had seemed to debate upon it a little while, he continued his words:

"Sixteen years ago, my brother Francis Jovanowitz was a servant of the Russian Government at Smolensk. Intrigue struck him down, and sent him to the mines. He who was fit to be a master of men was ground beneath the heels of the servants of slavery. The world forgot him in a month, he became a ragged wretch cringing under the sting of brutality and the lash. At that time, I was the representative of the Austrian Government in Poland; but I left my work and my ambitions to seek my brother, and after many weary months I traced him to Tobolsk—thence money and my yacht carried him and three of his companions in distress, through

Behring Strait to the waters of the Pacific. I left him to get his health at Tahiti, returning myself to Europe, full of the sights and sounds of misery which I had seen and heard in my journey from Orenburg to the Kara Sea.

" That was the hour of the first of my dreams. I remained some months in Austria trying to awaken my fellows to the full knowledge of the Russians and their prison systems; but the world is slow to pity the misfortunes of its neighbours, and no man listened to me. It was about this time that I first met Count Tolstoy, and found in his large Christianity a new impulse for my work. I began to ask myself if God had not called me to the help of all prisoners who suffered in the cause of man rather than the cause of crime? I found myself dreaming of a haven of refuge wherein those who had fallen for their faith in humanity should be sheltered from nations and from rulers. In the summer of the year 1880, I took my yacht to the Kara Sea again; and my money and my schemes carried therefrom nine more prisoners to the security of the British Isles in the Pacific. In the winter of that year, I was at Noumea in New Caledonia. Cruising with my ship in the northern channels of the islands, I fell in with several of those who were banished from France in the fateful 1871. These men I hid, and gave them passage to America; but a colony of refugees was now growing up around me; and I had to ask myself, What must be the outcome of it? where shall these outcasts ultimately find a home and a haven? how shall I shield them from the ill that must come?

" To that problem I had no solution until I fell in with Adam Monk at San Francisco in the beginning of the year 1882. He was then a wild, roving young fellow who had lost his money upon the English Stock Exchange, and had come to America with no aim and no ambition. But there was love in his heart; and when I was led to speak my thoughts to him, he offered me his life for the work. From him, the suggestion came that we should seek an island in the Pacific; remote, inaccessible, not marked upon the common maps; and there should set up a city of mercy and a refuge. And to this quest we went, but for many years we sailed the lonely waters of the Southern Ocean in vain; we pursued the work when all were weary with it; we set up our tents upon scores of islands, only to conclude after long weeks of trial that they

were not the homes we sought. At last, the
great storm in the year 1888 did for us what no
seeking of ours could do ; the finger of the
Almighty directed our eyes when blindness
seemed to have come upon them.

" When that storm struck the *Wanderer*, she
was a hundred miles from Easter Island in the
Western Pacific. But the hurricane carried her
like a match, and her decks were still white
with foam when the sun rose the third day.
Before it had set, the wind had fallen to a
whisper ; the lasting darkness of the storm had
given way to the golden sunlight ; the waters
shone like fields of silver ; the ocean went back
to her loneliness and her silence. And at sundown, my men, glad because their trouble was
ended, saw upon the ship's quarter the distant
line of a high shore, the black shape of a land
not marked on their chart. It was the shore of
the Isle of Lights ; the iron headland of my
home ; the great wall of the city which was to
rise up.

" I was then at Valparaiso, but when two
months had passed Adam came for me, and told
me with boyish exhilaration that the thing was
done ; that he had found a retreat for me, a

haven for my children. He had spent a month
surveying the channels of the inner reefs and the
land itself—for there was then a rude path to the
summit of the hills upon the western shore; and
he had no doubt that here was the one place in
all the world for us. I went with him to his El
Dorado, and found it to be all he claimed for it,—
but what it was you know,—and I gave half my
fortune to the work and the whole of such talent
as I have. In a year a city had arisen; in two
years it was peopled ; and to our united fortunes
there was added the gold we struck upon in the
igneous rock, in itself the ransom of a nation.

"In our new prosperity, in the blessing which
seemed to follow our steps, we did not forget
that we were in some part the enemies of many
nations, the disciples of a creed to which neither
kings nor courts could assent. From the first,
we busied ourselves about our defence; yet it
was not until our third year that a French
engineer, whom I had brought out of New
Caledonia, bethought him that we might use
the inner lagoon as our gateway. The tremendous sweep of water rushing into our island lake
at the flood of the tide, the irresistible suction at
the ebb, were to be observed at the height of the

chasm's brink. We knew that there must be a
tunnel leading from our lake to the lagoon without; and no sooner had we the notion than we
carried divers from San Francisco and began our
survey.

"The result of that you may anticipate. We
found the passage free except where the wide-
spreading branches of coral rose up in its channel. These we blew away with dynamite and
laid our cable for the lanterns—doing all our
work slowly, since it must be done at the slack
of the tide. But in three months we had a
clear waterway; and in six, I had received from
Sweden the flotilla of submarine boats which
had been designed for me. From that time,
and so soon as we had assured our safety by
running the boats through the tunnel with stout
cables attached to them, we blew away the lower
path upon the hill, and henceforth our island rose
above the sea like a solid pillar of rock. Do you
wonder that we called it 'impregnable'?"

I made no answer to his question, and when
he had sat a while, he, of a sudden, raised his
hand in emphasis, and his eyes glowed with the
fire of his mind as he continued:

"Nay, impregnable we were, a city of mercy

and a city of might. We had ears for every cry
of honest distress; eyes that looked upon all
countries of the world; hearts that beat the
faster when the angel of death came upon the
land and the voice of justice was stilled.
The hand of God raised us up to be a New
Jerusalem, the haven of the nations; the hand
of man cast us down and spread our ashes upon
the deep. But in this our night, let us pray for
the dawn when the light which we kindled shall
shine again upon our children, and the tears of
them that weep shall be wiped away, and the
people shall awake to the glorious dawn of peace,
the morning of the Eternal and of his reign."

.   .   .   .   .

Night fell upon the river, there were lamps
shining brightly in distant Henley town; I heard
a woman singing as she paddled herself toward
the lock. The sweet music and the spoken
words which yet rang in my ears called me back
to dreams; the face of the island home with its
lanterns and its gardens rose before me. It was
bitter to think that I had looked upon it for the
last time; that never again should I hear its
voices or find the shelter of its woods. As a
vision it had come into my life; as a vision it

passed from my sight.   But these it left to me—
the child whose warm tears were now upon my
face, the noble old man who had awakened to
this night of darkness.   And in love of them,
I shut the other picture from my eyes; and in
my fancy the city sank beneath the sea, and the
golden waves of the Pacific entombed her.

THE END.